HIS WAY
THE BRIAN CLOUGH STORY

PATRICK MURPHY

PAN BOOKS
LONDON, SYDNEY AND AUCKLAND

First published 1993 by Robson Books Ltd

This edition published 1994 by Pan Books Ltd

a division of Pan Macmillan Publishers Ltd
Cavaye Place London SW10 9PG
and Basingstoke

Associated companies throughout the world

ISBN 0 330 33687 8

1 3 5 7 9 8 6 4 2

A CIP catalogue record for this book is available from the
British Library

Typeset by Columns Design & Production Services Ltd., Reading
Printed and bound in Great Britain by
Cox & Wyman Ltd, Reading, Berkshire

Contents

Acknowledgements

Considering that Brian Clough's style of management was supposedly based on a reign of terror only surpassed by the Khmer Rouge, it has been instructive to hear so many of his former players fall over themselves to talk in glowing terms about him. The list includes some who would never place Clough on their Christmas card list, yet acknowledge that the man was outstanding at his job and often correct in the long run. My thanks to those players for their fairness, to those from the managerial and referees' worlds for different perspectives and to friends of the Clough family for valuable insights.

Without Clough, a few of us from the media would have sought alternative employment years ago. Perhaps he should have been given a Queen's Award for Industry. For sure, he was the subject of some fanciful claims on our expenses. If Brian Clough had consumed all the drink and food we are supposed to have pushed his way, then Chris Wootton *would* have had a story to tell the Sunday sleazies! My particular thanks to media colleagues – Gerald Mortimer, John Sadler, Ken Lawrence, Ron Jones, Mike Ingham, Audrey Adams, Sally Hayes, Lucy

Orgill, Phil Collins, Andrew James, Gary Newbon, John Dickinson, and Martin Fisher.

It is hard to imagine there will be another manager like Brian Clough, now that originality of thought among managers and players seems to be on the wane. The old chameleon brightened up many a dull day and turned out sides that gave a good deal of pleasure. He also spawned countless impersonators who never quite got that voice right. I hope this book gives some insight into the character of a man who has kept me in tales for a good few years.

PATRICK MURPHY

1

At the Court of King Brian

The eyes have it. They are part of an overwhelming personality, used to holding sway. Those hazel eyes may have become a shade rheumy in recent years, but they could still flash at the merest hint of weakness or a perceived character defect. The jabbing finger for extra emphasis, that distinctive nasally voice which launched a million quips – all part of the Brian Clough persona which has kept generations of night-club comedians and journalists in work. He has also given security and illustrious careers to countless footballers who would otherwise have been mere footnotes in club histories, known only to those who can recite the reserve side which started the game against Newcastle that frosty day many Januarys ago. The old alchemist knew the required potions very early in his career, and even if sometimes he appeared to have lost the prescription, it was fun watching him transforming the basest metals.

Everyone who has met him has a Cloughie story. That may not grant us the obligatory 15 minutes of fame decreed by Andy Warhol, but it can lead to a certain social cachet; your audience discovers a disciplined attention span while waiting for the details and the punchline. If the teller of the tale is honest, Brian Clough is usually the one who manages the devastating put-down, the baffling *non sequitur* that wrongfoots the opposition or disarms the intended aggressor. That blowtorch of a personality has been pressed hard for so many decades that the distinction between fact and fiction can be blurred. Yet one's pinching finger looks for the obligatory salt cellar when Brian comes out with comments such as 'I call meself "Big 'Ead" to remind meself not to be one.'

Brian has been perfectly happy to be the loosest cannon on the management deck for the past quarter of a century. As a player he was hardly a shrinking violet, glorying in his remarkable tally of goals for Middlesbrough and Sunderland, railing at the injustice of just two England caps, and so volubly convinced of his own rectitude that his team-mates led a successful revolt to sack him as Middlesbrough's captain.

He is an overwhelmingly generous man, touchingly loyal to those who show the same quality, and an assiduous, private worker for charitable causes. Ralph Waldo Emerson once wrote, 'Take egotism out, and you would castrate the benefactors,' and that is certainly the case with Brian Clough. He is an avowed Socialist, a creed nurtured in the North-East where his close-knit family was luckier than most to escape the ravages of chronic, debilitating unemployment. 'For me, Socialism comes from the heart. I've been lucky, I've made a few bob, got a nice car and house, but I think as many as possible should have the same. There are a few who've got on and made a few bob who don't think that way. Every bairn should have books, a nice classroom and the same opportunity to get on. I brought up my kids not to be greedy, to be generous with their time and their smiles. It's not all about money.'

Clough's many detractors call that simplistic Socialism, a convenient shibboleth from a man whose financial acumen would be acknowledged among the fat cats in the City, a *Guardian* reader who contributes his exclusive thoughts to the *Sun*, the newspaper that best embodied the Essex Man philosophies of the Prime Minister he despised, Margaret Thatcher. Clough palms off the contradictions with the risible comment that everyone should have the opportunity to be able to emulate him and drive a Mercedes, that the money from his newspaper column often goes to a charitable cause (undeniably true), and that the current standard of British journalism is so low that 'they'll all get you in the end'. Paradoxical maybe but Clough has been a consistent supporter of the Labour Party and particular MPs for many years, even if (another conundrum) he did not officially join the Party until the mid-eighties. At times he flirted with the idea of standing for Parliament, but the feeling persists that he was delighted to be asked, enjoyed the speculation, but rightly concluded that his craft was football management. Yet he is serious when he justifies his political credo: 'Of course I'm a Champagne Socialist. The difference between me and a good Tory is that he keeps his money while I share mine. I don't see why only certain sections of the community should have the franchise on champagne and big houses. A miner who has a good living, nice house and can afford a drink has a standard of living that helps the country. I paid income tax when it was 73 per cent and if a few more bob on our taxes now meant we could have more hospitals, better social services and give some treats to more underprivileged kids, I'd happily pay more. But I'd like those who can really afford it to pay more. And they don't, do they? I've never cared what the big nobs in football have thought about my politics, that's their lookout. Nobody will be able to prove it either way but when I went for the England job, I doubt if many around the table at the interview shared my beliefs. Perhaps that's one of the reasons I didn't get the job. I tell you what – it didn't go in my favour.'

Working with Clough has always been a case of taking him, warts and all. You fit in with his idiosyncrasies, whether player, club employee or journalist. As Geoffrey Boycott, long-time friend, fellow Yorkshireman, and another major achiever observed, 'Brian was always comfortable in himself because he knew he was talented and successful at his job. It was the others who were the problem, the ones who couldn't handle him or deal with his straight talking.'

David Pleat, a manager Clough admires for sharing the same footballing principles, describes him as 'the most amazing man I've ever met. I'm fascinated by him, and whenever I've talked to him, I find things he's said buzzing around in my head while I'm driving home. You find yourself telling your wife about him when you get into bed after getting out of the car.'

Pleat refers to Clough's 'frightening ego' in terms of wonderment, rather than censure. He recalls the time when he went to see Tony Bennett at the Barbican and tentatively agreed to go backstage to meet him after the concert. 'There was Brian, his wife Barbara and some friends. Brian was amazing, so relaxed, chatting away to Tony Bennett as if it was the most natural thing in the world that an English football manager should be on a similar level to a great American singer who probably didn't know the first thing about the game. Brian wasn't the slightest bit fazed.'

Pleat offers an analogy to the juggernaut that is Brian Clough's personality which may be hyperbolic but contains the kernel of truth. 'You know they're now going to charge for visiting Buckingham Palace? I reckon Cloughie could go up to the gates, persuade them to let him into every room for nothing and let him stroll around inside, inspecting every painting and every chair.'

This air of insouciance underpinned everything Cloughie did in his career. He was excellent at his job, and he and the rest of us knew it. In his younger managerial days, he felt that gave him the right to tilt at any windmill – all it needed was a Sancho Panza of a journalist to bring the thoughts of this particular Don Quixote to the nation. Like any other self-respecting hack of the time, this writer would be thinking 'This is good stuff,' while hoping that the biro or the tape recorder would keep functioning. Today, Clough concedes ruefully, 'I was good fodder for you lot at Derby', but it was a two-way relationship. He was as brilliant at manipulating the media as at galvanizing his players.

Cloughie knew about sound-bites 20 years before they became the subject of learned discourses on communications degree courses. A year before he won the First Division title at Derby, he was disarmingly frank about himself: 'Arrogant is a fair word – and conceited. I'm conceited that I've got them this far, having worked so hard with them. I think conceit and arrogance are part of a man's make-up. Perhaps I've got too much.'

Many years later, Cloughie would concede: 'Barbara says that I talked myself out of the England job and I think she's right.' Yet he knew that the cost of holding that most distinctive of tongues would have been too onerous and self-defeating. Emasculate the personality and you neuter the man's matchless ability to manage footballers. When you listen to the banalities from so many of the modern breed, as they witter on about '110 per cent', 'tucking in behind the front two' and 'sitting in the midfield', you thank the Lord you worked in the industry when Brian Clough's iconoclasm meant more to him than the chance of working his passage into an office at Lancaster Gate, then waiting for phone calls from other managers who did not want their injured players to join him on England duty.

He may have been the most self-indulgent of managers, with a calculating awareness of his own financial worth, but his incandescent self-belief brought him success and behavioural traits that were, to say the least, quirky. One Friday night, Neil Webb was settling down in his hotel room for the obligatory early sleep before the away match when he was tumbled out of bed by his manager. 'Hey, young man! Get downstairs now! You're having a drink with me, because the man down here can really play the piano!' Webb did as he was told – not an uncommon reaction at the City Ground – and after some admittedly handy work on the ivories by the pianist, the England international was told he could go back to bed. On another away trip, the Nottingham Forest team coach got to Luton rather too soon for Clough's comfort. He ordered the coach driver to stop on the hard shoulder of the motorway, and for the next half-hour, Forest's highly prized team and the most famous manager in the game walked up and down to kill time. 'It was so funny,' recalls Webb. 'We were still laughing about it when we got to the ground. As a result we were relaxed and we played well. He could really crack me up.'

I witnessed Clough's unorthodoxy at close quarters one wintry afternoon in the mid-eighties. Aston Villa were the opposition at the City Ground and at half-time I needed some information about an injury in the Villa camp for my BBC Radio report. Getting down into the dressing-room corridor just ahead of the players, I watched as Forest's captain, Ian Bowyer, tried to open

the door to Forest's dressing-room. It remained stubbornly
locked for a couple of minutes as all the Forest players bumped
into each other, gasping for refreshment and warmth. The door
suddenly opened, a ball was thrown at Bowyer and a familiar
voice rasped, 'Get back out there! You're playing crap! You
haven't entertained me, so go and give the crowd something
now!' The manager's assessment, though harsh, was accurate
and for the rest of the interval, the crowd was treated to the
sight of the Forest players disconsolately passing one ball among
themselves on the pitch, arms folded, teeth chattering, with a
palpable air of embarrassment. Less than an hour later, they
were being cheered off the pitch after an improved second-half
performance brought them victory.

By the late seventies Clough had become ensconced at the
City Ground. With trophies on a conveyor belt, he had taken
stock of his dealings with the media. His sacking after just 44
days at Leeds in 1974 had scarred him, and he knew a hard slog
lay ahead for managerial rehabilitation, despite his brilliance.
His wife Barbara and close friends advised him to tone down the
public comments, the braggadocio that the public and the media
enjoyed so much. It was wise advice. For the most part, Clough
concentrated over the next few years on what he did best. The
hunger for success was still there, his motivational skills were
impressively intact and with the incalculable assistance of his
partner Peter Taylor, he transformed Nottingham Forest. A
great story for those of us working in the area, but frustrating as
we tried to coax him out of his inner sanctum, to get him to roll
back the years and put on a few performances for us. He liked
to be asked, even though a polite 'No, thank you' was the usual
response. It was as unusual as Margaret Thatcher expressing
self-doubt or Joan Collins sporting laddered tights but for a long
time, Clough was an uncomfortable Greta Garbo figure.

He justified his self-denying ordinance with typical robustness:
'I stopped talking to the press when I found I was spending
more time with the press than I was with my players. I work
hard at my job and I don't see why I have to stand in draughty
corridors after a game, giving time to the Sunday papers, then
the Monday ones. Hell fire – if they can't do their job without
me, then they're poor journalists. I've earned the right to keep

away from the media. They over-react too much. We play an instant game and you can't always show your skills when someone is pushing you off the ball. How would you react if someone knocked that microphone out of your hand? Barbara says to me, "Do your job and go home," and she's right.'

Cloughie was shrewd enough, however, to ensure the lines of communication were not sealed off completely. An exclusive column with a variety of tabloids meant his thoughts were offered to some of the nation, while his personal bank balance and the interests of certain charities were not neglected. For those of us lacking the requisite financial clout, it was a case of digging in and establishing some basis of understanding, even if it was just a grudging acceptance of one's existence and the right to ask for the consolation prize of interviews with Forest players. I was always very careful to ask Clough's permission before approaching his players, many of whom treated media requests with the same wariness turkeys reserve for the month of December. They knew that an injudicious comment would spark off a lacerating dose of vitriol in front of their team-mates from a man uniquely qualified to dish it out – Brian Clough. After a while, this reporter moved from the bunker of 'What do you want?' to the sunny uplands of 'Nice to see you – but no thanks', then to the occasional Valhalla of 'Friday morning at 10.30 – you can work with me for five minutes.' You knew he would be late – he rarely wore a watch – but that was simply the basis for negotiations. Rock stars, actors and politicians specialize in the late arrival, so why not the most charismatic man in his profession? Yet you would get there early as a mark of respect, though that was not a reciprocal concept. Even though you knew he would eventually breeze in wearing his trademark green tracksuit top and aged trainers, you would glance down at your shoes, clucking if rather too many scuffs were visible. Other reporters with appointments who were partial to a fag would contain themselves, aware that Clough had developed the true fanaticism of the convert after kicking the habit himself in his early days at Derby.

After a time, the stalked quarry would materialize, the pass-code would be punched up on the outer door, and you would go through the *cordon sanitaire* to his office. He would decide on

the amount of pleasantries and hospitality before announcing
tersely, 'Come on, let's work.' Sometimes the hospitality was
fulsome, and as a massive mid-morning brandy was poured into
your tumbler, you would offer silent gratitude for remembering
to have a large breakfast, while casting around for a pot plant in
case the brain cells popped even more rapidly under the
influence of the drink and the man. The tape machine would
start to whirr round and you waited for the moments when he
would check if you were listening closely enough to him. When I
interviewed him before the FA Cup Final of 1991, he was well
aware I would be trotting out the obvious questions about at last
having his hands on the famous trophy after all those years of
trying. Cloughie flagged through most of that in understandably
bored fashion, pausing only to deliver the comment 'I should've
sold our Nigel to Terry Venables when he wanted him.' Double-
take from yours truly, a couple of gulps and the follow-up
question to check I had not misheard him. He proceeded to tell
me that Tottenham – the Wembley opposition later that week –
had put in a serious bid for his son four years earlier and that
Nigel was the one who had decided against the move. A good
little tale for BBC Radio but I might have missed it had I not
been as keyed up as he always expected his interviewers to be.

Testing you, always probing, looking for vulnerable areas.
Trying to put you on the back foot. I could see how he was so
effective in keeping his players on their toes. When he
celebrated his tenth anniversary at Nottingham Forest, Brian
granted me an interview. I found him in expansive mood, happy
to dwell on certain seasons that gave him justifiable pride. Yet,
at the start of the interview, he lobbed the ball back over my
head, making me chase hard.

'Brian, when you came here in January 1975, it was your
fourth club in 15 months. Did you think you were in danger of
not doing yourself justice as a manager?'

'What were those four clubs, please?'

'Derby, Brighton, Leeds – and Forest.'

Once he had established I had some grasp of the elements in
his career, we could proceed with the interview – but Brian liked
to stop you in your tracks. That same day, I had been chatting
to Nigel while Brian poured us a drink. It so happened that the

period of English history that Nigel had studied for 'A' Level was the same I had endured years earlier. After an inconsequential discussion lasting no more than a minute, Nigel left and Brian and I were alone again. Later, during the interview, we discussed the principles of management and Brian was warming to his theme. At the end of one typically trenchant observation on the subject, he paused, glared and said, 'And that's got nowt to do with all your "A" Level bullshit.' Game, set and match to the survivor in football's jungle who prospered without a single 'O' Level.

No professional on my side of the fence would ever dream of taking Brian Clough or his reactions for granted. After Peter Davenport scored a hat-trick against Sunderland, I made what I thought was a routine request to interview him on BBC Radio's Sports Report. As I stood outside the dressing-room door, I was stirred from my reverie by that distinctive voice. 'Tell him Big 'Ead says no!' was the riposte and that was the end of the matter. The player was very apologetic and I felt sorry for him until I saw Davenport speaking into assorted tape recorders and to all the press afterwards. I went looking for the manager and like a latter-day Macbeth 'screwed my courage to the sticking-place' and asked why I was the only one to miss out after observing the due courtesies. After a dusty exchange or two, I was told in no uncertain terms to go home and forget it. There was only ever one winner at the City Ground.

In 1989, when Forest at last reached Wembley for the first time in nine years, a hapless reporter from BBC Radio Nottingham experienced the essential Clough. Forest had battled through the second leg of their Littlewoods Cup semi-final to beat Bristol City after extra-time. The story, of course, was Clough, not his admirable players – and he and they knew it. Clough's response to the inevitable request for an interview was to present Phil Starbuck to the reporter. The fact that Starbuck was not in the winning team – nor even a substitute – was not lost on anyone! The manager demurred, as everyone knew he would.

A couple of years later, I experienced something similar. Forest had beaten Norwich City 6–2 at Carrow Road in a thrilling match with a display that triumphantly vindicated everything that was positive about Brian Clough's management. He was the obvious choice for an interview and when I was summoned to the Forest dressing-room, optimism coursed through my veins. Instead of the great man, I was presented with Scot Gemmill. 'It's his birthday today, Patrick,' I was told. 'This is a late present for him.' The fact that young Gemmill had made his first-team début that night – but only as a late substitute – was either irrelevant or yet another example of Brian's quirky humour. To be fair, Brian promised we would 'work' in a day or two and he duly obliged. He was always as good as his word and even though Forest had lost, he would still do the interview if he had promised earlier.

Gary Newbon, ITV's specialist in breathless touchline interviews, was once the grateful recipient of Clough's fidelity and the ensuing couple of minutes was a classic example of his skill at deflecting interrogation. Forest had just lost abjectly 4–0 at Everton, and with the Littlewoods Cup Final at Wembley a few days away, it was a worrying performance by Forest. Newbon was gratified that Clough had kept his pre-match word and he pressed him about Forest's pallid effort. Clough agreed they had been lacking in commitment, that the tackles were not firm enough. Rightly, Newbon harried Clough and with Wembley in mind, asked why his players had not been sufficiently committed. Clough fixed him with one of his baleful glares, then smiled and said, 'Because they're just like you and me, Gary – a bunch of pansies.' He smiled, kissed Newbon on the cheek and strolled off. The live exchange made the back-page lead next morning in the tabloids and left little room for a proper examination of the players' shortcomings. Once again, Clough had turned a damaging situation to his advantage by his flair for public relations. He also attended to the more important aspect of his job, getting the players motivated to win the Littlewoods Cup a few days later.

Cloughie would wrongfoot us for a pastime. In December 1986 he agreed to come on Sports Report with me, his first appearance on BBC Radio's five o'clock show for years. He had agreed to do it the day before and the show's presenter – hardly the most diffident of souls – banged the drum all afternoon that Cloughie would be on after the home game against Manchester

City. Journalistic acquaintances kept coming up to me throughout the afternoon, offering sceptical forecasts that Brian would renege if Forest played badly. I simply trotted out my sincere conviction that he kept his word in such matters, while privately acknowledging that the Barnum and Bailey treatment over the airwaves of the forthcoming interview was a touch grating and possibly misplaced.

In any event, Brian burst through the door of the interview room just after five o'clock and continued the chat we had been having the day earlier about England's prospects of bringing back the Ashes from Australia. A serious cricket student, Brian had indulged in a rare expression of envy when I told him I was flying out to Australia the next day to work for the BBC. We began the interview with a glass of Scotch in each of our hands and in customary fashion, he threw me straight away by asking about the other scores in the First Division, as if he had not already seen them. After a minute or two, it dawned on me that I had forgotten to tell Brian the interview was going out live – not just nationally but on the World Service – and that his salty vocabulary might be ill-suited to some of tender disposition. Mercifully he contented himself with a 'bloody' or two, talked publicly for the first time about Nigel's prospects in football (the sceptical listening hacks in the press box were grateful for that), and ended the interview with the cheering words, 'You come back from Australia a little more talented.' That was classic Clough: testing your resilience, offering something worthwhile after leaping the initial hurdle, second-guessing you throughout, and managing an effective put-down if you thought it was going well. It was the longest eight minutes of my life. It was also a fascinating insight into how he managed to get inside the minds of his players, to test the parameters of their resistance or co-operation, combining the stick with the carrot. Any sales director wondering how to galvanize his jaded sales force would have loved to see Clough work at close quarters.

Brian could be kindness itself. When my colleague Peter Jones died suddenly while commentating on the 1990 Boat Race he recorded a graceful tribute to a man he liked and respected, who had shared many a triumphant night with him in Europe. In 1987, when David Pleat was sacked by Tottenham after allegations concerning his private life appeared in the *Sun*, Clough took the opportunity of a pre-arranged interview with me to blast out his distaste for both club and newspaper: 'The standard of soccer journalism has gone down the pan. Too many of them are looking at the mud rather than up at the stars. The whole thing is unsavoury and a good man and his family have suffered the most. There isn't an editor or journalist who couldn't get himself on the front page for some indiscretion if they were important enough. Where is the moral courage from Tottenham to allow David Pleat to ride out the storm?' (Clough also wrote in similar vein to Pleat.)

This was not the glib, knockabout stuff that Cloughie would fire off almost in his sleep. He was genuinely outraged on behalf of David Pleat. For his part, Pleat has never forgotten Clough for that one gesture. 'It meant a great deal to hear the biggest name in football attack the paper that he in fact was working for. There was nothing in it for Brian but he stuck up for a principle.'

Brian liked his team to be praised. As he got older, his quest for manly sportsmanship from his players became more important as he saw other sides skirt the laws of the game, taking advantage of referees, while his own side carried on with flair and dignity. After a particularly enjoyable match at the City Ground, when Forest beat Coventry 4–1, my piece on Sports Report centred around the fact that it had been a pleasure to watch a match with just one offside decision, not one malicious foul, a doddle for the referee and a refreshing antidote to the increasing muscularity of English football. I concluded that the game was a credit to both managers – Clough and John Sillett – and that in particular Forest 'are a team to take your granny to watch'. Those sentiments were reported back to Brian and just as I was about to leave the ground, the summons came. He poured me a large brandy and, in front of several friends and members of his staff, he thanked me for my words. More than one player has told me that rare praise from Cloughie had them walking on air and that night I could see their point.

He disarmed me again at the start of the season that saw his team relegated. On 16 August 1992 such a scenario looked about as likely as Kenny Dalglish praising a referee, as Forest were due to take on Liverpool. Brian had prepared for the new season in characteristic style – nipping off to Majorca for some sunshine and arriving back the day before the first game. He stopped me in the corridor before the match to say he had heard me on the radio the day before saying that whatever happened in the next few months, Forest would remain a beacon of integrity, and that the referees all looked forward to their games. He was delighted with that and thanked me effusively. I waited for the sting in the tail and he did not disappoint. 'Mind you that stuff about Aston Villa winning the league was a load of bollocks!' I had also offered the opinion in the same piece that Brian would be a testing case study for any psychoanalyst, but he seemed perfectly happy with that opinion!

He is a caution, Cloughie. I have seen him demoralize another radio reporter by switching the 'off' button on his tape recorder and walking out without a word. Another turned up with a list of questions and after answering the first one, Cloughie leaned forward, screwed up his paper and said, 'Now young man – what else do you want to know?' Once he bewildered a camera crew who had asked to interview Gary Charles by sending out a young black apprentice who vaguely resembled the full-back. It took some time before the clipboard brigade realized they had been fooled. Yet when I asked if I could do an FA Cup semi-final preview with him fully two weeks before the match because I was flying out to walk the Alps with Ian Botham for Leukaemia Research, he readily co-operated. He not only showed his talent for making an interview sound immediate with comments such as, 'Now when you lot are listening to this, I'll be on my way to the ground, thinking of nowt but a win,' but he arranged to send out some videos of Forest matches to us, because we would be bored at night, killing time before an early start. The fact that one of the games was Liverpool's historic 5–0 defeat of Forest only enhanced his generous gesture. He was just as kind if ever I asked for some merchandise to raise money at auctions for the latest cricket beneficiaries of my acquaintance. He would always find an autographed ball or a piece of crystal, adding, 'Give him my love, tell him to make lots of money.'

Cloughie also told stories against himself. He loved to tell of the morning at Derby when he rang down to the dressing-room, looking for a cup of tea to be brought to his office. The exchange went like this:

'Bugger off!' and the phone was slammed down.

Clough rings up again. 'Do you know who I am?'

'Do you know who I am?' asked the apprentice.

'No.'

'Well bugger off again!'

Clough never did discover the identity of that particular artful dodger but he enjoyed his cheek.

He once ended an interview with Gary Newbon by thanking the cameraman 'for getting our two big heads in the same frame. I hope you keep that bit in.' They did and it made excellent television. Brian Moore, who worked with Clough for many years on commentaries and in ITV studios, feels his old friend mastered early on the exact requirements of his particular role. 'I think he had a real grasp of a good, graphic phrase with an everyday appeal. Geoffrey Boycott is the nearest to Cloughie today in the way he uses blunt terminology, but Cloughie was funnier. At his peak, Cloughie was fantastic and I just knew that people would be going to work the next day saying, "Did you hear what Clough had to say on the box last night?" Yet he loved to keep us on our toes, you know. He liked to be wooed when we needed him on the panel for the next World Cup and when we got him, he'd want to walk from his hotel through the Billingsgate Fish Market, chatting to the fish porters and leave it as late as possible before he got to our studio. You could never take him for granted and that's what he wanted you to think.'

Jimmy Armfield, a former team-mate of Clough at England level, felt he could have been a top-class sports journalist if he had decided not to go into management. Armfield, who works for the *Daily Express*, feels that the public would have become tired of Clough on television 'but in print, he would've been excellent value. I used to think his mouth was in front of his brain when he was a player, but if he had gone to college in his twenties, his natural intelligence and his outspoken manner would have set him up for an outstanding career in sports journalism. Now and then, when I needed a story from Cloughie, I'd go and see him and after a while, he'd say, "Get your pencil out" and he'd give me what I wanted in five minutes flat. He knew our business inside out.'

Alan Durban, who played for Clough with such distinction at Derby, has never been able to understand how Clough managed to sound so fresh in his comments for so long. An intelligent, eloquent man himself, Durban was aware of the need for a personable approach to the media when he went into management. 'I used to rack my brains thinking of something new to say when I was a manager. It's not as if I've ever been short of a word or two, but time and again I'd just resort to the same old stuff. But Cloughie kept coming up with provocative, funny thoughts, with a lot of commonsense in there as well. No matter how many years you've worked with the fella, and listened to that voice, you still turn up the volume when he comes on, because you know he'll make you laugh at some stage.'

Brian once told me during one of his reclusive periods, 'You media devour people.' He was right and he was advised sensibly when he realized that access to him was the commodity we all desired and that the rationing was entirely in his hands. Gary Newbon, in common with the rest of the media, was happy to play the game according to Clough's rules. 'At his peak, he was the one you wanted most of all on your show. And you had to be at the very top of your form to get the best out of him. The British public has this terrific fascination with their sportsmen like Boycott, Higgins, Botham and Eubank who have this streak of arrogance and ego, but Cloughie always had new patter for the punters. His ego was there for all to see, and he made no bones about it but we media people can't talk about egos – we've got the biggest ones around, haven't we?'

Hard to take issue with Gary Newbon on one of his specialist subjects, but it is clear that Clough read the runes of media dealings early on and mastered his brief. Consistently he said funny things: 'What is coaching? I'll tell you what coaching is – telling that McFarland to get his bloody hair cut!'

'Strike action by the players? Don't be daft, man! My players have been on strike for bloody weeks – we can't win a game!'

'Our team is so young, every game away is like a school outing. Our big problem isn't injury – it's acne.'

'I always tell directors and chairmen that they only have to

2

Annus Horribilis

Monday lunchtime, 26 April 1993. The day the music died. Brian Clough was retiring. Officially. Yet his players and backroom staff found out *after* the media who had been camped outside all morning in the club car park. Reporters queued up inside the Jubilee Club to use the only payphone they could find, mobile phones were coaxed into action by camera crews – everyone jostling to break the news.

The rumour machine had been clanking into overtime for a few weeks now, as Forest's astonishing decline towards relegation became an established fact and the pressure on the manager had become painfully discernible. The wheel had taken another spin the previous day when two Sunday tabloids had carried allegations from Forest director Chris Wootton that Brian Clough's ability to manage the club was being impaired by a reliance on alcohol. Wootton had claimed that the Forest board was in favour of sacking the man who had transformed the club in 18 years from second-rate to famously successful. It was significant that a director had popped his head above the parapet at the City Ground to voice criticism of a manager who

regarded most directors as little more than highly qualified
dispensers of drinks and pliant rubber-stampers of decisions. So
we gathered at the City Ground for the expected reaction from
the chairman, Fred Reacher, after a hastily convened board
meeting that morning. We did not expect anything other than a
vote of confidence for Clough and a routine public disembowel-
ling of the rogue director, who no doubt would have already
resigned from the board. After all, Clough had seen off a few
disaffected shareholders at the annual meeting a few weeks
earlier with his customary élan, and with just two games left for
Forest to salvage a Premier League place, what would be the
point in dropping the experienced pilot when the waters were so
treacherous?

Never underestimate the ability of human beings to make a
botch of things. The cock-up syndrome. It was fully operational
that morning at the City Ground. Mr Reacher began the press
conference with the anticipated denunciation of Mr Wootton,
revealed that he had refused to resign from the board and that,
until he could be removed at an extraordinary meeting of
shareholders, he was suspended from all duties. Yet he was still,
in essence, a director. As the media stared at their notebooks,
wondering about the line to take, the chairman offered another
piece of information that sharpened the focus. Brian Clough was
retiring at the end of the season. In a fortnight. The ego had
finally landed. Nothing to do with Chris Wootton's loud
whispering campaign. He was always going.

The media knew about it before Clough's players and
backroom staff. Another cock-up. As the players filed back
from training they wondered why so many camera crews were
limbering up to ask them questions. They were stunned to be
asked to give instant tributes to Clough. The backroom staff
were even more baffled. Alan Hill, chief scout and loyal back-up
to Clough for 16 years, heard the news when he switched on the
television in his office. Only an hour earlier, he had talked to
the manager about meeting for lunch and there had been no
mention of the impending announcement. Hill and the other
staff working close to Clough on football matters – Liam
O'Kane, Archie Gemmill and the assistant manager, Ron
Fenton – knew that he would be retiring at the end of the

season, but they were stunned at the timing of the announcement. The matches against Sheffield United and Ipswich had to be won to give Forest any chance of avoiding relegation, so why destabilize the club now and give some credence to the allegations of Wootton?

Fred Reacher, the chairman, now admits the matter could have been handled more tactfully: 'You can never select the right time for announcing the retirement of someone of Brian's calibre. We had talked about it for some time. A few days earlier, after our draw at Arsenal, we had toyed with announcing it then. The decision to retire was Brian's and there was no pressure put on him by the board. Despite Mr Wootton's allegations about having the necessary support, Brian would have still commanded the loyalty of the majority of the board – including mine as chairman.'

There is no doubt about Fred Reacher's sincerity. He had recommended Clough to the Forest board in January 1975 when they were looking for a manager to transform an ailing Second Division club, and over the years, the two had enjoyed a friendly relationship. In the previous couple of months, the chairman's expressions of public support had been models of their kind. No Chinese Whispers about sinking sands under Clough's feet had come from his chairman. He was also genuinely outraged at the insensitive timing of Mr Wootton's allegations in the Sunday papers. Yet despite the chairman's integrity, the Clough family was outraged at the way the story had been handled that April Monday.

Over the next few days, acres of newsprint speculated – did he fall or was he pushed? Eventually Barbara Clough and her three children – Elizabeth, Simon and Nigel – issued a rare statement attacking the Forest board. For Barbara to make public comment – even via a prepared statement – was as unprecedented as the Queen asking the paparazzi where she could buy the new Madonna album, and the sentiments were unambiguous. The statement deplored the fact that Brian could not break the news of his retirement first to his colleagues and players: 'He has such tremendous respect and affection for them that anything else would be unthinkable. We were therefore surprised and hurt when we heard on the one o'clock news on

Monday a statement of his impending retirement at the end of the season. We believe the timing could hardly have been worse. The word used most often in the press this week is resignation rather than retirement. After 40 years we feel disappointed that words like "hounded out" should accompany his retirement.'

A few weeks later as he finalized his move to Liverpool, Nigel told me that the interpretation of his father's decision had prompted the family statement. 'He had talked to us over the past five years about the right time to go. It always came down to his own decision, no one else tried to impose that on him. As we got more and more in trouble last season, it was then a case of him getting us clear of relegation, then announcing his retirement at the end of it. When you've been in the business as long as he has, fatigue creeps up on you around November and you start to think what a slog management is. He watched Forest games at every level as much as any other manager. He saw it as more important to watch the reserves and the youth team than being at the ground Monday to Saturday, nine till five. So in the end he just got very tired. And he was exceptionally worried about relegation, he felt that very badly. He didn't say as much to me – he had enough staff to discuss that with – but I could tell.'

For his part, Clough contents himself with a mild admonishment to the chairman he liked: 'He jumped the gun a little. I would've thought the tidy thing might have been to wait until the season had ended, but these things happen. I felt for the players – all that nonsense in the papers didn't help them as they were trying to stay up. I'd decided many weeks earlier to go. I talked about it with my family and I told my two grandchildren that they'd have me around every Sunday lunchtime for roast lamb. They seemed pleased enough.'

In fact, Clough had thought of resigning with just eight games left but Ron Fenton and Alan Hill had talked him out of it. Hill remembers how depressed he would be after yet another defeat. 'He'd come into his office, slump in the chair and say, "That was a load of garbage, I've never been associated with that in my life." He was depressed at the dearth of talent around. A lot of our performances scarred him last season and he thought he'd got too old to motivate his players. He asked us, "Would it help the club if I went early, so they could get someone in who's fresh?", but we told him to hang on till the end of the season, we needed his experience. He was often bewildered at our efforts on the field, yet somehow he'd motivate himself and next time the players saw him, he was his old confident self on the surface. I'm very sad that a man of his stature had to go out like that.'

Clough had been long enough in the public eye to know that the brickbats come with the territory when things are going badly. He did not shield behind convenient excuses like injuries to Neil Webb and Stuart Pearce that robbed him of international players for the last third of the season. Throughout the final season of his career, he shielded his players from public censure. Veteran Clough-watchers recalled the bizarre ways he would bring them back to reality when trophies regularly filled the Forest cabinet. This time he took the responsibility for failure: 'It's totally my fault. We haven't played enough good football that's also successful. As Eric Morecambe used to say, "There's no answer to that." It gave me a few sleepless nights, it was a position I'd never found myself in. I was perplexed we couldn't stick goals away after having dominated so many games. Just one example among many – we drew 0–0 at Chelsea yet we should've won 4–0. And how many times did a goalie come to the City Ground, play a blinder and see his team walk off with a 1–0 win? We lacked experience in certain key areas to cope with that. This last season Barbara used to say to me, "When you come up the drive, try and smile, because if you don't laugh, you cry." She was right – but it was hard.'

He soon became fed up with rival managers saying that Forest were too good to go down, as autumn merged into winter. He believed that, though. With 13 games left, I popped into his office for a chat a couple of hours before the match against Crystal Palace, an authentic six-pointer with Palace also down at the bottom. Other managers would have been twitchy, flicking through the dossier on the opposition, agonizing over team selection. Not Cloughie. He spent some time trying to throw his cap on to the hat-rack from a distance of ten yards, asking for nominations for the appropriate peg, all the while radiating bonhomie and voicing trenchant opinions about England's pathetic performances in the Test series in India. The day before he had signed Robert Rosario from Coventry for £400,000, a curious move considering Rosario's lack of goals in his career, an area that was proving dangerous for Forest. Fishing for his thoughts, I ventured the opinion that Rosario was an extremely personable chap. 'Is he? That's nice, I haven't met him yet. I'll see him soon when he plays tonight. If he's a success, he'll be one of my signings. If he blows it, he'll be one of Ronnie Fenton's.' There was an element of tongue exploring the inner cheek, but Clough had never been one for sitting in draughty stands, watching a certain player in a reserve game, panhandling for gold. That was the job of Peter Taylor, his excellent partner for so many years, and later the responsibility of Ron Fenton and Alan Hill. Cloughie was more interested in their attitude and readiness to learn on *his* terms once they were on his books. As he strolled off to meet Rosario in the dressing-room, he cheerily chided me, 'Don't be daft, man – we won't go down!'

Yet they did. A series of dreadful performances followed that upbeat encounter early in March. Two wimpish defeats in a row by Everton and Norwich, an inept home defeat by Blackburn (including the rare sound of Clough being booed by some season-ticket holders), and inevitable failure against the muscular sides like Wimbledon, Sheffield United and Arsenal. They were unlucky to lose at home to Aston Villa and deserved at least a point in a thrilling 4–3 defeat at Queens Park Rangers. It was not until that defeat at Loftus Road that Neil Webb realized Forest might go down. 'Such is my respect for the man that I thought Cloughie would still get us out of trouble. He took all the pressure off us by smiling and saying things like, "I must be doing something wrong, lads" and I admired the way he stuck to his principles of how to play. It's amazing to think we only got booed off the park twice at home – after the Norwich and Blackburn games. I think the true Forest fans realized what we all owed to him.'

This loyalty to Clough lasted till the last game of the season, on 8 May, another disappointing defeat at Ipswich, when the team continued to make pretty patterns, with little confidence and no end-product. Yet 5,000 had made the pilgrimage over to

Suffolk and they still roared out Brian Clough's name. The standing ovation from the Ipswich fans before the game, at the start of the second half and at full-time was even more touching.

A week earlier and the scenes at the City Ground defied logical analysis. Sheffield United, another side in the relegation mire, came to Nottingham and gave an object lesson in how to scrap for safety, play with boldness and composure, and carve out a precious win. It was the kind of disciplined performance one had come to expect from Clough's teams over the years, although United showed less finesse. Forest had played with their now familiar timidity and cluelessness, as if they had given up the ghost early on. They lacked pace in crucial areas, conviction at the right times and their sideways movement suggested they had modelled themselves on crabs. Sheffield United won 2–0 in a canter and Brian Clough had suffered relegation in abject fashion for the first time in a great career. Other managers would have crept away from public view and resorted to the bunker mentality. Not Clough. The kick-off had to be delayed while cameramen and well-wishers bearing flowers vied for his attentions at the side of the pitch as he acknowledged the salutations from the Trent End. In the second half, the Sheffield fans chanted Clough's name affectionately and were delighted at his recognition as he waved at them. The carnival atmosphere was totally at variance with the pusil-lanimous drift to relegation by a side that ought to have been in the comfort zone of the Premier League. Then, at the final whistle, Clough was persuaded out of his office to perform an emotional lap of honour. The rest is hysteria.

Just to cap a remarkable day, he even granted the press an audience, joshing them for claiming a stack of expenses on his account over the years. 'Modesty died when clothes were born' wrote Mark Twain and he would have enjoyed the way Cloughie turned what ought to have been a wake for his demise into a celebration of a glorious career. Hardly any credit went the way of Dave Bassett for the excellent motivational work on his team that spawned an impressive result to keep Sheffield United in the Premier League. No matter, it was Cloughie's day. It must be the first time a manager enjoyed the adulation of the home crowd after guiding them towards fixtures at Barnsley and

Grimsby, instead of Old Trafford and Anfield. Remarkably, gates at the City Ground for league games had risen to an average of 24,482 (only surpassed by eight other clubs in the division), compared to 23,721 the previous season, when Forest finished eighth in the table, got to two Wembley finals and the last eight of the FA Cup. All this after losing six league games in a row from August onwards. Life at the City Ground under Clough was never predictable.

Forest had started the 1992–93 season in some style, beating Liverpool more comprehensively than a 1–0 scoreline might suggest. Steve Hodge, a former Forest player, watched that game and thought his old club would easily hold down a top six place and challenge for a cup final. Hodge admits he misjudged Forest's inability to adapt to the athletic pressures of the modern game.

When he went to Leeds in 1991, Hodge had witnessed the attention to detail and insistence on physical excellence from his new manager, Howard Wilkinson, whose managerial credo was totally different from that of Clough. 'I learned that there are other ways to play the game these days. You need a mixture of the long with the short game, even though I prefer the Forest way as player and spectator. Forest also lacked that physical edge so many top sides have now. There was only Stuart Pearce to mix it if necessary and he was injured a lot in that relegation season. At Forest we never practised set pieces, it was all off the cuff, yet so many goals in the modern game come from corners or free-kicks. You also have to learn how to defend against those and Forest got more and more vulnerable at set pieces.'

Nigel Clough, the epitome of his father's approach to forward play, agrees it is becoming harder and harder to prosper the Forest way, unless you can find athletes who also know how to play constructively. 'It's harder to find the time on the field to play the way we liked at Forest, there's less time on the ball now and less room on the pitch.'

David Pleat grieves at the decline of Forest – 'I'd pay to watch them for their principles of wanting a controlled, passing game within the rules' – but he blames Clough. He feels it was wrong to play his influential players (Roy Keane and Nigel Clough) in defence for several games and that he should have been more adaptable to developing tactics. 'The line between success and failure at the top level is now so slender that you've got to do your homework on the opposition and work on set pieces. There are so many sides now like Arsenal, Wimbledon, Sheffield United and Crystal Palace who pack the team with athletes who press and press at you, denying space. Today the most common words you hear from the dug-out are "Get the second ball!" or "Squeeze out!" The coaches and managers are looking for possession from the knockdowns after the keeper has booted the ball downfield. Very depressing. From the Forest bench, you would either hear "Pass the ball!" or silence. It was up to the players. I know which style I prefer but it only works now if you have fast, athletic players to supplement high skill. They've got it at Manchester United and Aston Villa, but not many other sides in the top flight can marry the two philosophies attractively.'

David Pleat feels Brian Clough stayed a couple of years too long, a common consensus among those who respected him greatly and hated to see him veer towards self-parody. Pleat wonders whether Clough's backroom staff ever had enough power to change his mind over tactics or players: 'I was in his office an hour or so before the League Cup semi-final against Bristol City and they couldn't decide who the two substitutes would be. Brian asked Liam O'Kane, Alan Hill, Archie Gemmill and Ron Fenton for their choices and suddenly said, "You're right, Liam, it's those two." I just felt he was playing them all off against each other, having made up his own mind before. Was he just *playing* at giving them responsibility?'

There is some truth in that. Alan Hill says Clough wanted honest opinions at all times from his backroom staff and his bottom line was always 'Can he play or can't he?' In the end, Clough would make the final decision. The assistants used to push to play Nigel Clough in midfield or just behind the two front players, but his father invariably wanted him up front, with the number nine on his shirt, playing the way Clough senior used to relish.

Hill recalls a game against Crystal Palace in 1992 when Clough had finally been persuaded to try the sweeper system against his better judgement. 'We played five at the back with Darren Wassell sweeper and Gary Charles and Stuart Pearce pushing forward from full back. For the first ten minutes we pissed all over Palace. Then Brian started to say, "What are we doing? Wassell! Why aren't you centre half? Skipper! Where are you going?" We ended up drawing 0–0, yet we would have won easily if we had persisted with the new system. Brian lost contact with modern tactics. I agree his favoured style of 4–4–2 works but you need the right players for it. And we didn't have them towards the end.'

Ron Fenton, Clough's assistant in the last few years, kept trying to chip away at him, to make him try something different from two men up front, with two wingers in midfield, one of whom hugged the touchline and the other helped out with defensive duties, as well as getting down his wing and providing the crosses. 'But the modern trend is to put the full backs into midfield and get them raiding from wide positions, leaving three at the back and five in midfield. Sometimes our two wide men didn't occupy enough time in the middle of the park, so our young midfield players like Scot Gemmill and Roy Keane would get swamped. We've also been a little guilty of over-elaboration up front and that could be frustrating. I thought we could adapt our style of play without altering our principles but Brian wasn't ever really sure about that. He'd often say, "If you don't know what to do, then do nowt." But I always thought he was right to stick with his basic approach to playing football.'

Clough remained splendidly obdurate in his insistence on getting out of trouble his way. In his stubborn intransigence, his reliance on the game's simple verities, he was as defiant in adversity as Marshal Foch, who cabled his headquarters during a particularly bloody battle: 'My centre is giving way, my right is in retreat. Situation excellent. I shall attack.' Clough was sure he would unpick the lock of frustration at some stage in his final season, even though he was worried about the decline in his powers of motivation. 'I can't change and won't change. It's the way I've always played the game and managed teams. Get the ball, pass it, move, get ready to have it back again.'

Before every match he would go through the same ritual a quarter of an hour before kick-off. He would place a ball on a towel on the table and say, 'This is the tool you work with – treat it kindly and you'll be okay. If you whack it over the stand, that's not our style. Get hold of it and caress it.' Then he would tell his players to sit with their legs stretched out and smile. He liked them to feel warm and cheerful when they ran out on to the pitch. Frowns and deadpan faces were not welcomed in his dressing-room, because he was convinced that a relaxed footballer did himself justice. That may explain why Forest often went behind early on, then roused themselves. The plus side to that approach is that when they played to their potential, they were delightfully composed, looking comfortable on the ball wherever it was played on the field, an aesthetic pleasure in a game that was becoming increasingly hard-edged. If Clough is to be criticized for taking Forest into the uncharted waters of relegation by anachronistic methods, then he deserves the credit for consistent success over many years with an unchanging philosophy. Something else to be proud of was the fact that in the Premier League's Fair Play Table for the 1992–93 season, Forest collected fewer bookings than any other teams apart from Norwich and Aston Villa. They might have become a soft touch, but Nottingham Forest remained the team that referees noted in their diary with a justified sense of pleasurable anticipation.

So Clough could not change the playing style as his team continued flattering to deceive and under-performing. So why not bring in new players? In the space of four months in 1992, he had sold Des Walker, Darren Wassell and Teddy Sheringham to rake in around five million pounds, so the cash was readily available. Clough says tersely, 'The players I looked at weren't good enough to justify the sums of money the clubs were asking. I'd spent many years keeping Forest out of the red – I wasn't going to throw money away now.' Yet inflated fees were surely worth it if the new players kept Forest in the Premier League? An extra quarter of a million pounds would have secured Stan Collymore from Southend for a total of two million pounds, a ridiculous figure considering that he had cost Southend just £150,000 six months earlier. But Colin Murphy – at the time Southend's manager and a great Clough admirer – believes Collymore would have helped Forest survive. 'Two days before the transfer deadline, we'd agreed a fee of £1.75 million, but then my chairman wanted to push it up to two million because he thought that would look good. Forest jibbed at that and I was very sorry I never managed to sell Brian a player, especially Stan Collymore. He was just what they wanted to finish off their excellent approach work.' Ironically Collymore joined Forest after Clough's retirement for £2.25 million.

Clough's backroom staff also looked at West Bromwich Albion's Bob Taylor, but decided not to make a bid. They considered Neil Ruddock when he was at Southampton, and Andrew Cole before the young striker went to Newcastle from Bristol City. Each time the manager thought the clubs were asking for too much. When he bought Robert Rosario from Coventry, the player said, 'I don't think I can solve your goalscoring problems for you' but he was reassured that he had been bought to provide height up front and help create goals for others. Yet a total of 41 goals in 42 league games is a clear symptom of the malaise. So why sell a proven goalscorer, Teddy Sheringham? By the end of the 1992–93 season, Sheringham had scored 28 goals for Tottenham and was an England player. If he had stayed at Forest, how could they possibly be relegated?

Alan Hill says the club had no choice: 'He came to us at the start of the season and said it was driving him crackers going up and down the motorway to London to see his little boy, Charlie. He asked was there any chance he could get a move to London. Tottenham obviously knew about Teddy's domestic situation and came in with a bid. At no stage did Brian want him to go, but he's not one for hanging on to unhappy players.'

When Sheringham left, there seemed to be an ideal replacement just waiting to be snared. Dean Saunders was clearly not part of Graeme Souness's plans at Liverpool and this neat, busy, natural goalscorer would have been perfect for Forest, especially as he satisfied Clough's harshest demands by working to create chances for others as well as racking up an impressive quota of goals himself season after season. But Saunders had made the error of turning Clough down the previous summer in a manner that did not impress his suitor.

Alan Hill witnessed the negotiations at first hand. 'Dean was desperate to join us from Derby. A perfect move for him, and Arthur Cox, a good friend of Brian, was happy for him to go to

Forest. We met Dean at my house and Brian said to him, "Do you want to play for me, son?" Dean was very enthusiastic. He had been made a good offer by Everton but would prefer Forest. Brian said to me, "Okay, sort it out – match what Everton are offering and sign him." With that he went into my garden to look at my roses. A few minutes later I went out to give him some bad news. "You won't like this, gaffer – Everton have offered him seven thousand quid a week." He said, "That's more than *I* bloody earn! That just shows how out of touch I am these days." He reluctantly agreed to match Everton's offer and Dean left with his agent. We thought we had him. That night he rang up to say that Liverpool had come in, matched our offer and given him eight thousand quid a week! The gaffer was not impressed with Liverpool or Saunders.'

The episode had chastened Clough. As he said to Alan Hill, he was getting remote from the exorbitant sums players could garner these days; it seemed aeons since he had been the first English manager to pay a million pounds for a player, when Trevor Francis had behaved with such probity during the negotiations in 1979. Clough had never liked agents – he called them 'parasites' – and the Saunders episode hardened his resolve against the player and the perceived opportunism of other agents in subsequent discussions over players who might have saved Forest's bacon.

He seemed to stop winning in such negotiations. In 1989, Gary McAllister was all set to sign for Forest from Leicester City, but pulled out because he felt that Clough had been excessively rude to him. In retrospect that was a significant watershed. Not only would McAllister have been excellent for Forest – he went on to captain Leeds, and won a championship medal, playing with influential skill in midfield – but he was a secure enough individual to kick against the highly personal way that Clough conducted transfer negotiations. McAllister, an intelligent, sensitive man with a justified sense of his own worth, did not take kindly to Clough's relaxed attitude to time-keeping for their appointment, nor his pointed questions about the player's private life. It was rare for someone to turn down Brian Clough in 1989.

Kingsley Black nearly did so in 1991 and must still be

wondering if he was right to succumb to Clough's unique
method of doing business. When Black travelled up from Luton,
Clough made him stand back to back with him. 'You're not even
as big as me, son – take your shoes off.' An introverted young
man, Black did as he was told. He was then asked to hand over
his watch. He did so and at the end of the negotiations, he
plucked up enough courage to inform Clough that he wanted his
watch back. 'I'll give it back to you tomorrow when you sign for
me' was the reply. Clough then said, 'I'm told you're a coward,
son.' Understandably Black bridled at that, and when asked
where he liked to play, replied, 'A free role up front.' His
prospective manager replied, 'You've got to be brave for that,
son.' It was part of his familiar technique of testing out the
player's psychological weaponry, whether he was strong enough
to avoid being burnt by the furnace of Clough's ego. Black got
his watch back, and decided to come to Forest.

Alan Hill agrees that Clough sometimes misjudged the
character of some of his players. 'He got it wrong with the quiet
lads like Kingsley, who needed an arm around his shoulders at
certain times, rather than being bawled out. Tony Woodcock
was another – I've seen him shaking as he sat outside his office,
waiting to go in. Petrified. An England player! There were times
when Brian couldn't work those lads out.'

Hill feels that Clough would have retired if Forest had won
the FA Cup Final against Tottenham in 1991. Nigel Clough
agrees, 'but once he had lost, he didn't want to go out on a wave
of public sympathy, he'd rather go out as a winner.' The
manager thought the 1991 squad of Forest players was good
enough to challenge for honours the following season and that is
why he decided to keep Des Walker for another year, even
though Sampdoria were preparing a bid of five million pounds.
Walker eventually left a year later for just £1.5 million under the
terms of his contract, but Clough and his backroom staff felt it
had been worth the drop in money to keep him another season.
The money from two Wembley Finals and a good FA Cup run
helped subsidize the shortfall in the subsequent fee for the
peerless Walker.

By the time of Walker's departure, Darren Wassell appeared
a more than adequate replacement – fast enough to beat Walker

in training sprints and a clean tackler who played the game in a manly spirit. Yet manager and defender clashed in a reserve game with Rotherham when Wassell complained of an injured hand. At half-time, Clough grabbed hold of Wassell's hand, spat lightly on it, rubbed it and said, 'That's better.' Wassell was not impressed and as far as he was concerned that was the last straw in what he saw as a deteriorating relationship. His mother wrote to complain to Forest's chairman and when he was out of contract, in the summer of 1992, he readily agreed to join Derby, just a few weeks after Walker's departure. Clough remains baffled that Wassell should make so much out of an apparently trivial incident – as Alan Hill, a proud Barnsley boy, says, 'Mums and dads are always doing that to their kids in Yorkshire, there was no harm meant.' Yet if the relationship had not deteriorated already, the misunderstanding would have been smoothed over and Wassell would have surely prospered as Walker's replacement at the heart of Forest's defence.

Clough has always espoused the virtues of clean sheets, of building winning, attractive sides from sound foundations. On that basis, many Forest fans were baffled that he kept faith with Mark Crossley, undeniably a talented young goalkeeper but who had been suffering for a very long period from a severe crisis of confidence while continuing to play in the Forest first team. Just nine clean sheets in 42 league games in the relegation season suggests that Crossley ought to have been rested earlier.

It appeared to many good judges that an ideal replacement for Crossley was playing on loan to several clubs, yet was still available for first-team duty. Steve Sutton had been at the City Ground since 1978 and he had enjoyed an erratic relationship with the manager. Yet, for a time in the late 1980s, he was one of the most underrated keepers in the country as he approached his peak. He and Clough then differed over a new contract and ultimately, Sutton left Forest for good when he joined Derby in 1992. Yet for a long time the popular Sutton had to endure well-meaning supporters who kept asking why he was not in the first team. He had to smile, keep his own counsel and keep plugging away in the reserves, either waiting for a satisfactory move or his old place back. He has no personal axe to grind with Mark Crossley and it gave him no pleasure at all to see the manager whose principles he admired so much take Forest into the relegation quicksand. Yet he feels Clough lingered too long. 'I've seen relegation coming for four years. Remember how Sheffield United whacked us 5–2 the season before last at home? That was a bad one and it showed we couldn't cope any longer with the muscular teams. We papered over the cracks in recent seasons. When we won the Littlewoods Cup in 1990, we were mediocre in the league. Next season, we were again struggling in the League with games in hand and the chance of playing in the FA Cup Final motivated the lads to play for their places at Wembley. Yet when we won the Littlewoods Cup in 1989, I thought just a couple more players would let us compete with any side for the next five years. But Neil Webb and Gary Parker were allowed to go and we started to drift. Parker would've worked well with Roy Keane – Parker passing and Keane doing the running. We should've kept Franz Carr for his pace. He didn't really want to go, all he needed was a bit of care. There was a lack of leadership in the last few years. It needed someone to read the tea-leaves and spell out what was needed but the directors were spineless. There were times over the last few seasons when we would nick a game and I'd think, "How the hell did we manage that?" We became too predictable in our approach work – how often did you see a goal from outside the box, unless it came from Stuart Pearce?

'We never seemed to work at anything in training. We were living out a cavalier style in an age where we were being brushed aside. It was fine in the late seventies when we had class players at the back who were also experienced, but towards the end of my time, there was no sense of direction in training. Why didn't we work on set pieces, for heaven's sake? Every other team did. Usually we were still ready for more training when Cloughie said "That's enough" and back we'd go for a bath. He liked you to save your energies for match day but young players need guidance in training. Liam O'Kane would get an idea, and take ages to set up the cones in training to work on something, then the gaffer would come along and say "We're playing six-a-side today." All he ever wanted to do was play six-a-side. So Liam would have to pack up all his cones and wait for the chance to introduce something new when the gaffer was away.

'I'm really sad it's come to this, because what Brian Clough stood for was brilliant and when he was at his best, there was no one better. When I played against Preston reserves last year and I saw the way they were being brought up to play football, I felt sorry for them. At least we had the right grounding at Forest. But they'll struggle to get promoted next season, because they'll be competing against a lot of hungry, physical sides. Brian Clough has left Forest financially secure, with some good young players – but the club needs to be shaken to the core. It has coasted in recent years.'

Two other former Forest players who had frequent disagreements with Clough, yet retain great respect for him, also feel he stayed too long. Larry Lloyd admits that in common with most of the football cognoscenti, he was deceived by that early win over Liverpool in August 1992. 'Liverpool turned out to be mediocre, while Forest proved to be four players short of being average. They deserved to go down and I say that while supporting Clough's marvellous philosophy of how the game should be played. He was right not to change that, but he needed better players. For an intelligent man, he should've read the race card better. So he takes the blame – in our glory years at Forest it was always Clough's glory, so now he's stuck with the responsibility.'

Martin O'Neill turned down the chance to succeed Clough as Forest's manager. He decided to remain at Wycombe Wanderers because he felt the Forest board were unsure about his managerial capabilities. The board wanted Alan Hill as his number two or Frank Clark, while O'Neill felt he ought to be allowed to make those appointments without the directors telling him who he should have. The job went to Frank Clark so O'Neill continues his managerial education in the lower reaches of the Football League. He is sad to see Forest's demise and is convinced it would never have happened under the old Clough. 'Relegation would've been an impossibility under the man who managed me in the seventies – and with Peter Taylor alongside him. You always felt he knew what was going on, even if you didn't particularly like him. His ego about criticism blunted his edge towards the end – how else could you explain keeping Crossley in the side? He was ruthless about such things in his great days.

'I just think Forest got soft. I remember seeing Nigel Clough and Johnny Metgod wearing black gloves one freezing day when playing for Forest and I thought back to the evening in 1980 when we had to beat Dynamo Berlin in the European Cup, after going 1–0 down in the first leg at home. In East Berlin that night, it was the coldest I ever played, absolutely bitter, about minus seven degrees. We had to walk 100 yards from the dressing-rooms to the pitch in those conditions and if anyone had *dared* to put on a tracksuit or gloves to walk on to that pitch, Clough would've slaughtered him. We won 3–1 and went on to retain the European Cup, by the way. So perhaps the manager mellowed too much in his later years?'

Yet one final dreadful season should not tarnish the memory of a brilliant career, first as player and then as manager. John Sadler, who writes a column in the *Sun* with Clough, pleaded with him in the paper to retire, a month before the official announcement. 'It was one of the easiest pieces I've ever written. It was no more than what I'd said to his face a few times before. I was worried that the game he had given so much distinction to was beginning to destroy him.'

Nigel would have been happy to have seen his father stay on as consultant to Forest, rather than make a clean break, and it may well be that the gifted son would have remained at the City Ground if Chris Wootton had been persuaded to go quietly after throwing some hefty pebbles into the pool of rumour in April 1993. As long as he stayed on the board – albeit under sufferance – there was no place for Nigel Clough.

Neil Webb wonders if the old boy might do a Kenny Dalglish and bounce back at another club, while Brian Moore would like to see him pen his footballing thoughts for a broadsheet paper – say *The Times* or the *Guardian*. Lawrie McMenemy, who has shared many a discussion with Cloughie about the best time for retirement in club football, thinks weekly coaching sessions with youngsters at some club would bring him great joy, as McMenemy has discovered in working on the training field again with the England Under-21 squad. Cloughie will not be seen again behind a manager's desk, wondering who to pick for the next game. That door has firmly closed – for good. 'I don't know why you journalists don't retire, and stay retired like sensible people. I don't want to be seen anywhere near management now I've gone. You lot keep going too long and I did that for a time. Now I've got my grandchildren, my garden, my cricket and time to spend with Barbara. She deserves that. If you're not careful, football managers having a bad run come home and take it out on the wrong people. We've all done that. Now I can make amends.

'I'd like to see my son play now and again. It's right he's made a clean break. I said to him, "Go to Liverpool, get away!" But it'll be hard listening to all the chatter from the directors and their wives alongside me when I'll be thinking about what they're saying down in the dug-outs. I'll either get used to it or not come at all.'

Lawrie McMenemy felt for his old friend in that last season, as Cloughie's declining health became a subject of speculation in some tabloids and ribald comments on television. 'They take cheap shots at him, judging from what they see of snatched newspaper photographs. New-wave comedians who are millionaires inside two years, who have never met the guy, think it's a laugh that the man is suffering. I knew what Brian was going through in that last season. I used to take it personally when my club was losing, otherwise you're not doing your job properly. Cloughie's been managing with an injury, just like players have to perform with an injury. His injury was the burden of carrying a provincial club like Forest on his shoulders for so long. I had the same situation at Southampton, and so did Bobby Robson at Ipswich. To compete with the big guns, you have to get everything spot-on at your provincial club. When Cloughie was in at Forest, everyone moved a yard quicker, but in the end the weight proved too much for him.

'Football management is like a carousel. Some go up and down, some drop off, some stay on the horse for a long time, firmly in the saddle, both hands on the reins. Cloughie stayed on that horse longer than anyone. No manager in football history has stayed on a horse that keeps going up the carousel all the time. It just so happened that Cloughie's horse came off for the first time right at the end of his long career, whereas the rest of us have fallen off it and clambered back many times before.'

Perhaps those Forest fans who roared for Clough at the

moment of relegation were displaying a sense of perspective one rarely associates with diehard football supporters. The last of the actor-managers had gone, and for once the cliché 'end of an era' was justified.

3

Roy of the Rovers

For Melchester Rovers, read Middlesbrough and Sunderland. And – lest anyone forgets – England. Even if Brian Clough had never managed a Football League side, instead sliding into running a pub or running a sweets shop in his thirties, he should be remembered as one of the English game's greatest goalscorers (see Appendix, p. 227). He is proud that he remains the quickest to 250 league goals – and with defenders much more athletic now, goalkeepers more efficient and chances a good deal scarcer, there is scant likelihood that Clough's colours will be lowered. For much of Clough's short playing career, Jimmy Greaves was piling up goals for Chelsea and England and although playing rivals, the pair have always been on excellent personal terms. Even so Brian regularly reminds Jimmy when they meet that he reached the target of 250 league goals quicker than anyone.

'I accept the game is quicker now but it was bloody hard physically when I was a centre-forward,' Clough says. 'You'd get whacked from behind and never get a free-kick. It's not like tennis or golf where you can show your technical skills without physical pressure. In football you're all set to score when someone flattens you. Barbara often asks me, "What are you thinking?" and I'll say "nowt" and she doesn't believe me, but it's true. When I saw those goals in front of me, I thought about nothing but putting the ball in that space, everything else seemed to freeze for me. My kids often pull my leg when I talk about the goals I scored, that I wouldn't get all that many in the modern game. But are the goals a different size? Is there still a goalkeeper? An offside law? If it's in your blood, you can do it any time.'

Yet all but one of Brian's vault of league goals were scored in the Second Division. Was he an earlier version of Steve Bull, a predator against sub-standard defences, someone bound to be exposed if tested at the higher level? Not according to a string of good judges from that period who have observed the changing patterns and tactics of the English game. Jimmy Armfield has played, managed, reported and commentated in five decades of English football and he has no hestitation in placing Clough among the best of goalscorers. 'Players like Cloughie can do it wherever they play. He'd have made it in Division One, no question. He had the knack of getting into the right place at just the right time, not too soon. I once saw him score five for the Football League against the League of Ireland and none of them was from any distance, he just happened to appear in the most productive areas of the penalty area when necessary. He was only fair in the air, but strong and ready to go in hard for the ball when he saw the whites of the posts. And Cloughie was a good passer – he could receive it with his back to the goal and turn quickly. He played with his brains. There's a fair bit of his father's style in Nigel, you know – although Brian was a more robust player.'

Harold Shepherdson, Middlesbrough's coach at the time and trainer to the England team under first Walter Winterbottom, then Sir Alf Ramsey, saw many great goalscorers in a career that spanned 51 years. For him, Clough was outstanding, unlucky to have to compete against Jimmy Greaves and Bobby Charlton at international level: 'He was a gem. Half a chance and it was in the net. He was selfish in the penalty area but you expect that from great goalscorers. Because he was so confident he made a lot of enemies among the opposition and they tried to nobble him all the time, but he took the punishment and kept coming back. Brian was a hero in Middlesbrough.'

Football was in Brian's blood and the area where he was born and reared viewed the game with undiluted passion. When Middlesbrough played at home, the shifts at the local ICI factory were rearranged. Football was the opium of the masses and Brian's family reflected that. Even his mother Sally joined in the touchline exhortations if ever a game was played nearby. Brian was one of nine children, six brothers and three sisters (although one sister died young) and inevitably, the household talk revolved around football. Every Christmas, the boys would have new pairs of boots and although money was tight, the Clough children never lacked parental affection. Somehow Sally and her husband Joe would scrape together the money to take all the family to Blackpool every year for a fortnight. It was a typically close-knit family on a smart council estate, where families grew up proud of their standards, with spotless homes, a freshly cleaned doorstep and happy, boisterous children who nevertheless minded their manners when in the presence of their elders. Life at 17 Valley Road was no back-street saga of social deprivation, of pinched, drawn faces and meagre meals. Sally held the family together with a mixture of forceful personality, undiluted love and utter reliability, while her genial husband was happy to chug along behind the matriarchal figure. Brian loved his parents dearly and he was very proud of them whenever he brought them down to Derby to share in his successes at the Baseball Ground.

It was not uncommon for a party of around 30 to come down to Derby from the North-East when Brian's parents were alive. It is one of his more endearing traits that he remains unashamedly sentimental about the special kinship of an upbringing in the North-East, of the virtues of a warm, loving family and the necessity of showing respect to senior citizens. Stories of Clough buying coal or food for old folk in his village near Derby are legion. Queuing up in the local butcher's while an old dear wondered how much she could afford to buy, he would invariably lean forward and say, 'I'll get that, pet – have

the best.' Today he still makes sure his brothers and sisters are
looked after and charity workers are rarely spurned – particularly if Clough can ensure his participation remains private.

If young Brian was properly respectful to his elders, he
showed no such inhibitions while marching towards the
Middlesbrough first team. Although a naturally bright lad, he
showed no aptitude for books at school and proved to be the
only one of the children to fail the 11-plus. With the insouciance
that characterized his whole football career, Clough had already
mapped out how he would spend his adult life. His father had
become foreman at Garnett's sweets factory, alongside Middlesbrough Football Club's Ayresome Park ground, a quarter of
a mile from the Clough family home, and whenever possible,
Brian would pop down to see his dad and watch the Boro
players report for training. Clough senior was an avid supporter
and made sure the Boro players had a generous supply of
sweets. One day, Harold Shepherdson – by now Boro's assistant
trainer after retiring as player – was amused to hear a youngster
tell him, 'I'm going to play for the Boro one day.' He passed it
off as the usual day-dreaming of the local lad who would do
anything but work in a factory or stay on at school. Yet there
was something in the serene self-confidence of Master Brian
Clough that made an impression on Shepherdson. Within a few
years, he would be coaching him at Ayresome Park, listening to
the youngster forecast exactly how he would score 40 goals a
season.

For a time though, young Clough had to make do with work
as a messenger boy on part of the giant ICI complex. The idea
of the great egotist having to deliver messages at the behest of
better-educated clerks in suits beggars description: it must have
taken great self-control to button that precocious lip! Within a
year of leaving school, he was beginning to make a mark in
adult football, playing for Great Broughton in the Cleveland
League. It was hard and unrelenting football against narrow-
eyed, robust adults who gave the small youngster no favours.
An unspectacular start to a remarkable career and Brian was
glad to have four of his brothers and a brother-in-law in the
side. 'I thought I was the best player in the family, but the
others didn't necessarily agree with that then. I never got picked

for any representative side, you know, not even a regional schoolboys team. I was small although my head was big. I didn't grow until I was about 16 and by 19 I was up to five eleven. But getting into the school team alongside my brothers was my level of achievement for quite some time.'

Eventually, he scored a stack of goals for Great Broughton, then he played for Middlesbrough Juniors. Still the goals rained in, and at 17 he signed for Middlesbrough as a professional. His father was overjoyed; after watching the Boro on the terraces with his boys, one of them would now be out there on the pitch. But it was 1952 and National Service loomed for any fit teenager, who could not summon up fallen arches or urgent academic work to avoid the call-up. Clough played for his station side but never made it to the RAF representative team, much to his chagrin. By the time he was out of service, a good deal of pent-up aggression and frustration at thwarted ambition was swirling around inside his 20-year-old mind. He returned to Middlesbrough, determined to star in a side that would soar into the First Division and tilt at their North-East rivals, Newcastle and Sunderland. If that did not happen, he would be on his way. He had wasted enough time waiting for his appointment with destiny.

In his first full season with Middlesbrough, he scored 38 goals. Not just tap-ins, the staple diet of the striker, but fulminating strikes from the edge of the penalty area or deftly timed arrivals late in the box from crosses. The technique seemed finely honed in an astonishingly mature player. Most of the shots came from a powerful right foot and although he was no Tommy Lawton in the air, he seemed to time his leaps and hang long enough for the nod-in while his markers were on the descent from their efforts at shutting down the service from the wings. Clough had become a star in the North-East and at last the Boro fans had someone to mention in the same breath as the legendary Jackie Milburn at Newcastle.

Yet Clough was frustrated. The amount of goals zooming in at his end was more than matched at the other end. Clough began to think that he had to score a hat-trick to help Middlesbrough avoid defeat. After just nine games in the first team he asked for a transfer. Unlike most players of that generation, Clough soon mastered the art of manipulating the media, a skill that never deserted him. He made sure the local press knew of his disaffection and why he wanted to take his priceless talents elsewhere. The fans were desolate at the prospect of losing him and soon his manager, Bob Dennison, made him captain, partly to appease his vaunting ambition, partly to get his young star more money. Soon Clough's salty tongue had alienated most of his team-mates, as he continued to rail against their shortcomings, their lack of ambition and professionalism. 'As fast as I score, they throw them in at the back,' he used to complain. Hardened pros were not used to a lippy young player with the ego that gave him licence to organize matters on the field as he saw fit. Regularly on away trips, Clough would gather the rest of the forward line in his hotel room and tell them exactly what he expected from them on the morrow. To the wingers, Billy Day and Edwin Holliday, it was simple – 'get it over to me, I'll knock 'em in' – to his fellow-striker, Alan Peacock – 'to my feet, Peakie, don't mess about'.

The Boro trainer, Harold Shepherdson, had never worked with anyone with such a conceit of himself. 'He had that amazing aura of self-confidence. Every morning at training, he seemed to time his entrance for the maximum effect. He'd throw his cap on to the rack-stand in front of the others and then start talking to them about football. He was so dedicated, so desperate for success. To be fair, he wanted the others to do well also, and he was no back-stabber. A few of the others resented his blunt speaking, but at least you knew where you stood with Brian. Not a lot's changed, has it?'

Eventually, Bob Dennison, the manager, had a players' revolt on his hands. They held a round-robin, asking that Clough should lose the captaincy. Dennison, a quiet, amiable man, held firm in a gesture reminiscent of Lyndon Johnson's famous phrase about preferring to have a troublemaker relieving himself from inside the tent, rather than from outside, into the tent. Dennison thought he could get more out of his star player by giving him his head on and off the field, rather than risk alienating the folk hero of Teesside, whose hot line to the local media buzzed regularly and profitably for both player and reporters. Besides, Clough remained the best chance of a £2 win bonus for the rest of the players, many of whom seemed content to drift along in the upper reaches of the Second Division. Nevertheless, Clough was hurt by the reaction of his team-mates. Even his thick skin was penetrated, despite his protests that he was merely trying to get everyone in the team thinking more closely about their game.

In the late fifties, a group of enlightened coaches were gradually developing an influence in the English game, as the full impact of England's international isolation took hold following two humiliating defeats by Hungary in 1953 and the following year. Breaking free of the chains of conformity was all very well for top sides in the First Division, but clubs like Middlesbrough were still rooted in the conviction that the English way was best, with two wingers, a stopper centre-half and a strong man up front. If you scored enough goals, it did not matter so much that you shipped in a few at your end. That did not wash with Clough, nor does it today, despite his purist principles about the methods adopted. 'I was unpopular at Boro because I used to think I was a better player than I was. I also gave my defenders a bit of stick, just like I did when I was a manager. One year at Boro we scored 99 goals and only finished fifth in the Second Division! If we'd scored ten less and conceded 50 less, we might have got promotion.'

One of the half-truths about Clough that has snowballed over the years into accepted fact is that he was so selfish that he would unashamedly push colleagues off the ball if an easy goal was there for the taking. Alan Peacock, who played several years up front alongside Clough, disputes that. 'I never saw that happen. It was inevitable that he'd be in the right place to score, because he was more gifted at that than the others and he was better at sticking away the chances than the rest of us. So if a ball was bouncing loose near goal, you'd be looking to Clough to claim it. Any striker worth his corn would do the same. He was selfish in front of goal, but not to the detriment of the team. We beat Derby once 7–1 and I scored four. Brian got none and he wasn't too happy about that, but I don't blame him for that. I'm sure Rush, Lineker and all the rest would expect to get on the scoresheet if their team scored seven. I used to look up to Cloughie, even though I was only two years younger. He was an absolutely fantastic finisher: I can still see a goal he got against Bristol Rovers, lashing in a ball about three yards off the ground. Heavy balls in those days, mind you. It was still rising when it crashed into the net. His shooting was so powerful because he was an excellent trainer, building up his legs and thighs. When he scored, he was like a man on drugs – he just lived for that on the field. Every side needs a Clough.'

Alan Peacock picked up six England caps after Clough left Middlesbrough and he considers his mentor was ill-served by just two appearances for his country. 'He reminded me particularly of Roger Hunt and look at the caps *he* got. Definitely in the Greaves class as a finisher. Perhaps Brian's confident manner ruffled a few feathers. It can't have been because he played in the Second Division, because anyone could see he was a natural, whatever team he was in.'

Clough had an early inkling that the path to international glory would not run as smoothly as he wished when he was picked for an under-23 tour behind the Iron Curtain in 1957. He scored a typical predator's goal against Bulgaria, sweeping in a cross instantly with his right foot. England lost 2–1; but it never occurred to Clough he would have to stand down for the next game in Bucharest, against Rumania. Derek Kevan, the big, raw-boned West Bromwich Albion centre-forward took his place and Jimmy Armfield, one of the England players on that trip, recalls Clough's anguish: 'He was absolutely astounded when he cáme back to our room. Utterly deflated. He had done what he was picked for, scoring a lovely goal. That decision really rocked him and you have to wonder now about Walter Winterbottom's judgement, because big Derek never had Cloughie's ruthlessness in front of goal. His despair was all the more striking because Cloughie was such a confident lad, yet so young. He was much brighter than the average players on that trip and he was not afraid to pipe up and speak his mind in front of the manager. Even at cards, he was better than us – he gave up trying to teach us bridge!'

Harold Shepherdson, the England trainer at that time, believes that Walter Winterbottom was not biased against the brash young man with the effrontery to tell him who should play alongside him, when – not if – he was picked for the full

England side. 'Walter wasn't offended, he approved of players
who had minds of their own.' Yet Clough was not picked for the
World Cup squad in Sweden in 1958, even though Tommy
Taylor had been tragically killed earlier that year in the Munich
air crash, while Bobby Charlton also missed out through the
after-effects of that terrifying experience. Instead, the reliable, if
ponderous Kevan made the trip because Winterbottom was
impressed by his workrate. *Plus ça change* . . .

It was to be another year before Clough won a senior cap, and
two came and went in the space of eleven days in October 1959.
He did not play particularly well against Wales in Cardiff, nor at
Wembley, where Sweden won 3–2. Clough laid on a goal for
John Connelly at Wembley with an intelligent cut-back and
there lurks a tantalizing glimpse on film of his constructive skills,
where a lovely reverse pass through a crowded goalmouth set
Connelly free down the right – shades of Clough junior. Yet,
though he hit the bar against Sweden, Clough was starved of a
proper service. With two wingers and Clough, Greaves and
Charlton all cramming the centre, looking for the same service,
it would appear a rather ill-balanced forward line. That point
was put to the England manager by Clough with typical asperity
after the Sweden match, and it is hard to dispute his logic. It is a
moot point whether that exchange of views sealed Clough's fate,
but he did not play again for England, and he never played at
Wembley again. Just one match as a player at the stadium he
revered. He was only 24.

Years later, when he was excelling as Derby County's
manager and the banter would be flowing among his players
about the respective merits of current internationals, Clough
would say, 'Hey! I played for England, you know! Don't forget
that!' In training he would effortlessly display the skills that had
brought him so many goals a decade earlier.

Alan Durban used to watch Clough in awe in training. 'He
was a great technical header for a start. He would use a golfer's
stance to get strength in a certain part of his body without
needing to jump. Too many centre-forwards jump and in so
doing, they lose power in the header. But Cloughie would stand
there, really give it some oomph and his headers would rocket in
from 12 yards. He had a terrific right-foot shot but he was also

clever enough to place the ball when there was no need to blast.
"Pass the ball into the net, don't shoot," he used to say. You
could just tell in those Derby days what a terrific goalscorer he
must have been.'

After being dropped by England in the autumn of 1959,
Clough continued banging in goals for Middlesbrough, but he
was close to breaking with a club he thought lacked ambition.
He knew that his international career would have a chance of
resurrection if he moved into the First Division and with the
Boro defence still as profligate as sailors on shore-leave,
promotion remained a mirage.

In the summer of 1961, he took a Mediterranean cruise with
his wife, Barbara, whom he had married two years earlier ('Best
thing I ever did in my life – was I lucky!'). When he returned to
Southampton early one July morning, he was met by a man who
would eventually help shape him into a legendary manager.

At the time, Alan Brown was Sunderland's manager,
determined to get the club back into the First Division, and he
saw Clough's goals as the crucial ingredient. He was an
innovative coach, whose methods inspired countless players and
managers over a career that lasted more than 40 years. The
power of Alan Brown's personality imposed itself on every club
he managed; not for him the consensual approach, taking advice
from directors and ingratiating himself with the local press.
Among his players, Alan Brown's word was law. Punctuality
was compulsory, personal cleanliness essential, dedication to the
cause not a matter of negotiation. He studied fitness techniques
from other sports and readily borrowed new methods to make
his players fitter. He thought nothing of making them run
through the sea outside Sunderland's Roker Park, to develop
their lung power and calf strength. Leading the way would be
the tall, spare figure of the manager. As a teenager with enough
skills that eventually made him a 'B' international, Brown would
run at night along the river banks of Northumberland to
improve his stamina without distractions. At the age of 16, he
once ran the 17½ miles from his village of Corbridge to
Newcastle Bridge, paused for a short while and then ran back
home. Alan Brown was no ordinary football man. He had a
vision of the game and a messianic zeal given to few Englishmen

of his time. As a disciplinarian, he made the likes of Alf Ramsey and Bill Shankly seem pussycats.

Typically, Brown had interrupted a family holiday to track down his quarry on the Southampton quayside. Clough was the first off the ship at six in the morning and as he busied himself looking for his baggage, Brown introduced himself. He spelt out the details, told him Middlesbrough had agreed to the deal and that he would go back up to Sunderland with him to finalize matters, even though he was on holiday. Clough eyed Brown for a few seconds, then extended his hand, 'Done. I'll go and sort it all out. No need for you to come. You go back on your holiday, you've earned it. Now I'll try and sort out this bloody baggage.' Brown could not believe that a player of Clough's disputatious reputation could be so agreeable. 'There was no haggling, he never asked for anything extra, he was perfectly happy to be told he'd be on top wages. I never had an easier transfer in my life.' Perhaps one of the reasons why it went so smoothly was because Alan Brown's integrity was a byword in the game and Clough knew how lucky he was to be chosen by him. It was the start of a relationship that did not always run smoothly, but endured through mutual respect. Over the next three years while Brown stayed at Sunderland, Clough would be on a steep learning curve.

Sunderland only got a season and a half out of Clough the player and it was to be another three years before they achieved promotion, but he more than paid his way with 54 goals in 61 games. 'It was the happiest time of my life in terms of football. Sunderland folk are beautiful, much warmer and genuine than those at Middlesbrough and we had a wonderful relationship going. I was young, happily married, my first two kids were born in Sunderland, I was cracking in the goals. Lovely days.'

The new signing had the rudest of awakenings at his first training session under Alan Brown. After about ten minutes, an acquaintance of Clough's turned up on the touchline, waved and Clough sidled over for a chat. The manager was unused to one of his charges not hanging on his every word and he gave Clough a raucous piece of his mind, ending with the ominous words, 'Don't you ever dare do that to me.' Clough meekly accepted the public rebuke and another in the privacy of

Brown's office a couple of hours later. 'He accepted the dressing-down in a mature manner. He took it like a man. After that, I never had any disciplinary problems with him. We would argue about tactics and all the other things connected with football, but he was always a model of respect. I liked him, he was a fine man and a team player. Always clean and tidy, he'd knock on the door and wait before he would come in. I'd sometimes say to a player, "Isn't that a shocking pullover to be seen on an international footballer?" and they took the point. I liked my players to look smart, with short hair. I was the absolute boss at my clubs, but I cared deeply for my players. And Brian was compassionate. I remember we were having a bad run once and Brian knocked on my door, waited for me to let him in and then said, "I'm sorry, boss, I feel sorry for you. We're playing badly, but we'll put it right." Then he was gone. I was amazed that a player would think about his manager that way. Another time he admitted to me, "I'm bloody frightened of you," and I told him I knew. But I liked his kind of personality, he was bright and confident and full of ideas.'

Brian Clough still refers to his former manager as 'Mr Brown' and a measure of his gratitude can be gauged by the regular letters he sends to his retirement home in Bideford, Devon. He sent him a photo of himself and his two sons, Nigel and Simon, with the message 'They were born in Sunderland when I worked for you' and the framed photograph has pride of place on the Brown sideboard. When Mr and Mrs Brown went to California to see their daughter, Brian sent a handsome cheque because 'it would be nice for you all to have your first sandwich together on us'. When Nigel was featured in a Sunderland newspaper at the start of his Forest career, Brian sent the cutting to Alan Brown with the message 'I wish he could have worked for you. There's a bit of me in him, but he really looks more like his mother!' Before Connie Brown died, she regularly received huge bouquets of flowers from Brian and when he persuaded Mr Brown to attend a testimonial game at Plymouth, Clough took him into the Forest dressing-room and made it quite clear to his players how much he venerated the man.

Today, after several heart attacks, a stroke and with his sight impaired, Alan Brown is still straight-backed, immaculate and passionate about football. He cannot speak about Brian Clough for more than five minutes without tears welling up. Brian masters that with rather more success, but there are times when a tear creeps into the corner of one eye when he talks about the manager who taught him so much. 'Mr Brown taught me discipline. When I played at Sunderland, I was a bugger for cutting it fine and getting in for training just in time. He'd watch me from his window as I drove into the car park and by the time he'd got downstairs, I'd thrown my cap on to the hat-rack and was sat waiting for him. He'd burst in and say, "You . . . one of these days!" but it was said affectionately. I knew the score with Mr Brown, he was the boss.'

The pair were bonded further by the incident on Boxing Day 1962 that scarred Clough as a person and yet shaped a brilliant career subsequently. Sunderland, chasing promotion again, were at home to Bury on a foul day of sleet and hailstones. The game was played on a muddy, tacky pitch, an afternoon for sliding tackles rather than mazy dribbling. When Clough chased a misdirected pass into the Bury penalty area, he was left sprawling in the mud after his right knee made contact with the shoulder of the goalkeeper, Chris Harker. The ball ran loose and with his predator's instinct, Clough tried to get up and run after it. He could not get up off the ground. Thirty years later, Clough tries to make light of the incident: 'I had my big head down chasing a bad ball and I didn't notice the keeper was slow coming out for it, then making a lunge. Keepers are quicker out of their goals now. When I was carried off, our physio went to take off my boots but Mr Brown said, "Don't take his boots off, he might go back on." That's how we thought in those days.'

In his agony, Clough did not realize that Alan Brown was simply being kind. He did not want to tell Clough what he instantly knew – he was finished as a player. After just a split second of misdirected action. It was a torn cruciate ligament, in those days more serious than a broken leg. Alan Brown will never forget the sight that greeted him as he ran on to the pitch with his physio, John Watters. 'I was a qualified masseur and I knew straight away it was hopeless. Brian kept asking the physio what was wrong, but we decided to keep it a secret until it was confirmed by the doctor. We knew it was hopeless, but we

couldn't tell him, because it would've shattered him. He needed
to have some hope as the next few months went by.'

Brown insisted on supervising Clough's rehabilitation and
admits he drove him very hard, sometimes too hard. 'We'd run
up and down the 57 steps of the Kop at Roker Park 30 times and
I did every step with him. I drove him on, because he had to get
it out of his system, he had to be the one to realize he was
finished. Brian showed terrific guts. I was the trainer at Sheffield
Wednesday when Derek Dooley lost his leg after a playing
injury and I put Derek and Brian on a par for sheer
determination after a bad injury. I know I didn't endear myself
to Brian, he must have thought at times I was a sadist. But by
then, I looked on him as my own son and I worried how he
would cope with the mental strain.'

That strain manifested itself in erratic bursts of temper from
Clough as he lashed out in frustration at his team-mates and
coaching staff. At a time when he ought to have been nearing
his prime as a player, he was facing an empty, arid future. Even
though Clough had shrewdly saved his money and dabbled in
some newspaper work that brought in a few bob, he was hardly
set up for life. The best efforts of Jimmy Hill and the
Professional Footballers' Association in helping to abolish the
maximum wage were only beginning to make themselves felt
three years on, and many a player of that era would look on
running a pub or a newsagent's shop as the summit of his
ambitions. To Clough, that was anathema. Football was his
chosen career, he had been spectacularly good at it, and as a
married man with designs on starting a family, he had no formal
education to call on. All this after scoring 28 league goals by the
time Bury came to Roker Park that fateful Boxing Day; surely
dreams of an England recall and promotion to the First Division
were not over-fanciful?

All that adds up to some justification for the behaviour of
Clough over the next 18 months that saw his popularity with his
team-mates slump and a strong desire from the directors to get
rid of him. Len Ashurst was the Sunderland full-back whose
stray pass launched Clough on that ill-fated run at the Bury goal
and although he was sorry about the injury, he soon lost
sympathy for Clough the person. 'He's never forgiven me for

that bad pass. That moment has rebounded on me so many times whenever Clough's injury is mentioned. He was very low when he tried to recuperate. He kept away from the dressing-room because by then he knew he had no friends in there.'

Ashurst recalls attending a Round Table lunch with his team-mate Charlie Hurley soon after Clough's injury. The guest speaker was Brian Clough. He proceeded to go through the first team squad and after he had told the gathering that Len Ashurst was the man who caused his injury, Ashurst walked out in disgust. 'He was never the same person after he got injured, not that I thought too much of him before. He was always shouting, "Give me the ball, I'll stick it in," but you could just about deal with his abrasiveness, because he did score a lot of goals for us. But he manufactured his image after all those wasted months, trying to get back playing. He adopted that drawl we now know so well and started courting controversy, getting the press in his pocket. Fair play to him, he's up there with the greats as a manager, but not as a person.'

Ashurst only saw Clough twice more when they became managers. Clough bought Tony Parry from Hartlepools when he was at Derby as a favour to the club that gave him his first chance in management. When Ashurst, then the Hartlepools manager, arrived to finalize the deal with his chairman, he was told by Clough, 'You can f. . . off' and was sent down the corridor while the transfer was concluded. A few years later, Ashurst recalls a happier evening when his Sunderland side beat Forest in a League Cup replay. After the tensions in the Roker Park dressing-room 20 years earlier, it was a sweet moment for at least one of Alan Brown's former charges.

While Clough fretted in limbo more than a year after that Boxing Day collision, his morale took another dent when Alan Brown left to manage Sheffield Wednesday. It was not the warmest of farewells as the two men sized each other up. Clough felt bitter that Brown had not offered him some sort of coaching lifeline, he believed his manager's unrelenting work on his rehabilitation had been too dogmatic, too unfeeling. A job in football seemed a hopeless prospect to a 29-year-old with a shattered knee.

One day, Clough had overheard Brown doing a favour to

someone by using his status as Sunderland manager. He said fiercely, 'I just wish I could get the chance to do that.' Brown told him he would one day, but that was no consolation to someone whose self-pity was soaring out of control. Clough was unaware how much he was rated by Brown. 'I had visions of getting Brian on the coaching staff with me, but he had to get this thing of playing again out of his system. He was an honest fellow and I admired him. He knew the game and respected its traditions. I believe he would've made a top-class manager, irrespective of his injury. It would just have taken that much longer because he was still playing. He had so much personality, he would be big enough for a manager's job. The fact that he got there on his own was even more admirable, he didn't need my help to find an opening.'

Everyone needs help and luck in such situations, though – especially when your employers would like you off the payroll. That was the likely scenario for Brian Clough as 1964 came to a close, nearly two years after he collided with Chris Harker. He had forced his way back into Sunderland's first team and managed to play three games in the First Division at last – including a goal against Leeds. Yet he was limping during those matches, and his speed had gone completely. Clough was surplus to requirements, a thorn in the flesh of players and directors, when the new manager, George Hardwick decided to give him something to stop him moping around. He told him to start working with the youth team every afternoon.

Clough loved it. At last a challenge, at last something to take his mind off those wasted months running up and down those bloody steps, only to end up with a limp! He threw himself into his coaching sessions and soon he found he was bursting with innovatory ideas. He was young enough to show the kids just how things should be done on the field, his verbal fluency was overpoweringly inspirational and he convinced his young players they were better than in fact they really were. Within a few months, he had guided Sunderland into the FA Youth Cup semi-final and a delighted Hardwick made him youth team manager. Clough even sat still long enough to sit his FA coaching examination and to pass. One of those Sunderland youngsters was John O'Hare, who would play for Clough at

Derby, Leeds and Nottingham Forest over the next few years. 'When he took us over, he transformed the training. No more of those endless laps round the pitch, he got us involved in six-a-sides, in crossing and shooting – he did most of the shooting, he loved that! But he was so good at that we couldn't fail to learn from him. He was very confident with us. He knew he was good, but he wasn't arrogant about it. You could see he was so desperate to do well and he put his points over so well. He could grab our attention in a couple of seconds. He had this presence. Looking back on it, he had a hunger for management.'

Yet Clough's lack of diplomatic skills left him vulnerable at that early stage in his coaching career. Bright enough to read the minds of his young charges, imaginative enough to keep them interested, articulate enough to expound his footballing philosophies, Clough lacked the common sense to bed down in his new role, mend bridges with the club's directors and appear to don the cloak of maturity. Nothing really changed over the next few decades, did it? At 30, though, he lacked the power base and the stature of achievement to save his skin. In the summer of 1965, George Hardwick was sacked for the abject failure of steering Sunderland to a secure position in the middle of the First Division. A few days later, Clough was sacked as well.

The club pocketed a hefty sum in insurance on the player who was grievously injured wearing the famous red and white stripes – the same player who ended up with just £1,500 from his settlement. Yet another incident that shaped Clough's attitude to directors and to the cruel world of football politics. He would eventually become the leading exponent of 'get your retaliation in first' in such matters, but not even his most implacable enemy would deny that Brian Clough had been through some harsh years at Roker Park. The fact that more than 31,000 turned up for his testimonial only increased Clough's affection for the folk on Wearside, in contrast to those who ran the club.

It would be another nine years before Clough lost the feeling of financial insecurity that had racked him from 1963–65, as he wondered how his career would pan out with Sunderland. Not until Leeds paid him off handsomely for his disastrous 44 days as manager could Clough relax and look forward to prosperity in middle age, a concept very rare for men of his background from the North-East. He had learned some harsh lessons about himself and the football world at Sunderland, and countless players, directors and reporters would eventually smart under the lash of his experience.

He would always miss playing, however, always resent the years that were snatched from him. 'There's simply no substitute for playing,' he once told me. 'All the jobs you can get in football can never compensate for running on to the pitch when you feel fit and ready for it.' Sometimes the Forest players used to catch a wistful smile from their manager when the referee came in to check their studs before a match. Clough would playfully offer his trainers for inspection and say ruefully, 'If only . . .' One day, Neil Webb brought a book in for Clough to autograph alongside his picture from the early sixties as a player in his prime. The accompanying caption gave detailed information on Clough's goalscoring record and he proudly read it out to his players. It seemed that after an interval of more than 20 years, the memory of his achievements only partially obscured the pain of his early retirement. If that was one of the reasons why Clough sometimes took solace in a glass too many, it would be a curmudgeon who failed to understand the lingering emotions over a career that was snatched away from him by an accidental collision with a goalkeeper's shoulder.

By 1964, it was clear that Clough had designs on some form of coaching or even management as it began to dawn on him that he would never play again. It was probably swirling around in his fertile mind, indeterminate, yet tangible. When Alan Brown left for Sheffield Wednesday, Clough's tribute in his local newspaper column was uncannily prescient:

His approach to the game was often like that of a dictator. Not that I condemn this approach. If I am ever fortunate enough to find myself in a similar position I would like to inherit the same power. During the many hours I have sat at home and wondered about this man and his actions, I have asked myself the question, 'Does he ever find peace of mind for himself?' Not for a moment can I pretend I got to know Alan Brown in those years at Roker. In fact I wonder if anybody ever did. Alan Brown is a man who possesses powers which are almost uncanny. I can remember occasions when he made me feel so good, so elated that I would have tried to run through a brick wall if that had been his command. There were other times when I wished I had never clapped eyes on him.

Does that strike a chord anywhere? Similar sentiments ran through players' tributes to another colossus of a manager when he retired 29 years later. Brian Clough.

4

Clough and Taylor

The town of Hartlepool does not detain for long those peddlers of glowing prose who adorn the pages of the North-East's tourist brochures. You would need to be of a particularly Panglossian outlook to extol the virtues of an area dominated by ICI's Billingham plant, where the noxious fumes and desolate landscape evoke memories of the thirties' filmed adaptation of H. G. Wells's *Things to Come*. Tourists trawling for aesthetic pleasures along that coastline do not tarry at Hartlepool. Once you have pointed out that this is where Brian Clough began his managerial career, you are then casting around for other landmarks of interest.

Clough was at Hartlepools for just two years, from 1965–7, but the genesis of his unique managerial style was formed there before he reached his 33rd birthday. He recovered his self-respect, discovered he had a genuine gift for inspiring even mediocre footballers, honed his propagandist skills with the media, saw off the first of many chairmen hostile to his methods – and, above all, forged a partnership that became part of football history.

In many ways, Peter Taylor was the antithesis to Brian Clough. Taylor was six years older, a gambler with his money, where Clough was a hoarder. An average goalkeeper compared to the brilliant goalscorer. A tense, driven man, restless for new fields and challenges who sometimes had to goad Clough to shed his conservative instincts. A football man not especially bothered about playing the game for a living, compared to the young goal thief who never forgot the pain of early retirement, the loss of the joy of goalscoring. Taylor mastered the small print – the detailed contacts book and memory for particular players – while Clough's temperament was ideally suited to the expansive overview, the vainglorious gestures. Whatever the elements, the relationship worked. They would only be apart in football for two of the next 17 years and their record underlined the importance of joint management, of the art of the possible, of the need to exert mental dominance over players without inhibiting them. When Brian Clough retired, it was understandable that many tributes ended with the phrase 'There'll never be another like him' but it would be unfair to Taylor's memory not to add 'There'll never be another Clough and Taylor'. Clough's record of being the only manager to win the First Division with two provincial clubs is rightly lauded, but he would never have achieved that without the chivvying, restless assistant with the priceless ability to find good players, to separate the wheat from the chaff. Their acrimonious relationship after Taylor's retirement from Forest in 1982 cannot dim the lustre of their partnership in earlier years.

Clough recognized Taylor's contribution: 'The chemistry was absolutely brilliant. He saw things 24 hours earlier than I did regarding players, he was second to none at that. I remember once at Derby, he phoned me at 5.30 after a match and said, "Get in your car now and come and sign Archie Gemmill from Preston." You can't get more positive than that, can you? Sinatra told me once that the written word comes first, the music later and in football the one who picks the player comes first, all the bullshit comes later.' Check out that reference to Sinatra. Nice touch, Brian.

Taylor was more down to earth about his conversational partners, but he knew his worth. When we talked before his untimely death in 1990, Taylor set aside the sad rift between them which had festered since 1982 to speak with affectionate pride in their partnership: 'We just gelled together, we filled in the gaps. So much of it was off the cuff, instinctive, but we knew enough about things like tactics, having been in the game so long. Our temperaments were right for what we each had to do, we had some luck, some good signings and we disciplined the players. When I first met Brian in August 1955 he was brash and arrogant – every post had to be a winning post with him. I became a winner with him as well. It never bothered me that it was always Clough and Taylor, rather than the other way round. From day one, I accepted he'd be more famous than me and I accepted that, preferred it. My strength was buying and selecting the right material, then Brian's man-management would shape the player. He was brilliant at that. So many managers and coaches haven't a clue how to handle players, but Brian would bully one and cajole the other to get the best out of them. This game is solely about picking the right players for the right game and getting them in the right frame of mind. We used to do our homework during the week, not at 2.30 on a Saturday, when you can't really get the players giving you 100 per cent concentration. If you're wrong on a Monday, you'll be wrong on a Saturday, we used to say. The players knew what would happen if they kept getting it wrong – on your bike. I believe we were unique because in our early days together, we knew that management was a two-man job. Directors could never grasp that in the sixties, yet now everyone thinks it's natural to have an assistant.'

Until Clough and Taylor popularized the idea of joint management, there had been several managers who, by dint of ability, personality or cunning had ruled a club, without too much interference from directors. Matt Busby, Bill Shankly, Stan Cullis, Bill Nicholson, Alan Brown, to name a few. A reliable trainer/coach would fill in the gaps, but there was no doubt who was the number one. Many other clubs would expect the manager to dance to the boardroom tunes, executing a delineated policy towards transfers and playing styles. Clough and Taylor had no truck with that. They felt that if they failed, it was their responsibility. Jimmy Gordon, who had played alongside them at Middlesbrough, would prove to be a faithful, sympathetic trainer to them over the years, but they would stand or fall on their own achievements. Always conscious of the value of a pound note, they would be sidetracked sometimes by an obsession with money, at times paranoid that the other was pulling a stroke or that the directors were out-flanking them. Their years at Middlesbrough had toughened their skin, made them chillingly streetwise. Winning popularity contests in boardrooms and dressing-rooms was simply not on the agenda. Winning football matches was the priority, followed by financial security.

Peter Taylor was the only consistent friend Brian Clough had at Middlesbrough among the other players. Others treated him with wariness because of his enviable confidence and articulacy, while some resented his cockiness and his psychological hold over the manager, Bob Dennison. Taylor, Boro's goalkeeper, told Clough he could be the game's greatest goalscorer early in his first-team career and never wavered in his enthusiasm for the young man's abilities. Clough basked in Taylor's praise and soon the pair were inseparable. They spent evenings talking about football's intricacies and possibilities, coaching youngsters and dissecting Middlesbrough's players. Taylor, already married with a young family, used to josh Clough about his lack of interest in girls and he thought enough about his qualities to persuade Bob Dennison to give him a rise as he kept scoring goals. Both were warmly welcomed in the other's family home and still the talk revolved around football. To Clough, glorying in the supreme pleasure of scoring goals with such style, it was just an extension of his personality; he liked hearing Taylor praise him for his recent contributions.

Taylor was trawling deeper into the ocean. He did not share Clough's delight at playing – possibly because he knew the limits of his average ability as a goalkeeper – and he had mapped out long ago the preferred course of his football career. He had spent nine years at Coventry City under Harry Storer, a legendary martinet among managers in the days when most of them turned up for training in a suit and then wandered off for lunch in the boardroom. Storer liked hard, honest players who did what they were told and directors who kept out of his way.

He seemed to have the knack of finding brave, committed players from his scouting missions and Taylor – always interested in value for money – thought that was a particularly satisfying way to build a team. Pick them up cheaply, make them grateful to you for giving them a chance in the big time and give them hell if they foul up. Taylor took to studying the techniques and the attitude of individual players while working for Storer and gradually developed the eye for talent that proved matchless. Unlike many footballers who dread the day of retirement, Peter Taylor could not wait to start practising what the implacable Harry Storer preached.

By the time Brian Clough was clearing out his locker at Roker Park in the summer of 1965, bleakly contemplating life on the dole, Peter Taylor was already a manager at the age of 36. He had left Middlesbrough in 1960, leaving Clough even more isolated, and was an early success in the Southern League with Burton Albion. No one at that time would have forecast a great managerial career for the younger of the two, but it seemed as if Taylor was learning his trade impressively quickly. It was surely only a matter of time before the Football League clubs came knocking at Burton Albion's door. One did eventually. It was hardly a glamorous prospect. Hartlepools United had finished 15th in the Fourth Division in the 1964–65 season and its dwindling band of supporters had performed handstands of glee that, for once, the club had not needed to apply for re-election to the Football League. The burden of expectation was non-existent at the Victoria Ground and in retrospect it was the ideal place for a young maverick and an intense visionary to see what they could do.

The man oiling the clanking wheels that brought Clough and Taylor to Hartlepools United was one of England's greatest individualists as a player, Len Shackleton. Clough still laughs at the mention of 'Shack', whose impudent skills for Sunderland entranced Wearside. Occasionally Shackleton was selected to play for England; on skill and technique alone, he ought to have been an automatic choice for years but the committee which picked the team in those days was wary of a footballer who actually had a brain and a provocative turn of phrase. When Shackleton retired, he published a book that encapsulated his

cynical view of the football world and of directors in pa.
One chapter was headed 'What the Average Director Kn
About Football' and contained a single blank page. Clough
lapped up Shackleton's iconoclastic opinions and when he
became a soccer reporter for the *Sunday People* in the North-
East, he found a ready source of gossip and opinion from the
brash self-publicist at Middlesbrough. They were good together
and Shackleton also noticed the same applied to Clough and
Taylor. Bouncing ideas off the other, finishing the other's
sentences, they appeared to Shackleton to have an intuitive,
telepathic understanding. Shackleton saw them as a managerial
partnership long before Clough and Taylor and it was he, doing
the rounds of the clubs, who heard that Hartlepools was looking
for a new manager. Ernie Ord, the club's diminutive chairman,
was won over to Clough by Shackleton's persuasive tongue, who
then told Clough to appoint Taylor as his assistant. Clough
contacted Taylor, they met at an hotel in York and the older
man was persuaded that the offer of a new, three-year contract
at Burton paled in comparison to working together in the
Football League. Clough said he would not take the job without
Taylor. Somehow he persuaded Taylor to take a drop in salary
from £41 a week to £24 and to add insult to injury, Taylor would
have to be designated 'trainer' rather than assistant. Clough had
realized that even he would not be able to convince Ernie Ord
that two managers were better than one for an impoverished
club whose idea of progress was to avoid going cap in hand
every summer to the Football League to be allowed to struggle
on for another year. Manchester United managed without a
joint manager: what was so special about Hartlepools?

In an early example of his persuasive prowess, Clough
squared the circle of wooing Taylor and giving Ord the *fait
accompli* of Taylor, adding an extra burden to a meagre wage
bill. To Clough the job was a lifeline after several grim months
of wallowing in self-pity and worrying how to care for his
growing family. 'In the North-East, we have this fear of not
having a job and I couldn't do anything other than work in
football. I was absolutely thrilled and delighted to get the
Hartlepools job.'

He may have been the youngest manager in league football,

but Clough cut an unimpressive figure to Taylor when the pair met up after being apart for the last four years. 'He was overweight and had been drinking a bit after getting the sack. He was going to pot and worried about money.'

Clough needed Taylor's experience and deep knowledge of the game's highways and byways. He was reassured by Taylor's grasp of the essentials and at the treasure trove contained in his contacts book. Taylor expounded the credo of Harry Storer to him – the need to have strong defence, and to show moral courage on the field as well as physical bravery, the need to discover the psychological chinks in players' armour, spot the villains and weed them out. Alan Brown, Clough's former manager at Sunderland, recalls meeting up with Taylor and his family on holiday in Jersey at this time. Brown tried to slake his thirst for knowledge. 'I'd never met Peter before then but Harry Storer and I had been good friends for a long time, so it was absolutely natural that we'd sit and talk about the game. Peter pumped me, day after day, and I was perfectly happy, because I could see how sincere he was. At the end of the holiday, he shook my hand and said, "You've given me the A to Z of football" and I was very touched. It stuck out a mile that Peter would go places because his questions were so penetrating. And I knew all about Brian's qualities. Their success together didn't surprise me at all.'

So Taylor did most of the talking in the office in those early days, while maintaining the charade to the sceptical chairman that he was the trainer with the most magical of sponges at his disposal. Soon the partners realized that one could fill in knowledge for the other in certain areas and vice versa. Taylor would happily beaver away at the minutiae of finding good players, then convincing them that life at Hartlepools was just one remove away from the Elysian Fields, even though the wages offered would not have attracted the average foundry worker. Clough excelled at putting Ord and his fellow-directors off the scent and turning the state of the club to his public advantage.

It was at the Victoria Ground that Clough's public relations' antennae were at their sharpest. He knew enough about the media even then to be able to drum up interest in the revivalist atmosphere at Hartlepools United. It was not sufficient to tell the hacks that better times were around the corner, he knew they needed some tangible examples, some visual diversions. (In a more media-conscious age, we call them photo opportunities.)

Clough was aware that a good picture was worth several hundred words halfway down a page, tucked inside the paper. So when he conducted television interviews at the ground, he made sure he stood alongside the part of the stand's roof that was leaking and organized a bucket to catch the drips. When the tatty ground was spruced up at last with a lick of paint, the manager was there, with paint brush in hand and ready quip at the sound of a clapperboard. To save money, Clough decided he would drive the team coach, so he took his public service vehicle test. The cameras just happened to be there. He toured the working men's clubs, drumming up support for the 'Pool, rousing the punters with evangelical displays that smacked of Elmer Gantry. His breezy self-confidence, snappy one-liners and inexhaustible energy as he swept through the clubs made a heady cocktail for both media and public. He was brilliant at restoring a bloom to the cheeks of Hartlepools United and after he somehow beguiled a local brewery to sponsor the club, the supporters were marvelling at new floodlights and a stand without leaks. It was a *tour de force* in terms of column inches and items on television; no one else in football had contrived to garner so much public attention over such an unglamorous item, a Fourth Division club that managed to finish eighteenth, then eighth in the two seasons of Clough and Taylor's regime. Clough's original mind and feel for the journalistic exigencies proved invaluable and the renewed public confidence undoubtedly helped Hartlepools achieve promotion the year after Clough and Taylor left for Derby.

The Hartlepools experience was the first step towards Clough the manager getting more attention than his players. The cult of the manager that would reach its apogee a few years later with the likes of Allison, Docherty, Bond, McMenemy and Atkinson saw its origins at Hartlepools United. Clough knew he was more entertaining in person than his players and certainly the media had no qualms about dealing with someone of his verbal flair, gift of self-mockery and outrageous flights of fancy. Talk of groin strains and guessing who would be on the substitutes' bench next day was a mere bagatelle when Cloughie found a new angle for you.

The fact that he was excellent at his main job – managing football teams – was another justification for the media hanging around, waiting for him to grant an audience. Invariably it was worth the wait. Brian Moore noticed Clough's facility with the media as soon as he arrived at Hartlepools in 1965. 'I had to interview him for BBC Radio and he was terrific value for one so young. He was driven by the fear of unemployment, by self-preservation, and he put everything into those early years. He despised journalists who thought they could talk about the game but he loved football gossip, who'd fallen out with whom. He also liked to know what other managements were like in other walks of life. He's always been an amazing mixture of bombast, kindness, shyness, cheek and thoughtfulness. In those early days at Hartlepools, there was a deep conviction to do things in a strong, orderly way with Peter Taylor. They blended so well and they beat the system from deep in the Fourth Division. They changed the role of management from the most unpromising of situations.'

Although the Hartlepools public warmed to the new management team, the chairman was less than enamoured. Ernie Ord had a justified reputation for trying to reduce his managers to rubber-stamping status and he set about Clough and Taylor with his customary single-mindedness. Yet Ord had miscalculated with those two: they had been tested enough in the crucible of hard knocks before coming to Hartlepools and it would take more than him to deflect them from their aims.

The flashpoint came when Ord announced he wanted to sack Taylor; he cost too much for what he saw as a negligible return. Clough was outraged and refused to consider it. Ord told Clough he was therefore sacked as well. It was time for Clough to show his mettle. 'I said "I'm going nowhere" and stuck it out for the next 48 hours. I had a friend on the board and he organized a board meeting that got rid of Ord. It was either the chairman or me.' Taylor always stressed the importance of that first successful battle with a chairman: 'It was like winning the European Cup. Once we'd beaten Ord, we were on our way.

Brian had promised to fight him all the way after taking me away from that good contract at Burton and he was as good as his word. Whatever went on between us in later years, Brian always took my side when we argued with directors.'

The friend on the board that Clough referred to became the new chairman. John Curry had seen the quality of the couple at first hand and after rallying enough support, he managed to outmanoeuvre Ord. Yet Curry only enjoyed their managerial skills for one more year before Len Shackleton's recommendation took them to Derby County. A few years later, the Hartlepools chairman asked Clough a favour: would he buy Tony Parry to help keep Hartlepools afloat? Clough did not want the player, Parry did not want to go, but eventually the deal was done for £2,500, enough to save Hartlepools. Before Curry left the Baseball Ground, Clough told him, 'That's the last favour I do you – the slate's clean now.' Parry only played a handful of games for Derby.

Curry probably did not realize it at the time, but the boardroom coup he had engineered coloured Clough's judgement against directors. At times, Taylor would be troubled by some members of his club's board, but he tended to rub along with them, switching off mentally if any of them tried to talk football, often grateful if there was horse racing on the television as the discourse meandered on. Clough viewed directors in an altogether harsher light. His public observations on their general qualities over the years have been models of consistency: 'Directors have no idea about football. How can you ascertain if someone knows about something if the one asking the questions knows bugger-all about the subject?' Although some of his chairmen have been tolerated with grudging acceptance, tinged with a degree of respect, the overwhelming majority of directors for whom Clough has worked have been treated with disdain.

So Clough had relished his first taste of boardroom politics and Ernie Ord's scalp strengthened his natural inclination towards a rebellious attitude when directors came to call. He settled down to enjoy an Ord-free existence at the Victoria Ground, only to find Taylor getting restless. The older man felt they had gone as far as they could at Hartlepools. He wanted more money for himself – understandable, given what he had forsworn at Burton Albion – and to help him buy better players. A Nottingham man, he lacked Clough's sentimental attachment to the North-East and he had never cemented his relationship with the public in the same talismanic way as Clough, who had charmed so much money out of the locals in the pubs and clubs. Taylor felt they were ready to move upwards, to work with more skilful footballers, and to spend more of a chairman's money. Not for the first time, he saw the openings quicker than his younger partner and Taylor continued to nag away at Len Shackleton, to see if he could land them a better club. In the summer of 1967, he set up a meeting with Derby County to start a remarkable six-year period at the Baseball Ground, a leap of two divisions to a club with a great tradition of skilful football.

Soon Clough and Taylor would be joined at the Baseball Ground by another Hartlepools old boy, someone who would spend almost the next 20 years following them around. John McGovern was the prototype of the ideal Clough footballer – modest, polite, short-haired, with an awareness of his capabilities and his shortcomings. He was a one-paced player, but Clough could always find speed somewhere else in the team. He was a good, clean tackler who stood up in the tackle and did not telegraph his intentions to his opponent. An ideal, reliable man to have in midfield, doing the simple things well, not giving the ball away, establishing the solid platform to allow the more eye-catching players to display their skills.

At the age of 16, McGovern was spotted by Clough one Sunday morning in a trial match; he was frail, an ungainly mover, but he could pass the ball accurately with both feet and there was a composure about him that belied his lack of years. Clough liked him as a footballer and as a person. McGovern's father had been killed in a road accident five years earlier and his family was thrilled that such a vibrant local personality should take such an interest in their frail little lad. Eventually they reached a compromise over the boy's education and at 16, McGovern was playing in the Hartlepools first team. Brian was proud of his young charge and McGovern soon understood that loyalty with him was a two-way process. 'I had stick from the supporters of all the clubs I played for under Brian Clough. I remember a Nottingham reporter never mentioned me in 12 successive match reports when we were winning every game, but it never bothered me, because the manager thought I could play. Some suggested I was his favourite, but he never allowed himself to get too close to players. That way leads to contempt eventually and he was dead right. Clough saw things that others didn't and I'm glad he saw enough in me. I knew I could play football and that I wouldn't have survived under him if that wasn't so. I believe he was a football genius, the greatest manager ever in the English game. I think it's phenomenal that he retained the fire in his belly for so long. When I first played for him at Hartlepools he had concentration and passion coming out of his ears and that unpredictability which keeps people on their toes. He didn't seem to lose too much of that over the years, nor his grasp of the basics.'

When Clough and Taylor decided to leave Hartlepools, they had reassurance for McGovern: he would be joining them shortly at Derby County. More than a decade later, McGovern was raising the European Cup two years in a row as Forest's captain. All three men were good for one another.

5

The Dream Factory

Before Brian Clough breezed into the Baseball Ground in the summer of 1967, the supporters who recalled Derby's halcyon days were advancing towards middle age. Since the FA Cup victory in 1946, the only landmark had been winning the Third Division North Championship in 1957, hardly the kind of trophy to set the corpuscles racing. The club had coasted along dreamily for the previous five years under the benign managership of Tim Ward, but when they finished 17th in the Second Division in the 1966–67 season, Ward was sacked. He was happy to go; he had had enough of nit-picking from the directors, who moaned about Derby's reduced status without considering that a cash transfusion to buy new players might have been a good idea. Those directors would soon discover that Tim Ward's successor would prove less malleable.

Sam Longson, Derby's chairman, was putty in the hands of those two cheeky chappies, Len Shackleton and Brian Clough, when they started negotiations. Longson had remembered Clough's powers of leadership when he had seen him playing for Sunderland a few years earlier and he had watched his progress at Hartlepools with interest. This was before he caught the full blast of Clough's unstoppable sales pitch; Clough regaled the bemused chairman with the most colourful tales of the way he had revived the ailing Fourth Division club and outlined how he would make the good folk of Derby be proud of their side again. He neglected to mention that he would insist on bringing Peter Taylor with him as his assistant. For his part, Shackleton told Longson he had better move swiftly, because West Bromwich Albion were casting covetous eyes at Clough and were about to make a formal offer. Shackleton was being economical with the truth, but he rightly reasoned that the bluff old boy who made his fortune in the road haulage business would not follow up that piece of information. And Clough kept his counsel on Taylor until he could negotiate from strength – when he was offered the job. Once he knew that Longson had carried a sceptical board with him, Clough could state his demands. He won the day over Taylor and, for good measure, browbeat them into promising a substantial sum of money for new players. It was the first of many tactical coups by Clough over the Derby directors, yet they would triumph in the end, six years later.

Once Clough and Taylor knew that they had licence to bring in fresh faces, they were in their element at the Baseball Ground. Taylor, with his unrivalled network of contacts around the country, knew exactly who he wanted, while Clough concentrated on areas where he excelled – dispensing home truths, creating turbulence and readjusting attitudes. When he first met the Derby players, he told them, 'You've got three weeks to make an impression on me and if I don't rate you, you're out.' He announced that the photographs of great old players like Steve Bloomer, Raich Carter and Peter Doherty were to be taken down: from now on, the talk was of the future, not of the players who had performed with such distinction in the past. In his early team meetings, Clough noticed that the goalkeeper, Reg Matthews, was never there at the start. 'Where's Reg?' he would ask and he would not begin work until Matthews appeared. Clough knew why Matthews was usually the last to present himself. 'Reg, if you want a fag, don't go in the toilet. You've earned the right to have your fag in front of us. You've played for England. But the rest of you won't smoke in here – you don't deserve to!'

Within a few weeks, the turnover of staff at the Baseball Ground was remarkable. Of the first-team squad only Kevin Hector, Alan Durban, Ron Webster and Colin Boulton survived for any period after Hurricane Clough blew in. The groundsmen, the chief scout, the secretary and other backroom staff were summarily despatched – and a couple of tea ladies who were heard laughing and chatting gaily after a Derby home defeat. Clough expected everyone at the club to take defeats to heart, even those charged with pouring the tea afterwards to the players who had failed him. Clough had announced to the television cameras that he meant business – 'The things that are hard work to other managers aren't to me. Things like discipline, coaching and training. I've got my mind set on football and I know how to approach it. Doesn't matter whether it's Derby County or Liverpool.' No one could say they had not been warned. He was only 32 . . .

Derby's first signing was a Clough capture. John O'Hare needed no second bidding to leave Sunderland and join the man who had captivated him as a youngster a few years earlier. 'I just knew we'd be successful. Clough told me that we'd pass Sunderland on the way up and he wasn't far wrong. They were relegated in Derby's first year back in the top flight. Clough stuck me up front straight away, which suited me fine. I could've gone to other clubs, but the atmosphere at Derby was fantastic as soon as I got there. Clough and Taylor instilled this great team spirit and they cared for us. Once Clough found out that I was worried about my wife who had a lump on her breast. The next day he had her booked into a private nursing home at Ashbourne. A couple of other times he paid for my kids to have holidays in the summer when money was a bit tight.'

In the same week that O'Hare was signed, Clough and Taylor drove up to Merseyside to sign a young centre-half who played for Tranmere. Taylor had seen him a few times, could not believe that other clubs had not come in for him and told his partner that they had to move fast. It was a classic smash-and-grab routine on Roy McFarland and he eventually buckled. He was tumbled out of bed after midnight, and told by Clough,

'Take as long as you like, but we're not going anywhere till you make a decision.' When Clough made it clear he was not jesting, McFarland turned to his father for guidance. 'If they want you that badly, son, you'd better sign for them,' he was told. In a flash the forms were produced, the boy signed in a daze and Clough and Taylor were out of the door in the time it takes to say 'good night'. McFarland went to Anfield the next day, to watch his favourite team, Liverpool, wondering what he had done. He would soon discover: he won two championship medals and 28 England caps at Derby.

McFarland gives the lie to the opinion that Clough rarely bothered with coaching: 'If coaching is imparting common sense, then Cloughie was a brilliant coach. Alf Ramsey helped me a lot when I got into the England team but initially it was Cloughie who taught me how to defend. He said I was too impetuous, too easily wound-up, I chased the ball all over the field. He'd say, "Stand up! If you're a good defender, who's going to beat you? You're spending too much time on your backside. Peter tells me you've got a good brain – prove it to me!" Once he said to me, "Just occasionally, even good players have to kick the ball into the stand. When the ball bounces in your penalty area, you can't always pull the ball down and play it." He didn't rant and rave, he'd just throw things at you to make you think about your game.'

The third signing was John McGovern. So Clough would be happier about the midfield. O'Hare would hold the ball up front or flick it on to the quicksilver Hector – a player Clough had long admired when he was at Hartlepools and Hector at Bradford – and a pattern of constructive attack would be established. Alan Hinton was brought from Nottingham Forest to give the forwards a decent service from the left wing. Many thought Clough and Taylor had miscalculated, bringing in a player with little evident taste for the physical fray, but yet again the duo had spotted qualities in Hinton that were not readily obvious. They referred to Hinton's 'moral courage', his persistence in trying the imaginative pass, the cross from an unpromising angle when others would happily abdicate responsibility and roll the ball square or back. Taylor often used to ask about a player, 'Can he play the ball under pressure?' and Alan

Hinton could certainly do that. An expert on dead ball situations, a master at the swerving shot from the wing, Hinton proved as important for Derby's balance and attacking potential as John Robertson at Nottingham Forest a few years later.

Once Hinton was installed, Clough and Taylor knew they needed someone to win the ball in midfield, to ensure Hinton had a regular supply of it on the left wing. So Willie Carlin was bought from Sheffield United. Carlin, a small tough Scouser, was the identikit hungry fighter. He had played in most of English football's humbler outposts, so he was grateful for the chance to play at a higher level. He was a terrier of a player, on intimate terms with referees, and Clough soon acquainted Carlin with the realities under his new manager. Apart from occasional lapses from grace, Carlin acquitted himself with surprising restraint. More importantly, he gave Derby added steel and resilience, qualities needed to give the Hintons and the Hectors room to display their plumage. Balance was always the hallmark of the best Clough/Taylor sides.

They were still looking for that extra ingredient, however. Class, experience, know-how, leadership – all wrapped up in one player. They got it for £5,000. Within a year Dave Mackay had been named joint Footballer of the Year and his flagging career had been rejuvenated. It was a master-stroke by Clough to persevere in the chase for Mackay, who was all set to return to Hearts once he had found the pace of the English First Division rather too hectic.

Mackay had been a great wing-half in the Tottenham team that won the Double in 1960–61 and Clough remained a huge admirer of the granite Scotsman who could tackle, pass and cajole his team. In short, Mackay was a born leader, a winner, and Clough had to get him. He even subjected himself to the indignity of being kept waiting most of the day at Tottenham before getting to speak to Mackay – a rare case of the biter bit. When they negotiated, Clough agreed to Mackay's demand for £15,000 spread over his contract. It was a large amount for a man who was overweight and had his own relaxed attitude to training and fitness. He was even older than Clough. Yet Clough agreed and sold the package to his board. It was the best piece of business he ever concluded, in the opinion of Roy

McFarland, and Clough does not demur: 'David *was* Derby County, the cornerstone. A competitor at every level who lost his temper with himself and his team-mates whenever we lost. We were all impressionable young men – me included – and we stood back in awe of him. We decided to play him as sweeper and he took some persuading. He was used to covering every blade of grass but we wanted him to use his vast experience and talent to teach young McFarland a thing or two. At the time, he was definitely the best player in England, better even than Bobby Moore.'

McFarland still reveres Mackay and remembers a subtler side to Clough's man management: 'Dave was the best player I ever played with, and that includes England. A fantastic competitor, with so much skill. An absolute inspiration, he'd done so much in the game, hadn't he? Cloughie was very shrewd with Dave. He'd say, "What do you think, captain?" during team talks and he made it clear he respected him greatly. Dave was the only player I never saw get bollocked by Cloughie.'

Mackay was no ascetic, driven by a passion for hot chocolate and early nights. He was perfectly open about drinking through the week until Thursday evening, then he would dry out all Friday, sleep soundly that afternoon and be refreshed for the action by Saturday afternoon. Clough knew all about Mackay's self-indulgences, but never chided him. He was shrewd not to embarrass Mackay at training. While the others went through a series of punishing laps, Clough would shout over, 'David! I want to talk about something with you over here!' and Mackay's ageing legs and suspect stamina would be saved a stern examination. He knew how much the players respected and liked Mackay, not just for his authority on the field, but because he made them laugh with his bizarre bets: a favourite was to guess how many times he touched his brakes driving from his home in North London to the Baseball Ground! Clough even organized the first training session of the week to suit Mackay; because he still lived down south, it would be Tuesday afternoon, rather than morning. Dave Mackay must be the only player to have received such blatant preferential treatment in Brian Clough's years as a manager, but that probably reflects credit on the manager. Clough knew how to get the best out of his ageing warrior and he also realized that any iron fist treatment would lead to a rapid deterioration in their working relationship. Dave Mackay could look after himself on and off the field.

After a tricky first season – in which Clough's boast that he would finish higher in the table than the previous season rebounded on him – Derby romped to the Second Division title, playing a dashing, uninhibited brand of football. The players who remained at the Baseball Ground for a few years after that maintain that the team spirit was never better than in that 1968–69 season, because it was all so fresh. Clough has always agreed with that. 'I hadn't won anything till that. The memory is still vivid, more so than the European Cups.'

Alan Durban had seen the club transformed by Clough and Taylor and felt grateful that he had survived the bloody coup in those first few weeks. 'Clough converted me from a very mediocre midfield player to the captain of Wales. He turned us all from being part-timers to full-timers. Before, we had all found things to do in the afternoon – playing golf or snooker, selling insurance – but he then found things to occupy us. Football became the most important thing in our lives, but it was never predictable with him. If training had gone well, he'd knock it on the head after quarter of an hour, whereas other managers would just stand there, waiting for the allotted time to pass. In training, his methods were so simply expressed. He liked someone standing at the far post and another going across the front defender. John O'Hare would be told to hold the ball. I think Nigel Clough is an exact replica of O'Hare; with both players, Cloughie liked them to hold the ball long enough for the quicker guys to run on past them. All the while O'Hare, or Nigel, would have his back to the goal, then turn for the flick or killer through ball. The methods haven't really changed. But what he said was so good; he made me much more responsible for my area of the field, stopped me exposing my right-back as I ran all over the pitch, looking for glory. He drummed basic principles into us. He knew how far out of our penalty area he wanted us to defend, to head it as far out of our box as we could. Then get the ball down and play it.'

Clough had one major advantage over other managers in

training sessions, apart from his air of command and clarity of expression. He was still young enough to take part with the players and by common consent, he was the best finisher at the club in those early years. He would change in the same dressing-room as the players, enjoy the banter and he would score the best goals in the six-a-sides. Roy McFarland considers Clough to be the best volleyer of a ball he has seen at close quarters. 'He would make Alan Hinton smash the ball over low and hard and if they came over too slowly, he'd kick the ball away in disgust. He had solid legs, a short backlift and a terrific shot on him. I could understand why retiring early had left such a scar if he could finish like that.'

Clough's memory for incidents amazed the Derby players. In a training session, he would blow the whistle, stop the game and single out a player to tell him he had made a similar mistake a fortnight earlier in a match. 'Do you want to get better?' he would enquire, then re-start the session. If he was displeased with a result or a performance, the players would be hauled in for extra training on Sunday mornings. When Derby lost at home to Middlesbrough early in Clough's reign, he was furious and the players were made to run ten laps of the Baseball Ground the following morning. Clough stood in the centre circle, watching them sweat and curse as they eased aching limbs around the track and when the ordeal was over said simply, 'Thank you, gentlemen, see you at training tomorrow morning.' He had not mentioned the Middlesbrough performance at all but the players got the message.

Tactical talks from Clough and Taylor consisted of an amalgam of the iron fist, the velvet glove and the yawn of indifference if someone ever mentioned the opposition. Before a match against Wolves, Alan Durban was taken to one side by Clough and told: 'If Bailey finds Wagstaffe with one pass, you'll be sitting alongside me,' which ensured Durban worked hard in midfield trying to cut off Wolves' supply to their dangerous winger, David Wagstaffe.

In the fifth round FA Cup replay in 1973 against Tottenham, Durban was again put on his mettle by Clough's asperity. 'I was substitute and at half-time we were two down and Terry Hennessey was complaining about his dodgy knee. He said he couldn't go out in the second half and Clough told him, "You've got to, we've only got Ally as sub." That really did me, I was raging. I went on and played the best hour and a bit ever for Derby and we won 5–3 in extra time. At the age of 32, I could still get wound up by Clough.'

During Derby's European Cup run in the 1972–73 season, Peter Taylor had been to look at their next opponents, Benfica. Clough had suggested to Taylor that he should run through the opposition players, an unusual ploy, and after a few inconsequential remarks, Taylor screwed up his notes and said, 'There's nothing to worry about with that lot.' The Derby players later wondered if it had all been premeditated, but they had great faith in the ability of Clough and Taylor to find the right mode of preparation. Taylor was right about Benfica; they were hammered 3–0 on a vintage European night at the Baseball Ground when the cockpit atmosphere and the cauldron of noise overwhelmed the Portuguese. A spot of sharp practice from Clough also helped undermine them. He told his groundsman to water the pitch heavily before the game. 'They were very talented individually and I didn't want our home fans to see much of that ability. They were what I call Fancy Dans, who like to knock the ball around without any pressure but don't like away games too much, especially on a cold evening on a tight little pitch at the Baseball Ground. I wanted them to get bogged down in the heavy conditions. They were, and we pissed all over them.'

Final instructions before the game were always succinct and uncluttered. The game starts at 3 o'clock, not five past. The first thing you do in the game – a tackle, a shot, a pass – has to be done with 100 per cent efficiency. No dissent to the referees, it leads to wasteful bookings and robs you of your concentration if you stand there yapping when the free-kick is taken quickly behind your back. If the pitch is heavy be careful with your passing. Get the ball out to Hinton on the left wing and hold the midfield on the right side. Two wingers raiding at the same time leaves you vulnerable in midfield. All the time the opposition was scorned – 'We've seen them, they're not as good as you are, now go and prove it.' At half-time, discussion centred around what was to *come*, rather than a post-mortem of mistakes in the first half. If Derby lost, Clough did not berate his players in the dressing-room, as Alan Durban recalls: 'He was very good at either disappearing or picking us up. He wasn't one to wallow in self-pity and besides, he knew there was no point in slaughtering us because he would need us three days later to play for him and still have respect for him. I loved to watch him when we'd won and won well. He'd stand there in front of the mirror, getting his tie straight, checking himself out, squaring back his shoulders – and he'd walk out that door so proud, ready to brag about his boys to the press or tell some director he'd been vindicated again.'

A perfect example of the Clough/Taylor chemistry lay in the signing of Archie Gemmill. Taylor had checked out the little terrier at Preston and then Clough joined in the negotiations for his signature. Unfortunately, Gemmill's wife was impervious to the Clough charms that had gulled other parents and wives of players. She had seen Clough on television several times, going through his familiar hyperbolic routine, and was not enamoured with the prospect of her Archie having to cope with such turbulence. Archie played for time, telling Clough he would sleep on the offer, but he reckoned without the man's resourcefulness. Clough said he would sleep in the spare room – no invitation had been offered – and he proceeded to wash the dishes while the bed was made up. In the end, Gemmill's resistance was beaten down and he signed. In all Clough signed him three times – twice as player and then for his coaching staff at Nottingham Forest. With a neat sense of destiny, Gemmill's son, Scot was a first-team player in the last few years' reign of the manager who had signed his father from Preston.

Clough and Gemmill Senior would have some tempestuous times over the next 20 years. Gemmill resented being kept out of bed late in the team hotels when Clough demanded an audience for some anecdotal ramblings, and he could be thoroughly peeved when Clough tried to force a drink on him. Gemmill did not care for drink, especially on the eve of a match where he was expected to give everything for his hard taskmaster. Yet players like Gemmill kept coming back to Clough, aware that he could still coax good performances out of flagging limbs. Clough enjoyed baiting Gemmill over the years, capitalizing on Gemmill's rather intense attitude to his career, but he respected the little man. 'Archie was an absolutely brilliant player for me. One of the few players as nasty off the field as on it! Seriously, I dropped a clanger when I sold him a year too early at Forest. He would've been ideal at guiding some of the new players that were coming in. I thought his legs had gone but he proved me wrong.'

If Taylor saw the potential in Gemmill, it was the simple coaching skills of Clough that refined the player, made him such a valuable replacement for Willie Carlin. Alan Durban saw the transformation in Gemmill at first-hand. 'Peter saw the empty space to fit the chair into the room, but it was Brian who made him the player he was. When he first came to us, Archie was awful to play with – he'd run around like a headless chicken, leave you short with the pass and we didn't know where we stood with him. Clough told him simply, "Give it to Hinton and run past him." Now Archie loved that. It was difficult to run with the ball on that heavy pitch at Derby, but Archie could run forever to get the ball. His passing also improved and soon he was crossing some terrific balls.'

By the 1971–72 season, Clough and Taylor had assembled a fine side. Colin Todd had been bought from Sunderland a year earlier for £175,000 and the princely defender looked worth every penny, even though Sam Longson would like to have been informed of the deal before receiving a telegram from his manager while on holiday. It read: 'Signed you another good player. Todd. Running short of cash. Brian'. Another rebuff to the chairman's pride that was added to a catalogue of rancour which would be strewn all over the boardroom floor in the autumn of 1973.

Anyway, in 1972 Derby won the championship, with the considerable assistance of Colin Todd. The talent was there in the team, but the title would not have been won without unspectacular virtues like morale, teamwork and sheer stickability. When Derby lost a gruelling FA Cup replay to Arsenal, some pundits believed they would fade away for the rest of the season, leaving the title surge to Liverpool and the favourites, Leeds, who were involved in one of their perennial tilts at the league and cup double. Yet the mood of the Derby team in the

Highbury dressing-room after that defeat was an enormous
credit to the spirit instilled into the players by Clough and
Taylor.

John McGovern's back pass that stuck in the mud, allowing
Ray Kennedy to stride on and score the only goal, was a cruel
way to go out, yet amid the gloom, a positive note was struck by
the team's oldest player, Alan Durban. 'Never mind lads, that's
the cup out of the way,' he said. 'We'll go on and win the league
now.' From another player, that might have been dismissed as
windy rhetoric but Durban was an intelligent, resilient individual,
with his own designs on a management career. His confidence
transmitted itself to his team-mates and Derby only lost two
games out of the next eleven on their way to the title. They also
beat Leeds and Liverpool in that period, and, without the large
squad of players at the disposal of Bill Shankly and Don Revie,
it was a wonderful achievement, even if the title was won by a
meagre 58 points. On 1 May, Derby's last match, Liverpool
were beaten 1–0, and the goal came from the regular butt of the
crowd and perpetrator of that faulty back pass at Highbury,
John McGovern. Once more, the ugly duckling with the
distinctive waddling gait had vindicated his management's faith.
Even more remarkably, the Derby right-back making only his
second appearance that night was just 16 years and 9 months old
– Steve Powell. Clough and Taylor were never afraid to rely on
youth in testing circumstances, as the 18-year-old Gary Mills
would discover when he played in the 1980 European Cup Final
for Forest.

Although it had been an excellent win over Liverpool,
Derby's fans did not really expect it to lead to the title. If
Liverpool won at Arsenal or Leeds drew at Wolverhampton,
then the title would go to Shankly or Revie. With the prospect
of the Double looming for Leeds, the odds favoured Revie.
When Leeds won the FA Cup, it looked a formality. Wolves at
Molineux on the Monday night, with only one team totally
motivated. Yet Leeds lost 2–1 on a night forever shrouded in
allegations of bribes offered to the Wolves players. Arsenal held
Liverpool to a goalless draw at Highbury, so Derby won the
championship by a single point.

Glasses were raised among the Derby faithful in the East

Midlands, the Scilly Isles and Majorca. Clough had taken his family and parents to the Scillies for a holiday and when the news was phoned through to him, he bought champagne for the other guests in the dining-room. It was a sweet moment for Clough to have his parents with him at the time of his first great triumph. Sadly, he was to lose them both within the space of three years, but at least they had seen him take a giant step up the ladder to managerial greatness before they passed away.

The celebrations were rather more raucous in an hotel in Calla Millor than in the Scillies. The Derby players had flown out there with Peter Taylor a few days earlier, after beating Liverpool, and when they saw the odds of 8/1 against a Derby title on that Monday morning, a few bets were struck. Taylor had kept saying over the previous few days, 'We'll win it, don't worry – we deserve it,' and he had the great pleasure of breaking the news to the players as he listened to live commentary from Molineux over the phone. Cue alcoholic haze, interrupted by a phalanx of reporters and cameramen the next day.

The news was also marked in rather more muted fashion with a cup of tea in a London hotel by two of Derby's key players. Roy McFarland and Colin Todd had to report for England duty on that Monday evening and after listening to the Molineux game with their wives on the radio, the two drove to London. Tea and biscuits in McFarland's room just before midnight represented the sum total of their celebrations. They would enjoy a rather more animated evening three years later when Derby won the championship again.

As the champagne corks bounced off the ceiling in Calla Millor, Taylor shouted, 'You're in the record books, lads, no one can take it away from you – no hard luck stories!' and on a factual basis, it is hard to argue with that. Yet Alan Durban feels Leeds lost the title through their own fault. 'Don Revie kept them in their hotel on the Saturday night after they'd won the FA Cup. He should've let them have a drink, let their hair down and relax. They were good pros, those guys, and with the Wolves game on the Monday night, they wouldn't have abused their privilege. Revie tried to keep them psychologically screwed up for two major games for too long. Clough and Taylor would never have done that, they'd have had us round the table, swapping stories over a few beers or letting us see our wives or girlfriends. They were always spot-on at distracting us and then switching the light on when they thought we were ready. That was the great thing with those two – there was never any real tension coming back to us. They'd leap on someone occasionally just to remind us who was in charge, but there were very few rucks. They got us all together, as team-mates and friends. Cloughie saw us as his extended family.'

Interestingly, Durban felt Derby had played better in the 1969–70 season than the year they won their first title, and certainly they gave some thrilling, vibrant displays in that first season after promotion. In front of a packed Baseball Ground, with spectators almost able to reach out and touch the players on the wings, Liverpool were beaten 4–0, Tottenham 5–0 and Manchester United 2–0. Derby finished up going twelve games without defeat and fourth place in the table was due reward for a series of invigorating performances.

It was typical of Peter Taylor that he brought his partner down to earth quickly by mentioning the European Cup as the next target. Taylor was not one for resting on his laurels and he persuaded Clough to fork out a new British record fee of £225,000 for David Nish. Taylor thought a full-back with Nish's constructive qualities would be essential for games in Europe, against class sides who would not let you see the ball for minutes on end if you gave it away with a poor pass. John Robson, the full-back who played in all but one of the championship-winning games, was sold summarily to Aston Villa to make way for Nish in a typical example of Clough and Taylor's ruthlessness when they were at their peak. Taylor was right to try to broaden Derby's horizons and the achievement of getting to the European Cup semi-finals at the first attempt is often overlooked when the Clough and Taylor years are scrutinized.

The circumstances surrounding Juventus' 3–1 win on aggregate in the semi-final have long carried the whiff of corruption and Clough to this day refers to the *Sunday Times* investigation, which revealed that the referee for the second leg had been approached with a bribe. An investigation by UEFA swept the allegations aside, but there is no doubt that Derby were ill-served by the referee in the first leg in Turin. Gemmill and McFarland were booked for the most innocuous of offences early on, which automatically ruled them out of the second leg (because they had been booked earlier in the campaign) and it appeared that Helmut Haller, the Juventus substitute was on intimate conversational terms with the referee. He had been into the referee's room twice before the kick-off and at half-time, Haller again chatted with the official as they walked off the pitch.

All this was too much for Clough and after the game, he launched into a tirade to the Italian press that was a masterpiece of jingoistic vitriol. One of his few printable comments was: 'I don't talk to cheating bastards!' supplemented by some observations on the performance of the Italians in the last war. Observing the reaction of the Italian press while Clough's comments were translated back to them was one of the more hilarious vignettes for dedicated Clough-observers among the English media. After the return leg, when Derby were held to a goalless draw, the entertainment resumed in the press conference. 'You tell those fucking cheating Italian bastards . . .' was translated for the Italians along the lines of 'Mr Clough is not too happy', a state of affairs that was obvious as the bile cascaded from the most provocative mouth in football.

Clough's lack of diplomatic finesse at such times no doubt counted against him when the men in suits at Lancaster Gate ruled him out of the England manager's job four years later, but it was hard not to sympathize with a manager who deplored cynicism and sharp practice from any set of players. The very idea of Clough fraternizing with a referee before a match in order to curry favour was totally wide of the mark to anyone familiar with his genuine principles on that matter.

Whatever the murky waters swirling around that Juventus semi-final, Clough and Taylor had shown their adaptability to the European games, and their continuing knack of inspiring their players for the big matches. Those European nights at the Baseball Ground crackled with passion and electricity. The great Eusébio and his Benfica team were simply swept aside, going 3–0 down before half-time. Derby's away form in the ties was also impressive, with a disciplined defence and a positive outlook that did not spurn the breakaway goal. The same tactics that served Nottingham Forest so well on subsequent European campaigns. The Derby players I have spoken to who played in that Juventus game at the Baseball Ground are convinced that if Alan Hinton had not missed a penalty in the second half, and Roger Davies had not been sent off for retaliation, then the Italians would have been swept aside in that bearpit atmosphere. Certainly, Juventus were distinctly groggy at the time of the penalty award, but Clough and Taylor were never the type to bemoan missed opportunities and rail against the fates. Soon they would be facing a more durable foe than an inconsistent referee. Sam Longson.

6

Revolting Times at Derby

The handful of Tottenham supporters who brightened up many a dull newsday in the summer of '93 with their diatribes against Alan Sugar outside the High Court probably feel they were present at a unique struggle for the heart of a club. The 'I Was There' T-shirts only needed Terry Venables' signature to convince them it was an historic struggle watched from a distance by a captivated nation. Wrong. Brian Clough versus Sam Longson, with added vocals from the Derby Players' Choir – now *that* was a battle in October 1973. It had all the necessary ingredients for melodrama. A bitter chairman, a manager out of control, his players ready to follow him into oblivion if necessary, press conferences from either camp being held within a few yards of each other, the wives of the players taking to the streets in protest, the replacement manager faced with having no team, the streets beside the Baseball Ground choked with protesters. All conducted in the glare of television arc lights and in the presence of reporters glad they had brought along a spare notebook. Plus a surprising twist in the tail as the sharp, streetwise manager finds his bluff called by the stolid old patriarch. Within a fortnight, Brian Clough had swapped the manager's chair at the third team in Division One for one at a middling Third Division club on the south coast. The biggest own goal of Clough's career, and he had taken deliberate aim, it was not a fluke deflection.

The seeds of the bitter departure of Clough and Taylor had been sown over a number of years. At the heart of it was the deteriorating relationship between Clough and his chairman, Sam Longson, but other ingredients involved Clough's concern at the way the club was run, his burgeoning love affair with the media, his conviction that he had become semi-detached from the restraints of responsibility and the resentment lurking in the breast of other directors, to whom Clough was an insolent upstart. Not for the first time, Taylor saw the warning signals earlier than his headstrong partner. David Pleat, Taylor's close friend, rang him one day in 1973, bemoaning his fate in his new job as Nuneaton Borough's manager, only to be told, 'At least you've still got a job – Brian and me could be out of here within a week.' What chance of any managerial security if the pair who had taken Derby to the championship, then the semi-finals of the European Cup, were vulnerable? Yet in Lisbon, before the second leg of the Benfica game that season, Jack Kirkland, one of the Derby directors, had confided to journalists that he would be out to 'bury Clough'. Taylor knew he and Clough were walking on eggshells. He had confided in some of the players that 'The way things are going, we've got to keep winning games, otherwise that lot in the boardroom will slaughter us.'

Resentment had been simmering on and off since Clough and Taylor had arrived. After their first season, Longson had confided to his diary that he had to defend Clough, in particular from his fellow directors. They thought there was rather too much bravado and not enough that was tangible. The role of Taylor was also questioned, which infuriated Clough, who had fought to bring his friend to Derby and knew his value could not be appreciated by those living in the cloistered world of the boardroom, who only saw the team on match days. Clough's cavalier attitude towards signing players irked Longson, particularly when he was railroaded into buying Colin Todd. Taylor had to defend paying out £100,000 for Terry Hennessey and £14,000 for a non-league centre-forward, Roger Davies. One would have thought that a prospector of talent in Taylor's class would not need to justify his eye for a bargain but the steady dripping away at the stone seemed to be aimed at Clough in particular. He had over-reached himself when he paraded Ian Storey-Moore in front of the home fans in the autumn of 1972, announcing that the winger had been signed from Forest for £200,000. Storey-Moore was bewildered by the speed of the initial transaction, but soon discovered a darker side to Clough. 'I wanted to join Derby, but Forest insisted the administrative details had yet to be ironed out and Clough then got very nasty. He wanted to ride rough-shod over everybody and started taking it out on me. When it started to fall through, he threw the contract at me and shouted, "This is all you're fucking getting." I was holed up in a hotel for the best part of four days through no fault of my own.'

For once, Clough was beaten to the punch by Manchester United and Storey-Moore went to Old Trafford. Egg on the face time at the Baseball Ground after the player had been introduced to the fans, stoking further the fires of their European Cup dream.

There had been other disputes in the previous few months that all added to the momentum of the eventual breakdown in the manager/chairman relationship. A month before the title was won, Clough and Taylor resigned, saying they were going to join Coventry City. They left the door slightly ajar, though, and indicated they would stay for more money. The Derby board agreed, then discovered that Coventry, fed up with being stalled, had called off their part of the deal. So Clough and Taylor had got more money out of them while staying put! The board kept its collective powder dry for a month longer. Then Clough was told he could not take his wife and children on the pre-season tour of Holland and West Germany. Family life had always been of paramount importance to Clough – he used to ensure he was off work to be with his children at half-term time – and so he flatly refused to go on the tour. When the directors told him there would be little money available in the future for players, he began to discern some hostile straws in the wind.

Clough's unstoppable enthusiasm had created a whirlwind of activity and business at the Baseball Ground in the early years, and he was dismayed that the club lacked the administrative structure to cope with it. In 1970 an audit revealed various financial irregularities and Derby County was fined £10,000 for gross administrative negligence. Cruelly, they were also banned from European competition for a year – this after finishing fourth in the league, and qualifying for the Fairs Cup. That hardened Clough's resolve against those running the club. After the collapse of the Ian Storey-Moore transfer two years later, he sent a four-page protest letter to the Football League's secretary, Alan Hardaker, a martinet of Homeric proportions and not a man to take kindly to a blast from Clough. Sam Longson felt he had to apologize for his manager's intemperate outburst and he was hardly mollified when Derby were fined £5,000 for a breach of transfer regulations over the imbroglio.

So Clough/Longson was a derailment just waiting to happen. Most of the components would be thrashed out in circumstances which suited Clough far more than Longson. The chairman was totally unsuited to the public relations responsibilities inherent in reining in the garrulous darling of the media.

Longson, a blunt Derbyshire man, had made his pile in business with an iron fist and nary a sign of any velvet glove. Yet in common with many who earn vast sums of money from hard-nosed, unsentimental methods, such acumen seems to fly out of the window when they occupy the chairman's seat at a football club. The impression that it constitutes a hobby, a rich man's plaything, persists and Longson was perfectly happy to do Clough's bidding in the early days.

Soon Longson realized that he might be able to use his new-found prestige to become one of the game's power brokers, one of the movers and shakers that are seen regularly in the Royal Box on Cup Final Day, and on England trips abroad. He fancied a seat on the League Management Committee, breaking bread with the likes of Sir Matt Busby; to accomplish that, he had to keep Derby's collective nose clean and to be seen to stamp on his volatile, uppity manager. The signs were not good as the months slipped by in 1973: Longson was sure that some directors of other clubs were ignoring him because of Brian

Clough, while others would sidle up and ask what he was doing to still his manager's assiduous tongue.

There was nothing Sam Longson could have done. Brian Clough was now on automatic pilot, railing at all sorts of sacred cows in devastatingly entertaining fashion. For every person sick of the sight and sound of Clough, there were another 20 who could not get enough of him. That included all of us in the media. Any journalist who worked on Clough's patch at Derby in the early seventies will confirm it was the most exhilarating of times. As soon as he arrived at the Baseball Ground, he had revealed news management techniques that were beyond any other manager. 'Hey, young man!' he greeted the football writer of the *Derby Evening Telegraph*. 'What are your edition times?'

Journalists who came calling early on soon realized they had stumbled on someone out of the ordinary. John Sadler, the man in the North for the *Sun*, was one of the first, and it turned out to be the start of a fruitful friendship and association that has endured. 'Cloughie used to say, "If a reporter takes the trouble to get off his arse to come and see me, then I'll work with him." He was as good as his word. He had a great turn of phrase, a wonderful use of simile. Ten minutes with Cloughie and you'd have enough for a week. He was totally open about his massive ego. He wore it on both lapels, not his sleeve, but I found that amusing and at least honest.' Sadler admits that Clough influenced the way he has continued to view footballers and teams, and there is more than a hint of Clough in the polemical pieces Sadler still writes for the *Sun*. Toning down Clough's worst excesses was always a worry for Sadler, as the comments became more and more strident.

Ken Lawrence shared the same problem. He wrote Clough's column for the *Sunday Express* during the Derby days – typically Clough insisted on dealing directly with the sports editor, rather than any of his perfectly competent writers. The partnership yielded a series of hugely entertaining rants at various targets. 'I had to water it down at times,' admits Lawrence, 'because Brian felt very strongly about cheats in the game. His standards of discipline among players haven't changed. He would've been a good journalist himself – "Take this down, young man," he'd say. He always had a line for you, often about Don Revie or Alf Ramsey's latest selection. Cloughie was a remarkable man to work with, I learned so much from him. He was so clear in his thinking in those days. I never knew anybody with a bigger ego, but you could warm to him because he was generous and loyal if he liked you. He was always on the point of resigning, always scuttling off to Scarborough to think about his future. He held directors in total contempt.'

In later years, Clough would never be seen at a post-match press conference at Nottingham Forest but his sightings in the Derby press room were regular and relishable. He would stand there, flicking through the Green 'Un, rubbishing the quality of the Derby match report, sipping a beer, offering gems off the top of his head – 'That Corrigan didn't have much of a game, did he? Like a journalist without a pencil he was!' He gave generously of his time, and again the following lunchtime, when he would hold court at the Kedleston Hall Hotel. He was informative, witty, stimulating and free with his hospitality. He could not resist the banter with the media, even on Sundays. No wonder Barbara mapped out a no-go area when her husband arrived at Nottingham Forest a year or two later. At Derby, a few journalists actually had his home phone number! That was one area that was understandably sealed off in time.

Just a random glance at the press cuttings for the autumn of 1972 confirms what amazing value Clough gave the media. One day he was suggesting that the FA Cup should be suspended for a year to give England the best possible chance in the World Cup, the next he was hinting at making a move for George Best. Then Clough revealed he would soon be leaving football and getting a job outside the game, to spend more time with his family. A week later, he graciously offered to swap jobs with Sir Alf Ramsey! Then, after failing to convince Sam Longson that he ought to be allowed time off to follow the England cricket tour of the West Indies, Clough announced he would like to be the supreme dictator of English football. Part of his remit would be to halt league football in March to give the national side three months' preparation for the World Cup Finals. As Derby advanced on the later stages of the European Cup he announced the players would only get £100 each if they actually won the trophy! Then, in August 1973, he came out with an astonishing attack in the *Sunday Express* on Leeds United. The Football Association had just fined Leeds £3,000 for bad behaviour on the pitch and suspended the fine for a year. Clough, who had been infuriated over the years by the Leeds approach to football, said they should have been demoted into the Second Division and their manager, Don Revie fined. 'The men who run soccer have missed the most marvellous chance of cleaning up the game in one swoop.' Today's football journalists having to beat up spurious stories about whether Ian Wright *did* give the 'V' sign to a section of the crowd would gladly give up a month's expenses for the kind of stories that Clough poured out, accompanied by some gloriously trenchant invective. John Sadler and Ken Lawrence performed splendidly in those years by not only giving us vintage Clough, but ensuring his essential character shone through all the vituperation.

Sam Longson did not necessarily share the enthusiasm of the media and the public for Clough's outbursts. The old boy saw his chances of puffing cigars throughout the corridors of power fading fast. When television made Clough an even bigger star, smelling salts became a constant presence in the Longson pockets. In the summer of 1973, Jimmy Hill left London Weekend Television to present the BBC's football coverage and LWT offered the job to Clough. He was tempted and eventually agreed to work for them on a part-time basis. This invariably meant frantic dashes down the M1 on Thursday or Friday afternoon, back up the motorway for Saturday's match, then every Sunday in the TV studios in London. Not only was the patience of the admirable Barbara Clough stretched, but the relentless flow of characteristic comments from her husband angered his chairman. Brian Moore, who worked alongside Clough in the studio at that time, has fonder memories: 'He was at his extravagant best then and he knew how good he was. I'll never be able to thank him enough for filling in for us when Jimmy Hill left and he was tremendous value. I just don't know where he found the time to do it all and the Derby directors wanted to know that as well. There's no doubt that Brian took his eye off the ball around that time – which was managing Derby – but we weren't complaining. Nor our viewers!'

Sam Longson did, though, and at last he saw a means of curbing Clough. He presented him with an ultimatum. Clough's appearances on television had to be curtailed and allowed only with board approval. His newspaper articles had to be vetted by the directors before being published. Clough and Taylor said they would resign if Longson insisted. At a board meeting on 15 October, their resignations were accepted by a majority. Clough and Taylor were out. All the petty quibbles and major sores from either side had merged into a boil that could not be lanced.

For Taylor, the last straw had come the previous Saturday at Old Trafford. Derby had just beaten Manchester United 1–0 to go third in the table when Jack Kirkland had pointed a finger at Taylor across a desk and said, 'You – I want to see you on Monday morning.' Kirkland had not been a director for very long, but clearly saw himself in the role of dispenser of home truths to Clough and Taylor. He could not understand the role of Taylor, nor why he was being paid so much, and had set out to make life difficult for him. Taylor stormed out of the Old Trafford lounge, saying no one had crooked a finger at him since schooldays, and sought the support of Clough. That was readily forthcoming and they were spoiling for a showdown with Kirkland as much as Longson.

Till his dying day, Sam Longson maintained that he had called the bluff of Brian Clough, that Clough was simply testing the waters to see how far he could go. Certainly Clough did not want to leave Derby County and regretted resigning. 'I should've made them sack me. I'd signed a five-year contract only a year earlier but walking out meant I got nowt.' Clough was soon at work, though, trying to engineer a counter-revolution with the assistance of his friend, Mike Keeling, who resigned from the Derby board at the same time as Clough and Taylor left. Two days later, amid remarkable scenes, Clough arrived at the Baseball Ground for the match against Leicester. With a borrowed ticket, he took up his position a few seats away from the directors' box and acknowledged the acclaim of the crowd. A few yards away, his former chairman, aware of being upstaged, attempted something similar and although some gave him a sympathetic hand, it was obvious who was the hero. Thus buoyed up by the public support, Clough slipped away to appear on the Michael Parkinson show and plan his next move.

Clough felt the players would be his trump card – and he was understandably optimistic. A Protest Movement had been hastily formed and marches, banner-waving and unsubtle threats from some of the more headstrong supporters heightened the explosive atmosphere. The players had decided to remain aloof from the protests until after the match against Leicester which Clough had briefly attended, but a few days later Roy McFarland handed the directors a statement on behalf of all the Derby players. They wanted Clough and Taylor to be reinstated. Clough had met the players at an emotional reunion at his local, the Kedleston Hall Hotel, and the statement came out of that meeting. He wanted to come back, with the hint of an olive branch of compromise.

Unknown to the players, the board had already decided on a replacement manager. Dave Mackay, the man who had done so much to inspire Derby County a few years earlier, had been recruited from Nottingham Forest. Clough's best signing was now to fill his chair at the Baseball Ground. When the players heard about the appointment on the grapevine they decided to go to the Baseball Ground in an effort to change the directors' minds. Further pantomime conducted in the glare of the television cameras. As the police were forced to disperse a highly excitable crowd of protesters, the players refused to leave until they had seen the directors. It was called the Siege of Derby in the papers next day, but Roy McFarland takes a rather more downbeat view of the animated proceedings: 'All we wanted to do was see Sam Longson and plead with him to take Brian and Peter back. Why throw away all that good work? We were worried about our careers – we were losing the best in the business. It's true we were close to them, but there was never any doubt who was the boss. But Brian especially wanted to come back and he was pleased we were so much involved. When we got to the ground, the only officials left were one of the directors, Jack Kirkland, and the secretary, Stuart Webb, but they wouldn't come out to see our deputation. All we wanted was a constructive discussion. But the door to the boardroom was locked and we had to leave. There was a confrontation between Kirkland and a couple of our players afterwards and it all got out of hand but I think we were 100 per cent right to make our views known. We were shocked and hurt and Kirkland didn't understand that.'

McFarland and his team-mates then adjourned to Archie Gemmill's house and the captain tried one last gambler's throw to restore Brian Clough. He rang Dave Mackay at the City Ground, Nottingham, and asked him to reconsider his decision. Mackay declined and vowed to take the Derby job the next day.

Still the dispute rumbled on. The players threatened not to play for Dave Mackay, their wives got involved in the Protest Movement, taking the stage at one meeting to rapturous acclaim, and amid all the mayhem, Clough announced he was going to Brighton as their manager. If the Derby board thought that would be the end of the matter, they were mistaken. Clough still hankered after a return to the Baseball Ground, still nurtured hopes that Mike Keeling would engineer a boardroom coup, still kept the lines of communication open with his former players. Easy when you are still living in Derby and show no signs of looking for a house in the Brighton area.

At about this time, Brian Moore stayed with Clough and was struck by his lack of spark. 'He was like a little boy lost. The offer of full-time work from LWT was still on the table and he was agonizing over that. "What shall I do?" he kept asking me and I went so far as to look at houses in the Surrey stockbroker belt for him. But I knew that at heart he didn't want to leave Derby, or his team.'

Five weeks after the resignation of Clough and Taylor, the new Derby manager was still facing enormous problems. The Protest Movement had been given renewed life by the involvement of the players' wives and then their husbands decided they would rebel against Mackay. They decided they would not report to the Baseball Ground until one o'clock before the home game against Leeds, because of their desire to see Clough and Taylor reinstated. Mackay called their bluff as successfully as his chairman had called Clough's a few weeks earlier. He told them he would play the reserves against Leeds if necessary, and Cliff Lloyd on behalf of the Professional Footballers' Association told them they would be in breach of contract if they carried out their threat. Eventually the rebellion fizzled out and Dave Mackay got on with the task of managing an extremely talented group of players.

Mackay has never been given the credit he deserved for his work as Derby's manager, a view with which Brian Clough heartily concurs. In Mackay's three seasons in charge, they finished third, first and fourth in the table and a series of clever signings (Charlie George, Francis Lee, Bruce Rioch) built on the tradition of flowing football established by Clough and Taylor.

McFarland, back at Derby as assistant manager, admits he was wrong to ring Mackay and ask him to refuse the manager's job and he agrees the wives ought to have kept out of the dispute. He has heard the rumour that at one stage, a plane was standing by at East Midland Airport to take the players to Spain, thereby avoiding Derby's next league game, but he doubts that such a scheme was ever feasible or sensible. 'Brian was pulling the strings in the background, but why not? We were his lads and he never wanted to go. Going on strike was never going to solve anything, but the directors had left us totally in the dark. Why wouldn't they speak to a deputation of players? Had they seen us early, all the hysteria might never have happened. Peter Taylor was right when he said, "There's no going back, let's get on with our lives", but the rest of us were very agitated.'

Clough admits he was wrong to resign, that he should have hung on, or wait to be sacked and then pocketed handsome compensation. He felt frustrated that the excellent squad of players gathered by himself and Taylor brought success to another manager, even to someone he admired as much as Dave Mackay. He believes the crux of the issue was the personality change undergone by Sam Longson. 'He wanted me to project Derby County in those early days. He used to push me down the motorway to go on television. But once he'd done a bit of rubbing shoulders with the big-nobs he decided he wanted a vegetable in the manager's office. Just like all directors, they change the rules when it suits them. For a few years we got on like a house on fire and I was like a son to him, he couldn't have been kinder if he had been my own dad.'

He has no problems with the players threatening to go on strike. As a dedicated Socialist, Clough does not deny the working man the right to strike, as he demonstrated in 1972, when he gave 200 miners free tickets for the stand to watch Derby County, a gesture which did little for his stock in the boardroom. Not many *Tribune* readers in there! Clough knew that talk of strikes would be dissipated once the wives sat down to examine the mortgage repayments and the need to feed and clothe their children. He had miscalculated the obduracy of his truculent chairman, and the amount of goodwill for him in the boardroom. Clough had lost in the final minute, after dominating the match with any amount of brilliant approach work and shots that had thundered back off the woodwork.

Gerald Mortimer, who covered the events for the *Derby Evening Telegraph*, feels that Clough was bitter about the local press's role: 'He thought we should've done more to sweep him back to power, but there's only so much you can do. We would all prefer Cloughie to have stayed, because he was not only great for us, but he was a terrific manager. Things had been pretty quiet for a long time at Derby before he and Peter pitched up. Today people go on about Derby being a football town, but it wasn't till Clough and Taylor that we had those great nights at the ground, when you could feel the electricity. Sam Longson was a jealous old man who came to resent Cloughie's fame and the amount of stick he was getting in other boardrooms, but it was the supreme naïvety of Brian's career that he thought he'd be reinstated. Once Dave Mackay was installed, there was no going back.'

Or was there? On at least two other occasions, Clough toyed with the idea of returning to the Baseball Ground. In 1982, he met Peter Taylor to discuss his return after Taylor had already gone back. Clough dismissed the idea fairly swiftly and decided to stay put at the City Ground. Five years earlier, Clough got as far as a press conference at the Baseball Ground only to announce he was seeing out his contract at Forest. That was a day in the best traditions of Derby drama. Forest had an outside chance of promotion in the spring of 1977 when the new Derby chairman, George Hardy, thought he had managed to woo the pair back. It is a moot point whether Clough simply allowed himself the luxury of toying with Derby, a club in danger of relegation from the First Division, but certainly Taylor was very keen to go back. He often used to rhapsodize about the great games and players he had seen at Derby, long before he ever went there to work, and he had the same sentimental attachment for the club as Clough had for Sunderland.

By the time Clough arrived characteristically late for the press conference at the Baseball Ground, the whiff of intrigue and bathos was unmistakable. The formality of Clough and Taylor's expected reappointment had been long delayed and we were treated to the bizarre sight of Colin Murphy, the caretaker manager, peeking out of his office, and asking us if we had heard anything. The same question was being hurled at every reporter over the phone by our departmental heads as the air in the cramped press room became even more acrid with cigarette fumes. At last Clough breezed in, strode down the narrow corridor avoiding all questions, and closeted himself in the boardroom with George Hardy. He told the chairman he was not coming, gave a short statement to the media, then drove away – but not before he knocked on Colin Murphy's door and said, 'Take them for all you can get, there's no way I'm coming back.'

A few months later, Murphy was sacked and Clough, of all people, helped negotiate his pay-off with Hardy. Colin Murphy explains: 'I was having troubles over my settlement and I was due to see George Hardy for further discussions when Cloughie turned up at the ground. Derby Reserves were playing Forest Reserves and it was an ideal chance for him to put a word in for me. He did more than that. He said point-blank to the chairman, "Has he got his money?" and then hauled the three of us down to an office and organized my settlement! He really laid into the chairman on my behalf, talking about honest virtues and the value of a contract, and he did well for me. Next day I sent Cloughie a Bible, because the things he had been talking about were straight out of the Good Book.'

Who else would have the chutzpah to deal in such a manner with a chairman he had crossed swords with a few months earlier? Only the same man who persuaded Tommy Docherty to bring his Derby team to the City Ground to play a testimonial game for Clough and Taylor a month or two later – with Derby having to pay their players appearance money because Clough refused! Docherty was greatly taken by Clough's cheek. 'For a start, I loved the idea of the pair of them getting a testimonial from Forest when they'd hardly been there five minutes. That's class, and so was the Dom Perignon Cloughie poured me at 9.45 in the morning at the Midland Hotel, Derby when he put the proposal to me. I was all in favour, I didn't know all the politics that had gone on, so we turned up at the City Ground. He gave me, my assistant and my physio lovely presents and when I said, "What about my players?" he said, "Fuck them, that's what they're paid for, to play football!" The Derby directors had gone spare in the first place when I told them the plan and when they had to fork out for appearance money, they banned all mention of Brian Clough. What a stroke he pulled! Typical Cloughie – I loved him, you always knew where you stood with him, unless you were a director. If he walked into a room I was always pleased to see him, because he made me laugh.'

Clough had earlier launched another pre-emptive strike on Derby by spiriting Alan Hill away from Dave Mackay and installing him at the City Ground to run his youth policy in 1976. Despite Hill's insistence that he was under contract to Derby, that he did not like what he had heard and seen of Clough, he would brook no opposition. Clough said, 'I want you here, Jimmy Gordon's told me all about you.' Clough airily waved away Hill's doubts and simply battered him into submission. It ruined the close friendship Hill had enjoyed with Mackay and his assistant Des Anderson but Clough – yet again – had worked the oracle, in the process wounding his old club once more.

If, as the Sicilians say, revenge is a dish best eaten cold, then Brian Clough ultimately enjoyed making a meal of Derby County. He still lives a handful of miles from the Baseball Ground, and he has not moved from the area since he arrived there in 1967, with Barbara and three young children. Whenever the Derby ex-Players' Association organize a social get-together, Clough invariably comes along and yarns happily with the likes of Durban, McFarland and O'Hare. He may have achieved an enormous amount 15 miles down the A52 at Nottingham Forest,

justly lauded, his ability to motivate players. Clough's man-management skills were the most durable arrows in his quiver during his 28 years in management, but they missed the target time and again while at Leeds.

Those man-management qualities had lain dormant for some time before he arrived at Elland Road in July 1974. There had been hardly a sight of them during his eight-month stay at Brighton. The players saw little of him at the Goldstone Ground. When he signed for Brighton on 1 November 1973 the melodrama at Derby still had a few acts to play and although the Brighton faithful saw Clough as their messiah, he had no intention of putting down permanent roots on the south coast. He did buy a house in Brighton, but kept in touch with his former Derby players and the leaders of the Protest Movement. The King Across the Water only needed to hear the skirl of the pipes and he would be back at the Baseball Ground. Brighton's chairman Mike Bamber was unaware of that as he cranked up the hyperbolic machine, calling Clough's appointment 'the greatest day of my life', and the home crowd trebled for the first game under the command of Clough and Peter Taylor.

Typically, Taylor viewed the new job as a fresh challenge; he was glad to get away from all the intriguing at Derby and he set to his new revivalist task with his customary professionalism. Several of the Derby coaching staff were wooed away to join Taylor's list and soon he was scouting for new players. The club certainly needed them. In one week in December, Brighton lost at home in the FA Cup by 4–0 to the amateurs Walton and Hersham, and they trumped that a few days later, losing 8–2 at the Goldstone to Bristol Rovers. Clough knew a bone had to be tossed at the slavering hacks after that defeat and he announced he was ashamed and that some of his players lacked heart.

The following day, he had recovered sufficiently to appear on television, alongside Brian Moore, as chipper as usual. He brought seven-year-old Nigel along to the studios and the boy made his début in front of the cameras, perched on Moore's knee. That was a shrewd move by Nigel's proud father. He once gave Alan Durban a fascinating piece of advice on dealing with tricky situations as a manager: 'When you're in trouble, bring your children along to the meeting if you can,' he told Durban. There was a better chance of disarming your critics that way – especially if the offspring were as polite and delightful as Clough's three 'bairns', as he always called them. 'Never worked for me, though,' said Durban. 'Cloughie obviously knew the secret.'

While Taylor brought in new players, his partner continued to savage the survivors for their disappointing performances. He said they did not know their trade and were shirking their moral responsibilities. Lacking the necessary clout to reply as individuals, the players turned to the Professional Footballers' Association, whose chairman Derek Dougan had long been happy to fire salvoes at a man his equal in both ego and an eye for a good headline. 'He shouldn't criticize his players publicly,' said Dougan, 'unless he allows them to answer back.' The list of players who have done that in Clough's time is about as full as the Margaret Thatcher Book of Humour, and the atmosphere at the Goldstone Ground became sullen and defeatist. A few months earlier, Clough had been working with the likes of McFarland, Todd, Hector and Gemmill; the lads at Brighton were just journeymen, willing enough if they were shown the way, but Clough was just marking time for better offers. The hunger to improve players that was so impressive at Derby in 1967 was dormant on the south coast.

So Clough took drastic remedial action: he left the shop to Peter Taylor to run and went for a few trips. New York to watch the momentous fight between Muhammad Ali and Joe Frazier, then to Iran where the Shah of Persia indulged him and offered him £400 a week to manage the national side, double what he was getting at Brighton, plus endless perks. He turned it down and yet a few days later, tossed a substantial pebble into the pool of mischief when he said, 'Of course I wanted to go to Iran, but the board vetoed the move. I am not saying I'm happy here.' That was patently obvious. He had also spent a good deal of time away from Brighton, canvassing during the General Election campaign for Labour's candidate in the Derby North constituency, Philip Whitehead. Clough threw himself into electioneering with messianic zeal, electrifying a series of public meetings with impassioned, witty speeches. The predicted collapse of the Labour vote did not materialize and Whitehead's return to Parliament had much to do with Clough's magnetic canvassing. It was a far headier challenge at the time than managing Brighton and Hove Albion. Peter Taylor could deal with that. 'Now, pet, can we count on your vote tomorrow?'

Clough now admits that he took the Brighton job for the wrong reason – money. He says Mike Bamber was a marvel in putting up with all his shenanigans, his frequent absences from the ground and trips abroad. Clough agrees that he ought to have gone to Brighton to re-establish his managerial credentials, to show he could still mould a set of individuals into a coherent whole.

When Sir Alf Ramsey was sacked as England's manager in April 1974, that set off a train of events which brought Clough a more stunning reverse than the realization he did not fancy the Third Division any more. When Don Revie was appointed Ramsey's successor, the Leeds board acted swiftly. They felt they needed a major figure, someone big enough to handle established, mature internationals, someone gifted enough in public relations to satisfy the media, a man experienced enough to lead the League champions' challenge on the European Cup next season, a big personality unlikely to be intimidated by the legacy and the memory of the man they called 'the Godfather', Don Revie. So they chose Brian Clough. To be fair to the Leeds directors, Clough possessed all those stated qualities in abundance and with Peter Taylor alongside him to smooth away the expected rough edges, they could be the dream ticket.

There were two major drawbacks, however. Peter Taylor was happy at Brighton, having installed his family in a sea-front apartment and got his teeth into the job of doing a Derby at Brighton. Taylor would not be coming north. (After nine years together, the Clough/Taylor juggernaut would be off the road for the next two years.) So why did Leeds persist in the appointment when Clough's invaluable partner was not to be part of the package? The answer to that lies in Clough's quickness of mind. The Leeds chairman Manny Cussins had arrived at a Brighton hotel to finalize the deal when Taylor told him he was staying put. Cussins was taken aback by the news; he was well aware of Taylor's importance to the success of the

partnership. Unknown to Cussins, the media had gathered
downstairs and Clough was not going to pass up the chance of a
new start with the League champions. He strode into the foyer
and as Cussins gathered his thoughts in the face of the media
onslaught, Clough announced, 'Gentlemen, I've just been
appointed the new manager of Leeds United.' Short of saying,
'Oh no, you haven't' the hapless Leeds chairman had to go
along with the *fait accompli*. A few weeks later, Cussins would
be equally uneasy as he tried to justify the sacking of Clough in
front of another clamorous media throng.

The other reason why the appointment was doomed lay in the
man himself, Brian Clough. He simply brought too much
provocative baggage with him. He had made no secret in the
past that he despised the methods Leeds had used to gain
success. Clough's suggestion the previous summer that Leeds
should be demoted for their disciplinary record had cut deep
and no amount of emollient bluster from Clough when he took
the job would smooth that one away.

Don Revie's bunker mentality when anyone dared to criticize
his beloved players was common knowledge, especially in
newspaper offices where a chiding reference in print would often
lead to a phone call from Revie himself, threatening to ban the
offending reporter from Elland Road. Paranoia oozed from
Revie's office at Leeds United – a deep resentment that his
teams had never received the credit they deserved for their
consistency over the previous decade. Why home in on his
players' problems with referees when they were playing so
effectively? Revie had a point, particularly when his later teams
are examined. They had won the League title in 1974, playing a
brand of soccer not far removed from Holland's concept of
Total Football, the buzz theme at the time. Yet Leeds remained
respected, feared even – but not loved like Busby's Manchester
United, nor revered emotionally like Shankly's Liverpool. The
earlier emphasis on over-physical play, laced with the kind of
cynical gamesmanship that would be admired by the likes of
Juventus and AC Milan would prevent Revie's Leeds from
winning over the nation. Strange that two proud managers, born
eight years apart, hailing from the same area of Middlesbrough,
would be so diametrically opposed in their footballing philosophies. And it was the expansive Clough rather than the

suspicious Revie who echoed successfully the public consensus
about Leeds United.

Clough says he admired what Revie had achieved at Leeds,
that he was thrilled to take over the best team in the country.
He wanted to win the championship in style and manage
something Revie had not done – win the European Cup. Clough
feels his own frankness was his downfall at Leeds: 'I was so
naïve I used to think that people could take criticism if it was
true. By hell, I got a rude awakening at Leeds. They resented
me so much that from day one it was absolute agony. If you
can't get your players on your side, you've got no chance.'
Agreed. Yet there are certain ways to get players on your side
when you come into a new club. One way to alienate them
immediately is to go straight back on holiday to Majorca, after
signing the contract, without even meeting them.

The players were due back for pre-season training, a vital
period for any club, even more so with a new manager, bound
to have a different approach after so many years working for
Revie. Yet Clough chose to slap on some extra Ambre Solaire
at Calla Millor, rather than meet his new charges to try to build
bridges after his intemperate comments about them. When
Clough returned, he was very late for an important event at
Leeds, the traditional pre-season get-together of wives, players,
directors and other staff. Don Revie had prided himself on the
family atmosphere at Leeds, and although his relationship with
some of the directors was far from harmonious, he had built up
a genuine loyalty among players and families. Unlike Clough –
apart from his early and final periods at Derby – Revie was
happy to be close to his players. They could ring him any time,
he would offer his advice on any subject. No player I have
talked to ever had Clough's home phone number, although the
amount of personal favours he did for many of his lads is not in
doubt. In arriving late for that get-together, Clough was making
it clear that there would be distance between himself and the
rest at Elland Road.

His first team meeting with his players was even more
provocative. Anxious to grab their attention, Clough announced
they should throw their medals in the bin, because they had won
them by cheating! He then singled out the players individually

and told them what he thought of them. To Norman Hunter, the scourge of forwards and referees, he said, 'You've got a terrible reputation in the game and I know you'd like to be liked.' Hunter, an experienced international, highly popular, and coveted by most other managers, delivered an understandable riposte: 'I couldn't give a fuck.' John Giles, who had riled Clough for years with his sly fouls behind the referee's back, was told, 'You're another with a bad reputation, even though you've got so much skill.' Giles shrugged his shoulders: 'So what? If they kick me, I'll kick them back.' Giles had been recommended by Revie as his successor and Clough was aware of that. 'It's not my fault you didn't get the job,' he said, unaware that Giles did not want the job, that he was happy to carry on playing. Then Clough tried the disarming approach after the blitz on Hunter and Giles. He told Gordon McQueen and Allan Clarke that he rated them, and was looking to them to push on to better things. The rest of the Leeds players groaned. They prided themselves on their professionalism, their refusal to allow any player to think he was above the constraints of playing for the team, yet McQueen and Clarke were the two vulnerable ones in that area. Giles told me: 'McQueen was often floating on air, thinking he was above it all while Clarke thought he was the bee's knees when he first came to Leeds. We'd spent a lot of time knocking that ego stuff out of him and there was Cloughie telling him he was a star! Why single out those two – that was the last thing we wanted.'

So relationships between manager and players had started badly – and they soon deteriorated further. Training sessions were haphazard. Clough was often late, as he drove up every morning with Jimmy Gordon, his faithful retainer whom he had lured as trainer/coach from Derby. Travelling up the M1 every morning from Derby was hardly the ideal preparation for winning the Leeds players over and they were unimpressed at hanging around for 20 minutes or so, waiting for the manager. They were experienced professionals, used to punctuality and precise guidance and Clough's *laissez-faire* approach seemed calculatingly disrespectful to them. After the Charity Shield at Wembley against Liverpool, Norman Hunter mentioned he was concerned at the way Leeds had been exposed at corner kicks.

'We've got to get that right next time,' said the arch-professional, only to be told by Clough, 'You're professional footballers, sort it out yourselves.' Turbulence seemed to be Clough's chosen method of establishing himself. When Allan Clarke scored in a game after a fine pass from John Giles, Clough blew a fuse when he heard Norman Hunter praising the pass. 'Never mind the pass,' he shouted. 'Did you see the way Clarkey stuck it in?' Giles insists he was not perturbed: 'I felt sorry for Cloughie, really, because it was such a silly, childish thing to do. I'd been playing long enough to know when a pass is a good one and I didn't need a manager to say so.'

The Leeds players, accustomed to Revie's almost obsessive attention to detail, would have been perfectly happy to be allowed to play with freedom in a more relaxed framework, as long as they knew the playing pattern. Yet Clough bemused them by saying little about how they should play. He rarely made a point to them in training and hardly ever before a match. When Leeds played Huddersfield in the West Riding Cup, Mick Bates was picked to play. Normally a midfield player, Bates realized there would be a glut in that area and said, 'Shall I play further up, ahead of Giles and Bremner?' Clough turned on him and shouted, 'You'll do what I tell you and play where I say.' Yet he did not tell Bates where he ought to play, it was left to Giles and Bremner to sort it out during the match.

Soon Clough realized he needed some familiar faces around him. Peter Taylor refused another emotional request to leave Brighton so he went back to Derby and signed John O'Hare and John McGovern. Traffic from Derby to Leeds every morning became heavier. Then another player was signed from the East Midlands – Duncan McKenzie from Nottingham Forest, for a club record of £250,000. It was difficult to see how those signings would strengthen the side. O'Hare and McGovern had been in Derby's reserves for some time – O'Hare had been injured – and they would surely just be squad players at Leeds. As for McKenzie – gifted but wayward, he would be a severe test of patience for the Leeds players who regarded giving the ball away as a finable offence.

McKenzie, a genial character not suited to the Byzantine

complexities of dressing-room intrigues, was told by Clough that he was to be his eyes and ears in what he increasingly saw as the enemy camp – the players. Clough appeared insecure to McKenzie. He talked of splitting up the team, selling David Harvey and Trevor Cherry, and buying Peter Shilton. He wanted John Giles to take the manager's job at Tottenham, and when that fell through he was keen for Giles to join Bobby Collins at Huddersfield. Giles says Clough had totally misread the situation from the start: 'There were devils in his mind. I'm sure he felt embarrassed by his earlier comments about us, which were not that far off the mark, by the way. We weren't bothered by all that because professional footballers have a strong streak of self-preservation. Once Revie had gone, it was a case of getting on with the next manager, whoever he was. There was a close relationship with Revie, but he still kept his distance. Clough misread the atmosphere as soon as he arrived. His way is to dominate the company, to make people fit in with him, but we were mature, intelligent adults as well as experienced footballers and his rudeness backfired on him. It was just silly mind games that impressed nobody.'

After six league games, the champions had gathered just four points. Clough had been booed at home after the 1–1 draw against Luton. Leeds were not playing well, but as Giles says, they were professionals, they wanted to do well and win trophies for themselves, irrespective of their feelings for their new manager.

Not even the most demanding president of an Italian club would fire a manager after only 44 days in the job, but that is what the Leeds directors set out to do. First they needed others to fire the bullets, to pass the responsibility on to a group who would be able to sell it to the disaffected supporters. The players! Of course! Manny Cussins and his vice-chairman Sam Bolton organized a meeting in the players' lounge, the significance of which has been a matter of speculation for nearly 20 years. Clough was present, aware that some harsh words were about to be exchanged. Cussins and Bolton initially said they simply wanted to clear the air, but Clough knew that after the previous night's board meeting, they were looking to the players to find a palatable way out for them. Such a proud, individualistic man as Clough could not stomach the charade for very long and he slipped out of the meeting, leaving the players to twist the knife *in absentia* if they so wished. Clough knew he was finished at Leeds and set to work on the amount of his compensation with a degree of exactitude and pertinacity that would impress any accountant. Leeds United would pay for this humiliation.

When the chairman and the sacked manager gathered on the steps at Elland Road, a cursory glance would make one believe that Clough had come out on top. Clough was beaming broadly, wisecracking with his usual gusto, while Cussins looked as ill-at-ease as Sam Longson the previous October. Fielding impertinent questions from chaps toting clipboards was not on the agenda for the ageing chairman who would prefer club policy to be conducted *in camera* or, at worst, with the aid of a pliant hack. With as much dignity as he could muster, Cussins told the media: 'What has been done is for the good of the club. The club and the happiness of the players must come first. Nothing can be successful unless the staff is happy.' So it was the players who got rid of Clough, Mr Chairman? 'We've been spoilt by Don Revie.' With that, Clough absented himself from the throng with a cynical smile and returned to his negotiations. He contented himself with the comment that it was 'a very sad day for Leeds and for football'.

But not for Brian Clough's bank balance. He had learned his lesson at Derby: never resign. Leeds would have to pay a hefty sum for hiding behind the players. Colin Lawrence, a good friend of Clough since he came to Derby, sat in on the negotiations in case his business expertise was needed. 'Brian had the advice of a friend who worked for the Inland Revenue and he took them apart. They not only agreed to pay up his four-year contract, but also to pay the tax. He also got to keep a new Mercedes they'd just given him. Brian handled the details very well indeed; he was more than a match for the Leeds directors. When we drove away from Leeds, he put his feet up on the back seat and said, "I've just come up on the pools." He then got straight on to his bank manager and made sure the cheque was presented at a Leeds bank. When it was cashed there, he could relax.'

Even though Clough had not signed the contract, Leeds honoured it, so a total of 44 days cost them over £100,000. Small wonder that the directors were anxious to hide behind the players in selling the sacking to the supporters. More than £2,000 a day for the services of Don Revie's successor was hardly the essence of financial acumen.

Although Leeds reached the European Cup Final later that season, the cost of paying off Clough hampered the transfer dealings of his successor, Jimmy Armfield. Armfield says that when he took over, no Leeds player breathed a word of criticism of Brian Clough. The subject was never mentioned in his presence as the players simply got on with the job. Yet if they had been the sole agents of Clough's fall, would they not have alerted Armfield to their latent power? Perhaps they had been unwilling pawns in the boardroom game as the directors covered up their error in appointing Clough in the first place. That is the view of Billy Bremner, the Leeds captain at the time. Until now, Bremner has resisted invitations to discuss the significance of that meeting between the players, chairman, vice-chairman and Clough. 'We've been the fall-guys for Clough's sacking for all those years, but it wasn't true. Players don't sack managers, but it was convenient to use us. We only had one meeting about him, and that was on his last day when Manny Cussins and Sam Bolton were looking to us to do their work for them. It was their fault we were in that state, not ours. It was a complete mystery why they appointed Clough in the first place, but you know what directors are like. In his later years, Don Revie told me what a battle he'd had with the board at Leeds and after the Clough affair, I could see what he meant.

'Clough was not good with his man-management at Leeds, but the chemistry was wrong, the vibes were bad. Who's to say that it might not have been the perfect mix a few years later, when his harsh words about us had faded? This may surprise many, but I really admired what Brian Clough stood for in his teams. I liked the way he'd say to us "Go away and forget about it" if we played badly. One of his main priorities was to entertain, just like we were doing at the time at Leeds. If more managers had his attitude, the game wouldn't be in such a state.'

John O'Hare thinks it is 'twaddle' to suggest the players

would have been happy for Clough to stay at Leeds. He sensed a change in the man as soon as he arrived at Elland Road, a month after Clough. 'The players didn't want him, they wanted him out. I was amazed that they were so open about it in front of me and John McGovern, but at least they knew we wouldn't be spies in the camp. We weren't isolated but Clough was frightened to manage the way he wanted to.'

Clough maintains the ship was not on the most even of keels when he took over the champions. Several contracts were up for renewal, including that of Bremner and he had the feeling that some of the established players had not given of their best. A turnover of players was necessary for a serious assault on the European Cup. He makes the sound point that it is often harder to continue the run of success than achieving it first time, that he tried to do far too much too quickly. 'I lived by the rule that in the first three months you're at your strongest as a new manager. Do all the unpleasant stuff early while you've still got the power.' He asked Manny Cussins to give him more time, but the chairman did not want the wounds to fester. Clough takes an upbeat view of the experience: 'Good came out of that because I was financially secure for the first time in my life. I always knew I was a good manager, but now I could really go for it and put my ideas into operation. There was tons of work around, but chairmen were wary of me. They knew I'd want to run the show. They were dead right.'

His good friend Geoffrey Boycott is sure that Clough concealed the hurt with his usual bravado for a long time. 'For a year it crucified him inside, he'd never been told before he wasn't good enough. It hurt the club more in the long run and I'm glad about that, because it was terrible of the directors to take him on, knowing his character – and then give him no time to do the job. It's a shame for the supporters that they had all those managers afterwards and that it took so long to get success again, but the directors were totally at fault. They knew about his criticisms of the players, but they chickened out of their duty to stand by him. Forty-four days is a long time to prove yourself, isn't it?'

Should Clough have trimmed with the wind early on, got his

feet under the table, instead of rampaging around, with his usual policy of *Stürm und Drang*? After all, he was taking over the League champions and the bedding-in period was bound to be a little sensitive, given his previous strictures about Leeds. John Giles believes that if Clough had handled the early stages differently he would have exorcised the ghost of Revie surprisingly quickly. 'If he'd given himself three months of sensible dealings, he'd have been there for the next 20 years. It was set up for him. I know he hates me, calls me "a shithouse" but I couldn't care less. I really admired the way Cloughie turned out his sides, I think the man's been a genius, a great football man. He'd have won everything for Leeds if only he'd handled it better, but he never allowed himself to get off first base.

'He blames me for getting him the sack at Leeds, he thinks I was after the job. I wasn't – not when Revie left or after Clough. When they were considering Clough's successor, I told the board I didn't want to be considered. I was enjoying playing too much. Three years later, I was still playing in the First Division. Cloughie got rid of himself, not the players. You could tell he was a bright guy, but where was the common sense? Why couldn't he do what Bob Paisley did when he took over from Bill Shankly? Why all the calculated rudeness? He could've built a dynasty at Leeds, but he left the field to Liverpool. Leeds were never the same after that. He could've replaced a player every year, like Liverpool and just tinkered with a very successful machine. In the end, I think it was insecurity that did him – he was worried what the players thought about him. He thought it was either us or him. He forgot about the directors.'

The Leeds experience will always be held against Clough when his suitability for the major clubs is discussed. Wonderful achievements at provincial clubs like Derby and Forest, yes; but how would he have fared at Liverpool or Manchester United? Leeds was the only club he managed that did not need his distinctive root-and-branch treatment right away. A period of retrenchment, then selective weeding would have been enough. Leeds had won the championship by five clear points, playing football of a quality no current side could match. Clough had told Giles, 'It was your arrogance I didn't like when I was at

Derby,' and he was often frustrated that Leeds normally triumphed in their epic battles of the time against Derby.

Perhaps Clough simply wanted to do it his way, a recurring theme in his career. He suggested as much in a highly entertaining encounter on television with Don Revie, when the body language of both men spoke volumes. Revie, hunched in his seat, barely able to look at a man he disliked intensely, kept referring to his record at Leeds, asking how could Clough improve on winning the title in 1974 with the loss of just four games. Clough, at his most dynamic, leaned forward poking his index finger and said, 'I wanted to do it better than you, Don – and lose three games instead of four.' He never got the chance and it hurt him.

Aldous Huxley once wrote, 'Experience is what a man does with what happens to him', and Clough certainly learned from his 44 days at Leeds. Directors would be marginalized and ultimate power would, as far as possible, reside in his office. If the board did not like it, Clough would walk away and find another club. He could now afford to be as self-indulgent as he wished. All he needed was a club that would accommodate him. Preferably one without a dressing-room full of internationals, with minds of their own.

8

Stirrings in the Forest

Napoleon liked his generals to be lucky as well as successful. He would have liked Brian Clough. The call from Nottingham Forest in January 1975 was perfectly timed and the deal just right for his particular skills. Forest were 13th in the Second Division, and falling. Gates were down to an average of 12,000, the club was virtually bankrupt and not one player on the books was interesting any other managers. Their best players had been sold in recent years – Hennessey, Cormack, Storey-Moore, Newton, McKenzie – and their replacements and the youth policy were inadequate. Just eight years earlier, Forest had been within a game or two of the Double, playing attractively under Johnny Carey, but now they were in a backwater, going nowhere. A prospect guaranteed to appeal to Brian Clough; he had revived the somnolent Derby County and had no doubts he could do the same again by the banks of the River Trent. No need to move home, no worries about dealing with internationals who missed being molly-coddled by their previous manager. This time he would really make that first three months in the job count.

By a neat twist of fate, the man who began the moves to bring
Clough to the City Ground was the same one who announced
Clough's retirement 18 years later. Fred Reacher had just joined
the Forest board when he suggested that, with Clough out of
work, available and living nearby, an overture to him might not
be spurned. Four members of the board immediately said they
would resign in that event, so Reacher thought, 'I'd better keep
quiet, I'm the new boy.' Stuart Dryden, the vice-chairman,
mulled it over, though, and suggested to Reacher he raised the
subject again at the next meeting. The vote was carried
unanimously and Dryden began the negotiations with Clough. It
was the start of a genuine friendship that shows the generous,
loyal side to Clough's nature. Clough relied on the support of
the postmaster and magistrate in those difficult early months at
the City Ground and when Dryden later needed moral support,
it was given unstintingly. In 1980, Dryden was convicted of
fraud and sentenced to six months in prison. At the trial, which
lasted seven days, Clough sat beside Dryden's wife, comforting
her, and later kept in touch with Dryden when he was sent to
Sudbury Open Prison.

So Clough was ready for the fray and he showed he had lost
none of his flair for dealing with the media. The quips tumbled
out on his first day at the City Ground: 'I'm leaving the human
race to rejoin the rat race. At my age I'm too young to retire,
football is my job. Now there is only one thing in Forest's favour
– the club has me.' On the same day, the kitchen staff were told
they would be getting a new cooker and fridge and the
physiotherapist was to expect an ultrasonic machine. All paid
for by Clough's awareness of the media's needs, with the money
coming from exclusive deals with a newspaper and a television
company. Outside, the car park was full. Forest fans were
clamouring to become lottery ticket agents and within a few
days, £4,000 worth of season tickets had been sold, even though
the season's campaign was half over.

The players did not need to be clairvoyant to know that they
would be on trial at once. Barry Butlin, the striker who had
played at Derby, had first-hand knowledge of Clough's style and
he said: 'Whatever happens, it'll be different.' It was. There was
to be none of the bombast and insensitivity that permeated his

first team talk at Leeds. This time, Clough knew the players were looking to him for inspiration and renewed confidence. It came within two days. Luckily, Forest had to go to Tottenham for an FA Cup replay, so that gave Clough an early chance to assess the players. They scraped through 1–0, but the result was more important than the performance and it gave Clough some breathing space. The papers latched on to his success at White Hart Lane, suggesting that it would only be a matter of time before Forest soared back into the First Division. He was by now too old a dog to swallow all that, but he was happy for the media to concentrate on him and allow the players time to get used to him.

Clough says he was surprised at the untapped talent at the club when he arrived. In fact, five of those players would still be at Forest during the club's massive success towards the end of the decade. One of them was Ian Bowyer. He recounts: 'My first encounter with him came when I was sat on the treatment table. He stormed in, gave me an icy look and asked how much training I'd missed and what was the problem. Then he was gone, no rapport at all. He made it clear to all of us that we'd be judged on what was to happen, not on what had gone on before he came. And we were expected to conduct ourselves in a professional manner. From that first game at Tottenham, I never felt pressure from Clough to win a game – but I always felt under pressure to give my all for him. If we lost games and he was happy with our efforts, that became a managerial problem. His in-depth knowledge was amazing: he just knew if you'd ducked a tackle or a header in the match and you dreaded the sharp edge of his tongue. But he could praise as well. In that first season, we lost at Bristol Rovers but I scored, playing up front. He said to me, "You couldn't have done any more, son," and that filled me up, getting the carrot from Clough, instead of the stick. Mind you, there was a lot more stick around in those early days.'

There needed to be. Forest took just 14 points from 16 matches in the rest of that season, finishing 16th in the table. Clough concedes, 'We were lucky not to be relegated,' but he had already taken steps to ensure the foundations would be more secure. Jimmy Gordon was enticed back as coach; with

Peter Taylor still happy at Brighton, Clough needed the loyal Gordon to act as a buffer between him and the players, to tell the manager quietly that there were other options. Clough respected the self-effacing, loyal Gordon and his contribution to the great Forest years should not be overlooked – a point publicly acknowledged by Clough and Taylor when Gordon was chosen to lead out the Forest team at Wembley before the 1980 League Cup Final.

Clough continued his usual policy of bringing in reliable staff by snapping up John McGovern and John O'Hare from Leeds, for half the money he had forked out for them six months previously, a piece of business Clough enjoyed enormously at the expense of Manny Cussins. This was the fourth time McGovern had signed for Clough and this time he noticed that Clough's energy was not as demonic as before, he seemed to be channelling his efforts more constructively. John O'Hare believes Clough had lost some of his amazing self-confidence: 'To the Forest lads, he was brash enough, but we knew him when he had been really full of himself. He wasn't breezing around so much, picking on anyone for the hell of it. He was more subdued. I think it took him some time to get his confidence back after Leeds.' Clough says he signed McGovern and O'Hare to show the others how he wanted to play. He was finding it hard to graft awareness and intelligence on to players who had developed bad habits, or in some cases, had never had any good habits.

A particular problem was a dumpy little Scot called John Robertson. He had talent, a sweet left foot, but he needed a good football brain to compensate for his lack of pace. Clough set to work on him. 'Early on, he gave me a real roasting at half-time. He hadn't seen me once in their penalty area, I wasn't timing my runs, I was just running around. He wanted me to take responsibility for the ball, to do something worthwhile with it. Moral courage, he called it – he said ten-yard passes were fiddling, farty things. In the summer of '75, he worked on me during the tour to Ireland and it all panned out in front of me at last. He told me to get wide on the left, stop rushing around and hang on to the ball. He said there are lots of players who can't tackle but can cross a ball – Alan Hinton for a start. He made me realize the things I wasn't good at and cut them out. From the age of 15 I'd been told to play the early ball, but Clough thought that was just passing the buck. "If there's space in front of you, go into it," he'd say. It was the best bit of business Forest ever did when they got Clough. I loved playing for him and Peter Taylor.'

Robertson became a revelation and a rarity – the man who orchestrated Forest's attacking moves from the left wing. Most sides have their playmaker in midfield, setting up the options on either wing, but Robertson would take up residence wide on the left and expect the ball. His ability to cross the ball under pressure was matchless and the calm way he would accept a pass when tightly marked and then wait for support gave Forest an ideal platform for their stunning counter-attacks. Peter Shilton's throw out to Robertson, then the overlap from the full-back or from Archie Gemmill in midfield or Tony Woodcock or Gary Birtles further upfield – that was a trademark Forest attack in their palmy period. John Robertson was the most influential player in that side.

Robertson is the first to admit he owed a great deal to the man on the other side of the field. Martin O'Neill eventually settled into a semi-defensive role on the right side of midfield, a role that made great demands on his morale and resilience, not least of all because Clough insisted he had to do so much donkey work. O'Neill's job was to get tackles in on the opposition full-back or midfield players and cover for Viv Anderson when the rampaging full-back went on one of his thrilling, leggy surges. Clough used to tell O'Neill, 'What's the point of giving you the ball when there's a genius on the other wing?' and that was hard on a skilful player who would have thrived as the constructive presence in midfield, an area where he played his best football after leaving Forest. It was understandable that Forest's fluid 4–4–2 style would not permit them the luxury of allowing two wingers to hug their touchlines and simply wait for the ball to be delivered; one of the wingers had to be a fetcher and a carrier as well, and that was O'Neill's bad luck. His occasional frustrations led to a testy relationship with Clough, but O'Neill concedes he was lucky still to be at Forest, after the former university student had started off on the wrong foot back in January '75. 'We were sat round a table, talking about ordering new boots and I came out with a tatty, cynical aside. "I've just got a new pair, does that mean I'm staying next season?" I said and Clough took a long, hard look at me. In those early days, I was anything but special – I couldn't even get in a bad side – and I must have seemed a real little smart-arse. Clough gave me a hard time after that – he used to say, "You may have 'A' Levels, but you're thick as a footballer." This lippy Irishman never stood a chance with Clough.'

O'Neill, Robertson, Bowyer and Anderson were all at the City Ground when Clough arrived in January 1975. O'Neill and Robertson were transfer-listed, drifting. So was Tony Woodcock, a mild-mannered local lad who was struggling to make any impact in midfield. He was loaned out to Lincoln City and Doncaster over the next year and finally Clough played him up front, telling him to time his runs, schooling him in the art of turning with the ball, with his back to the opposition goal. Essentially a left-footed player, Woodcock had an intuitive understanding with Robertson and proved a calm finisher. Within three years of Clough's arrival, he was playing for England. The fact that five players who appeared in European Cup Finals for Forest were already at the City Ground on Clough's arrival does bear out his contention that the outlook was not as bleak as it appeared, yet it needed vision and tenacity to lay down the guidelines of a reliable, attractive pattern of play. When Forest finished in eighth position in the table after Clough's first full season, it was clear that consolidation was not enough. He needed a spark to inspire him again, to rouse himself for the challenge of getting into the First Division. He needed Peter Taylor.

Clough was lucky. Taylor had missed out on promotion with Brighton by one point and felt he could not go any further, much as he liked working for his chairman Mike Bamber. He needed a new challenge and Clough, who had monitored Brighton's progress from afar, sensed it was the right time to move. He flew out to Taylor's holiday apartment at Calla Millor, and spent the next few days turning on his persuasive charm. It worked. Clough and Taylor were back in business. It was to be Clough's best signing for Nottingham Forest.

Taylor recharged his partner's batteries as soon as they returned to Forest. Clough rediscovered his sense of humour as Taylor's brilliant mimicry and sense of timing often had him rolling around on the floor, begging him to stop. It was the happiest of times for them, they were rebuilding a club again, their forte.

Clough concentrated on wheedling money for players and a new stand out of the directors, while Taylor delved into the trusty black book and scoured for new blood. He signed Peter Withe from Birmingham, a rough diamond with only 50 league games to his credit, but a hungry individual who had gone to South Africa to try to make a career in the game. The ball would stick up front with Withe, as he proved receptive to the Clough credo of the centre-forward holding the ball, waiting for support to come pouring through at speed. Taylor felt that Forest needed some bite in the back four, the kind of rugged, bloody-minded commitment that allows you to escape with a draw on a wet evening away from home when you have been battered for most of the match. Larry Lloyd was his next target. Lloyd was a stopper centre-half of the type who used to try kicking Clough up in the air when he scored so many goals but he was good enough to have played for England and won trophies for Liverpool. But he was now at Coventry, wasting his career and aware of it. Lloyd was not popular at Highfield Road, he felt he had made a mistake going there after Anfield and he wasted little opportunity in saying so. When he was asked to join Forest in November 1976, he thought it was preferable to marking time at Coventry – besides, this Clough bloke might be interesting. That was the start of a tempestuous five years for Lloyd at the City Ground, during which he became one of the few players who left Liverpool to win major honours and a recall to the England team. It also led to some seismic rows with Clough that brought hours of entertainment to the other players and a steady flow of fines for Lloyd. He has never hidden his dislike of Clough, telling him once, 'I think you're a brilliant manager, but if you walked into a pub, I'd walk straight out,' but even Lloyd agrees there were times when he had to trim his adversarial sails. 'I'd been terrible at Coventry, slagging off everybody, but I soon knew I had to watch it with this guy

Clough. At times I bit my tongue when he had a go at me in front of the other players and that's something I'd never do usually. I rowed with him more than anyone, but come Friday morning, Lloyd was number five on the team sheet. He never let our rows dictate his team selection. Without doubt, he was the best manager I played for when he was at his best – and I played for Bill Shankly and Bob Paisley.'

By the time Lloyd arrived, John Robertson had discovered that Clough's partner could also hand out the abuse. They first met on Forest's pre-season tour to Germany and Taylor brusquely told him to go back to the hotel after one match, while the rest of the team stayed at the ground. Taylor met him at the hotel pool, accused him of being a disgrace to his profession, told him to stop living out of a chip pan and that his idea of warming up before a match was standing at the centre circle, scratching his backside. For the next game, Taylor made him substitute and when Robertson came on for the second half, he played well, showing he had at last digested Clough's impassioned pleas for moral bravery. For the next seven years, Robertson was never out of the Forest first team, apart from injury. He acknowledges: 'Cloughie had been the one to show me the way, he was always onto me about my smoking, but it was Pete who kicked me up the arse at the right time. My mum used to get upset when they said in public that I was a tramp and a boozer, but it didn't bother me. If it hadn't been for those two, I might have ended up a tramp and a boozer!'

Certainly Clough used to enjoy himself at Robertson's expense. 'Whenever I felt off-colour, I'd sit next to Robbo because then I looked like Errol Flynn. But if you gave him the ball and a yard of grass he became an artist. He was the Picasso of our game. It never worried him if there were five players around him when he got hold of the ball. He had so much quality.' Clough and Taylor's hilarious double act at team meetings would skirt around trivial matters like marking at corner kicks, or who to look out for in the opposition. 'Just give it to Robbo,' they would say, or by variation, 'Keep playing to the fat man.' The genial Robertson would smile, hope the meeting would soon end so he could sneak a fag behind Clough's back, and count the hours until the match.

Clough the striker. No English player has beaten his ratio of goals per games (*Colorsport*).

The proud wearer of an England shirt. It remained a source of irritation to Clough that he only played twice for the full England side (*Colorsport*).

Essentially a right-footed player, Clough was a deadly finisher – with a powerful shot from a short back-lift, the bravery to pitch in where the boots were flying, and the selfishness all top strikers possess (*Evening Gazette Middlesbrough*).

Another goal for Middlesbrough. Clough knew he was supreme at his job and he never lost the opportunity to remind Jimmy Greaves that he was the quickest player to reach 250 league goals – not Greaves (*Evening Gazette Middlesbrough*).

...ough in Sunderland colours. He ...as happiest as a player at Roker ...ark, playing for a manager (Alan ...rown) he respected so much (*Colorsport*).

...oxing Day 1962, and Brian Clough's ...laying career is effectively over after ...olliding with Bury's goalkeeper. A ...plit-second accident that led to a ...reat managerial career (*Sunderland Echo*).

The heady, early days at Derby County. Sam Longson (*centre*) was the chairman who viewed Clough as the son he never had, even though initially he did not want Clough's invaluable assistant, Peter Taylor (*left*) (*Raymonds*).

The brash young manager in his office at Derby County, where every photographer was accommodated (*Raymonds*).

The year is 1972 and Clough and Taylor proudly watch Derby's championship trophy being displayed by two players who were to follow them around to four clubs – John McGovern (*left*) and John O'Hare (*holding the trophy*) (*Raymonds*).

Derby's playing squad, who won the First Division in 1972, display the spoils of victory to an adoring Baseball Ground. Clough always maintained he had more friends in this squad of players than at any other time as manager and still attends social gatherings of Derby's Former Players' Association (*Raymonds*).

Brian Clough with his family, the pillars of his life and profession – wife Barbara, Simon (*left*), Libby and Nigel. A few years later, Barbara put a stop to this kind of exposure and she and at least two of her children settled into deserved anonymity. Nigel wasn't so lucky (*Raymonds*).

Peter Taylor was never as comfortable in the public eye as his partner, who considered the media attention at Derby to be their just reward. Different personalities, but a brilliant partnership at its best (*Raymonds*).

August 1974 and Clough leads out Leeds United at Wembley for the Charity Shield match against Liverpool. It was one of the few occasions that Clough showed any signs of leadership during his 44 days with Leeds (*Colorsport*).

Brian Clough's first day as Nottingham Forest's manager – 6 January 1974. Forest's chairman, Jim Willmer, welcomes the man who would transform the City Ground and blow the dust off the trophy cabinet (*Nottingham Evening Post*).

Celebrating the League Cup Final win over Liverpool in 1978 with Kenny Burns, one of Clough and Taylor's most inspirational signings. Within a couple of months, Burns would be voted Footballer of the Year and in the next two years he would help Forest to four more major trophies (*Colorsport*).

Clough and Taylor suffering during the 1979 European Cup Final against Malmö, a poor game won by Trevor Francis's header, but a wonderful achievement for a club that had been in the Second Division just two years earlier (*Empics*).

Two 'number nines'. The father's public mask slips when he expresses pride as another award comes Nigel's way. Maurice Roworth, then chairman of Forest, presides over the family gathering (*Nottingham Evening Post*).

A playful touch from Clough as he and Terry Venables lead out their sides for the 1991 FA Cup Final. Venables had the last laugh, exhorting his Tottenham side to greater glory just before the start of extra time, while Clough remained impassively on the sidelines (*Nottingham Evening Post*).

Clough's eye for a photo opportunity never left him. After signing another extension to his contract at Forest, he suggested this angle to the photographer – 'to show I'm caged in again by the buggers!' (*Nottingham Evening Post*).

A rare sighting of Barbara Clough with her husband, on the Nottingham Council House balcony, before the civic reception to recognize Forest's Littlewoods Cup win in 1990 (*Nottingham Evening Post*).

Clough shows his political allegiance towards the miners as he takes part in a rally in protest at pit closures in November 1992 (*Empics*).

How many of the modern managerial brigade would be able to laugh at themselves like Brian Clough? In March 1993, on the day he received the Freedom of Nottingham, he pleases the photographers looking for an unusual picture (*Empics*).

Pity about that last-minute equalizer, granddad. Susannah Clough represents a substantial consolation for a retired manager (*Nottingham Evening Post*).

The confidence and high spirits oozing out of Clough and Taylor were becoming addictive. The team that won so much so quickly was taking shape in 1976. Frank Clark was signed on a free transfer at the age of 32 and remarkably he was still there in 1979, winning a European Cup medal. Gary Birtles, who had signed a petition in a Nottingham night-club two years earlier, calling for Forest to appoint Brian Clough, was signed for £2,000 from Long Eaton United. Birtles had never met the first team and yet he was thrown in straight away. Clough knew he had signed a striker, yet he played Birtles in midfield on his début. After the game, Clough said to him, 'If I ever play you in midfield, tell the chairman to give me the sack.' Birtles says that actually boosted his confidence, he felt it was Clough's way of telling him he would play up front. Over a nine-year period, split by a move to Old Trafford, Birtles was to become the quintessential Clough forward – reliable, honest, aware, no Fancy Dan. Clough used to tell Birtles, 'Defence starts with the attack, it lifts our defenders to see you tackling back. If you give me 100 per cent, I'll carry you off the pitch.'

In the 1980 European Cup Final, Birtles gave the perfect display as the lone target man up front, with Forest using a five-man midfield to stifle the threat of Kevin Keegan, who was playing for Hamburg. Birtles ran himself to a frazzle that night, selflessly pulling defenders to the left, holding the ball long enough for support to arrive, scrapping for it 30 yards out to nick the ball back to John Robertson, who scored with a low shot to win the Cup. Without the wholehearted efforts of Birtles that night, Forest must have buckled, with Hamburg getting so much possession. It was the kind of unselfish centre-forward's display that Ian Rush has given for Liverpool over many years, and Clough was very proud of the man he had signed when he was a 20-year old carpet fitter, and who became his squash partner over at Trent Bridge. Birtles explained: 'I enjoyed playing squash with Cloughie, because he'd often let me off the last few minutes of training so we could get over to Trent Bridge for the game. He was as hard on the court as in his office, but I learned how to get round him. If there was any doubt in one of our matches, I'd always say, "Play a let, gaffer." Perhaps that's how I stayed in the team.'

Birtles, O'Neill, Robertson, Woodcock, Anderson - all became internationals within a year or so of enrolling at Clough and Taylor's finishing school. Larry Lloyd won back his place in the England side, unwittingly providing Clough with a priceless gibe at his *bête noire*. Lloyd had a poor game against Wales, who won 4–1, and Lloyd wondered if his manager had watched the game. The next time he saw him, he soon found out. 'Hey, Big 'Ead! Tell me, who was the player who won his fourth and last cap in one day? It was you, against Wales!' It was no more than Lloyd had expected. In a recent blistering encounter, he had ended the proceedings with the withering comment, 'Just remember Clough, I got twice as many England caps as you!' before storming out of the dressing-room. Clough had simply kept his powder dry, waiting for the right time for his riposte.

A couple of years after the 1976–77 season, Forest would start collecting notable scalps like Liverpool, Ajax, Cologne and Hamburg on their way to successive European Cups, but Clough has always insisted that the first trophy he won at the City Ground was just as important. It was the Anglo-Scottish Cup, and to win it, Forest beat such illustrious clubs as Ayr United, Kilmarnock, Orient and Bristol City. Clough is convinced winning that trophy in December 1976 was a turning-point. 'Those who said it was a joke competition were absolutely crackers. Most of my players had never won a thing in their careers till then. If you enter a competition, you enter it to win the thing. In my early days at Derby, we won the Texaco and the Watneys Cup before we were League champions, and it did a great deal for our confidence. Forest hadn't won a thing for 17 years before the Anglo-Scottish Cup.'

It seemed to galvanize the players as well as the management because Forest put in a late push for promotion. Although they put together an unbeaten run of four matches to end the season, it looked as if Forest would just be edged out: *déjà vu* for Taylor after his disappointment with Brighton the year before. *Déjà vu* in other ways, actually. Wolves came to Clough and Taylor's rescue, just as they did five years before when handing Derby the title by beating Leeds. This time, Bolton only needed a home draw against Wolves to get the third promotion spot, but

Wolves beat them. In another reminder of 1972, the recipients of Wolves' bounty were on holiday in Majorca when the news was officially confirmed. Forest were in the First Division and Clough was the bearer of glad tidings. 'We were flying over northern France when the pilot gave us the half-time score and a few of our players and friends started celebrating. I wanted to wait and then we lost radio contact. So when we got to Palma Airport, I ran to the phone and rang Stuart Dryden's wife. Her first words were, "I suppose congratulations are in order" and then the line went dead, I'd run out of change. But I knew we'd cracked it and so were a few bottles soon after. I remember at the time that some crackpots were saying we had fluked promotion. It may have looked like we crept in, but you don't fluke it over 42 games. You battle away from August onwards and make your own luck.'

And good managers do not rest on their laurels. At that stage in their careers, Clough and Taylor were at their peak. They were about to show the ruthlessness and clarity of vision which set them apart from other managers who would have stayed loyal to the players who brought them promotion. 'Observe and replace' Clough had told Taylor the previous year when they had been reunited. Taylor was now ready with his replacements. A year later they would be running around the City Ground, brandishing the First Division trophy.

9

England Rejection

In December 1977, Nottingham Forest were top of the First Division, defying all pre-season forecasts, yet Brian Clough was set to leave the City Ground. This time it was for reasons other than boardroom wrangles, antipathy from the players or a tempting television offer. Clough wanted to be England manager. He had been short-listed as Don Revie's successor and he was excited at the prospect. When Clough joined Forest, he had a clause inserted in his contract that he could be released if offered the England job; he might have been thwarted as an international player, but the ambition to run the England set-up was fierce throughout the seventies. He took soundings, asking the advice of his politician friend, Philip Whitehead, and checking up on the background of the crusty chairman of the Football Association's selection committee, Professor Sir Harold Thompson. Clough, hearing that Sir Harold was a former professor of chemistry at Oxford University, asked for information from Gerald Mortimer, the Oxford-educated football writer at the *Derby Evening Telegraph*. Mortimer's answer was frank: 'I don't think you'll like him, Brian.'

Sir Harold had an attitude to the new breed of media-friendly managers that was almost semi-feudal. He saw the likes of Clough as a *nouveau arriviste* and would have great pleasure in sending the brash upstart back to the East Midlands with a stinging rejection. It took a week before Clough was officially rebuffed, with the job going to Ron Greenwood. The conformists decided to trust in the safe pair of hands, rather than the hugely gifted maverick, as so often happens in British public life.

Clough has no doubts about the main stumbling block to his candidacy: 'That Thompson – what a bad job he did for English football. No wonder Alf Ramsey couldn't work with him. I took it as an insult that someone who knew nothing about football was in charge of the interview. How Thompson got to that position in the FA makes me want to scrap democracy. I was at my peak then – building a good side, winning things, happy and fulfilled. I was absolutely ripe for the England job in 1977. They were wary of me. I was never one for hob-nobbing in boardrooms, so some of those around the table didn't know me too well, only my image. They had a sneaking suspicion that I might have tried to run the FA and change a few things. They were right about that. I had a superb interview and I should've got it. You always know if you've had a good match as a sportsman without anyone telling you, I assume you know when you've done a good interview. I was spot on that day.'

Clough honestly thought he had the job when he walked out of the interview room at Lancaster Gate – with one caveat. He rang Peter Taylor for a debriefing and said it was in the bag 'if it's straight'. He felt he had outflanked Sir Harold with his distinctive charm, that Sir Matt Busby was very accommodating when they discussed football matters, and the rest of the committee had been won over. The other candidates were Lawrie McMenemy, Bobby Robson and the Director of Coaching, Allen Wade. In fact the job went to Ron Greenwood, who had not even applied. Perhaps short-listing Clough was just a sop to public opinion. All the public opinion polls conducted by the tabloids came out overwhelmingly for Clough. Don Revie's surreptitious dealings with the United Arab Emirates that culminated in his defection had outraged the majority of fans who were looking for dignity from an England manager. Now that is not a quality one associated with Brian Clough at that stage of his career, but the public perception was that of a passionate patriot who won more football matches than most managers. He was also fun – anarchic, wilful, articulating the thoughts of the punter in the pub. There's the rub, as a famous Danish procrastinator once said.

Since joining Nottingham Forest, Clough had broadly heeded the advice of his wife and close friends to tone down his public comments. The old recidivist would never be the apostle of circumspect banalities and, realizing this, he often chose to demur when the media tried to wind him up. Better to say nothing than waffle platitudes was his laudable view around that time, and the constructive side to his management was correspondingly illuminated as his Forest side took the First Division by storm. The hubris that had led to his setbacks at Derby and Leeds seemed to have faded, as the old roaring rhetoric was replaced by impeccable observations by Clough on the need for Forest fans to cease obscene chanting and appreciate the fine football being played.

Yet timing often let Brian Clough down in his career and just a few days before the interview at Lancaster Gate, the moth could not avoid the flame of controversy. Clough railed against West Bromwich Albion for failing to offer their manager Ronnie Allen a contract. It was a familiar theme of Clough's – the insecurity of tenure endured by many managers – but his outburst was particularly ill-timed. The chairman of West Brom was Bert Millichip, later to succeed Sir Harold Thompson as FA Chairman and at that time an increasingly influential figure inside the portals of the FA. Millichip tartly told Clough to mind his own business and no doubt his anger was communicated to the august members of the selection committee.

Even when Clough was waiting inside Lancaster Gate to be called for his interview, he could not resist a dart at the Establishment. Looking closely at a series of photographs of England teams, he told Ted Croker, the FA Secretary, that the current England strip was 'hideous'. Certainly there had been a fair measure of public disquiet about the new strip, a busy concoction with red and blue stripes at various angles on a white background, and Clough told Croker that the old white England shirt was the ideal and should return. When Croker offered the mild comment that the FA ought to move with the times, he was told, 'Bullshit – a Rolls-Royce is always a Rolls-Royce and it's the same with an England shirt.' Strange that the FA selection committee never realized that the scourge of the Establishment was rather conservative himself in his football philosophy.

Peter Swales, who was part of that selection committee, says that Clough was impressive in the interview. That is no surprise to anyone who had dealt with him when he was at the peak of his profession. Swales says that Clough would have landed the job if Greenwood had not been available. That begs the question – why choose Greenwood? There is no doubt he had been one of the foremost tactical thinkers in England for many years, yet he was now 54, 12 years older than Clough. His West Ham side had won the FA Cup in 1964 and then the European Cup-winners' Cup the following year, but nothing after that, despite the presence of Bobby Moore, Martin Peters, Geoff Hurst and, in later years, Trevor Brooking. Greenwood had been eased out by John Lyall three years earlier, and as West Ham's general manager, was hardly at the nerve centre of the English game any more. Yet he was safe, as Clough acknowledges: 'They gave it to Ron to quieten things down. In his later years I started to listen to what he said compared to the early days and we got close enough to respect each other. But I was the one for the job. They dropped a clanger.'

Greenwood shrewdly tried to keep Clough inside his new England family by offering him and Taylor the job of running the youth team. It was just a sop to defuse public anger and spike Clough's guns. Clough and Taylor had a big enough job winning trophies at Forest in the next year without spending time teaching the kids how to play football Greenwood style, rather than their way. Not that Greenwood differed greatly from Clough and Taylor in such matters, but it was rather optimistic to expect a manager of Clough's stature to knuckle down. After an uneasy year, Clough and Taylor resigned the post, pleading a heavy workload at Nottingham Forest.

To be fair to Clough, he was less critical of subsequent England managers than he was of Ramsey when fulminating regularly from his manager's chair at Derby. Whenever I got him on to the subject during interviews he was a model of restraint. It was either, 'Ron's the best man for the job,' or 'Bobby's the ideal choice,' and later 'Graham Taylor is clever, he's served his time and the best thing he's done is to appoint Lawrie McMenemy as his assistant. Good luck to them.' Apart from an occasional mild criticism of Taylor and Robson for not picking his son more often, Clough has been very supportive of England. He used to say that he pushed his players out the door at Forest to go on England duty and when they became full internationals he was proud of them and pleased that he was still able to educate them. As Neil Webb says, 'He turned good players into internationals.'

The feeling persists that once Clough failed to land the prize in 1977, he got over it fairly quickly. The role of the People's Choice being shafted by the wimps of the Establishment is one he will play with a degree of relish, as one would expect from any proud Yorkshireman. It is a role that also suits his friend Geoffrey Boycott, another high achiever who has been the archetypal blunt Yorkie in professional sport for almost as long as Clough. Boycott captained England just four times, and that was only because Mike Brearley had to come home injured from Pakistan in 1978. By common consent Boycott was the best cricket brain in the England team for years but his quirky individualism was often construed as selfishness, a trait that does not sit well with the demands of captaincy. The quiet skills of diplomacy were never the forte of either man, but Boycott feels his friend was unlucky. 'Like me, he was never one for being what he isn't. He's very frank but he's a traditionalist and the FA should've been proud of that. It was England's loss, not his. You ask the man in the street and the overwhelming majority always came down for Cloughie. They knew he'd have given everything to the job and got the right response from his players. Brian Clough's values were dead straight and the fans knew that those who didn't play their heart out wouldn't get picked again. That's how it should be with England.'

Clough shares with Boycott a healthy awareness of his financial worth – 'brass' as they term it – and it would have been diverting to see how much Clough would have winkled out of the FA had they offered him the job. Taking into account all his ancillaries at Forest, Clough would have been faced with a substantial drop in salary had he been appointed England manager. He would not have been able to command such high fees for his exclusive column in a newspaper, although that did not inhibit Bobby Robson who had a similar arrangement for much of his eight years in the job. However, the thoughts of Cloughie come rather more expensive than those of Bobby Robson and money might have been a stumbling-block. Would he have turned it down if the FA had taken a leap into the unknown? That has been a favourite ploy of Clough's over the years. Like Deborah Kerr, one of his favourite film actresses, he *did* like to be courted, and the list of clubs who thought they had ensnared him is almost as long as Geoffrey Boycott's memory of his best innings. Yet the fierce patriot in Clough would have held sway and his ego would have been stroked at the thought of being chosen on merit by the men in suits who palpably preferred a quieter life. Besides, Manny Cussins and the Leeds board had ensured that Barbara Clough was light years away from taking in washing to make ends meet. Just as no England cricketer turns down the chance of captaining his country, no football manager would spurn the challenge of matching Sir Alf Ramsey in winning the World Cup.

The nagging doubts over Clough's suitability for the diplomatic nuances kept surfacing. The hilarious, splenetic outbursts after the two Juventus matches in 1973 evoked memories of Alf Garnett at his most vigorous. His late arrival at a press conference in Munich before the 1979 European Cup Final, stemming from the coach driver losing his way, brought forth the withering observation, 'No wonder you lot lost the War.' In 1981, Forest went to Tokyo to contest the World Club Championship Final and their manager was not impressed by the bumpy, bare pitch. He asked, 'Why is it that a nation with the technology to put a television in my wristwatch can't grow some bloody grass in its Olympic stadium?' It was a test for the famed Japanese inscrutability as Clough's words were translated, but Clough enjoyed playing up to the image of the Englishman Abroad.

Lawrie McMenemy, also short-listed in 1977, thinks his friend was vulnerable when considerations veered away from football. 'If it was just about handling the players, he'd have done it with his eyes shut, he'd have them in the palm of his hand. But you can't tell the FA officials they can't come on your plane, or please yourself when you talk to the press. On the international stage, you play tournament football every two years and the media interest is massive then. Brian might have had to take a few deep breaths. Would he have been too bored without club football? Well Jack Charlton isn't. I think Tommy Docherty would have been a better international manager than club manager because he would have been fresh to his players, his snappy one-liners might not have been stale. Brian would've been the same, telling his players they were the best in the world. The man's got the Union Jack on his chest. I can understand why they went for Ron because the job's also about how you handle a foreign referee, how you wave the flag abroad, how you cope with the pressure of running the side that everyone in the world still wants to beat. Brian would've had to be careful outside the dressing-room. You can't tell the Germans that we've beaten them in two World Wars and the World Cup Final in '66. Having said that, Brian's an intelligent man and he did mellow. If he'd really wanted to do the job, he'd have compromised.'

That is also the view of the man who played for Clough longer than anyone, John McGovern. 'He'd have astounded them with his diplomacy if they'd bitten the bullet and given him the job. The responsibility would've made him bite his tongue and he's such a patriot that pride would've forced him to tone it down. And in the dressing-room he was such a genius that he'd get the results.'

There would have been no disciplinary problems for England if Clough had been the manager. In his early days at Derby, he would rant at the referees from the dug-out as much as anyone, but he soon realized the futility of that and for the next 25 years, he was a model of supportiveness to the law enforcers. Clough would encourage referees to book any of his players who showed dissent and such mental rigour was an important part of Forest's success in a series of combustible affairs in European competition.

One incident at the Heysel stadium in 1984 captured Clough at his best. Forest had gone to Brussels, defending a 2–0 lead from their first leg in the UEFA Cup semi-final against Anderlecht. The club was desperate for a money-spinning final and Clough, conscious that he had blundered in the transfer market in recent years, was fully aware of that. Before the game, he had expressed doubts over the Spanish referee's ability to handle such a potentially explosive game. His fears were not unfounded. Anderlecht were awarded a dubious late penalty when one of their players fell over Kenny Swain's outstretched leg and yet, with a minute to go, Forest thought they were into the final when Paul Hart headed what looked to be a perfectly good goal. The referee ruled an infringement by Hart and Forest lost 3–2 on aggregate. The travelling army of Forest fans contained more than a few hotheads and at the end of the match, the atmosphere was poisonous – this in a stadium that tragically proved inadequate to cope with those intent on mayhem a year later, in the European Cup Final between Liverpool and Juventus. As the final whistle blew, Clough defused the situation immediately by rushing on to the pitch and shaking the referee's hand. He no doubt wished he could shake his neck instead, but contented himself with a meaningful stare. That apparently respectful gesture from Clough was clearly visible to everyone in the stadium and helped calm a dangerously inflammable atmosphere. It was a test of diplomacy handsomely surmounted by Clough, even though he admitted years later that the referee had got his revenge for those pre-match comments.

Presumably Clough's failure at Leeds was relevant when the FA's selection committee ruled against him. The one chance to work alongside established internationals and he blew it by totally misjudging the chemistry. That fuelled the conviction that Clough could only prosper on *his* terms, at a smallish club, with mediocre players being inspired to play above themselves and no stars bucking the system. Yet Dave Mackay was a star when he came to Derby and Clough handled him superbly. Players of the calibre of Roy McFarland, Colin Todd and Archie Gemmill never felt inhibited by the indiscriminate lash of Clough's tongue. Just before he left Derby, Clough had been

very close to signing one of English football's biggest names –
Bobby Moore. Clough had excited Moore's interest in winning a
championship medal and he would have signed for Derby had
West Ham not proved so obstructive. Clough also wanted
Trevor Brooking in that abortive deal – hardly the strategy of a
manager uneasy with star players.

Brian Clough has never been averse to informing his star
players just who is the boss, but apart from that nightmare at
Leeds, he has created the proper, relaxed framework in which
his teams can perform at their best. He misread the situation at
Leeds, wrongly assuming he was bound to face an initial wall of
hostility from the players. If Peter Taylor had been there for
their good guy/bad guy routine that was usually such a winner,
the earlier, significant exchanges would not have happened and
Clough would have shown how he could work with top players.
With Taylor part of the proposed England package in 1977, the
conclusions drawn by the FA from the Leeds affair were
superficial and damaging. Larry Lloyd is not a man to let his
professional judgement be clouded by his personal animus
towards Clough and he is convinced that his old sparring partner
would have enjoyed a fruitful relationship with the country's
best players. 'When he walked into a room, you *felt* him there,
even if you had your back to him. Clough had that aura and the
players would've sat up and taken notice of him immediately. I
played for Alf Ramsey and he knew his own mind, didn't care
about being popular and stuck to his own system. Clough would
have done the same and he'd have made it work.'

Trevor Francis – 52 caps for three England managers – agrees:
'He was by far the best manager I played for, a unique talent
with a magnificent record. His presence transformed players. He
made me a better player by teaching me how important it was to
incorporate my style of play into the team pattern that was
unchanging. Play it simple. Look at all his good sides – they play
attractive football, but play it simple.'

Clough's insistence on a reliable basis of play was also
Ramsey's creed. He had spent a couple of years tinkering
around with formations, before settling on the 4–3–3 that won
England the World Cup. While England supporters have
endured successive managers chopping and changing patterns,

answering the media's clarion call for various players, and giving an overall impression of confusion, Ramsey's reputation has undergone a welcome rehabilitation. Clough would have approached the job in the same cold-eyed way as Ramsey. Jettisoning a player like Jimmy Greaves was not as important as sticking to the accepted playing formula, as Clough did at club level for so long. Roy McFarland played for both managers and accepts that they were very similar in approach: 'Cloughie was more volatile but he inspired loyalty just like Alf. I used to laugh when one of the England lads said, "How can you play for that Clough?", but all they saw was the stuff on television, where he was just playing it for laughs. The real Brian Clough was fantastic in the dressing-room, so the England lads would've loved playing for him. He would've looked at about 20 players for England and stuck with them, just bringing in a new player now and then to have a look at him. The press wouldn't have picked Cloughie's team for him, that's for sure. The players would know how he wanted them to perform and then they had the freedom. Not one of Don Revie's dossiers in sight; the opposition wouldn't have had a mention.'

The point about dossiers is well made. Under Revie, the England players were told so much about their opponents that they must have lacked self-confidence at times, especially as the manager chopped and changed the team with bewildering frequency. In 1981, Ron Greenwood changed the tactical formation five times in 12 games as England struggled to qualify for the World Cup; he also asked the players for their opinions while surrounding himself with advisers. Under Graham Taylor, there hardly seems enough room on the touchline to accommodate the phalanx of coaches decked out in England tracksuits, pouring advice into Taylor's ear. Ramsey only had his trainer Harold Shepherdson alongside him and some great players out on the pitch who were expected to take responsibility for making the system work. That has always been the Clough way. Neil Webb has experienced contrasting styles of management as he moved from Nottingham to Old Trafford and back again, while still playing for Bobby Robson and Graham Taylor and for him, Clough's methods are the best. 'Cloughie treated you like an adult as a footballer and he was brilliant at not cluttering up our game. When I went to Manchester United, Alex Ferguson was so intense. There was a dossier for each game, the scouts had the opposition watched several times and then we'd have a half-hour team meeting on match day. On my first England tour, Bobby Robson made us watch videos of the opposition for an hour – it was worse than Fergie! Clough simply relaxed us and told us we were good. I'd have loved to have seen him manage England. Players who didn't know him would've been startled at the way he prepared us. They'd have been queuing up to go on England trips – no slight strains that meant you had to withdraw at the last minute. No one would want to miss out.'

Clough never believed that he would have fretted at the lack of England matches and pined for the glut of games that prolong an English season. 'I remember Len Shackleton making me laugh in the old days up in the North-East when he said that if he could, he'd get away with working one day a week for his newspaper for the same money as six days a week. I understood that. I wouldn't have missed attending 40-odd first team matches, 30-odd reserve games and watching the kids 40-odd times in a season – not one bit. The England job would've suited me down to the ground. I'd even have learned to ski!'

If there had been any reconnaissance needed for the next international, the passport of Peter Taylor would have been the one that was regularly presented. At his best, Clough was matchless at deciding what was vitally important, as distinct from peripheral. Recent England managers have set great store on visiting hotels and training camps abroad, where they would present themselves in a few months' time; trusted English chefs have been brought on the payroll to ensure no repetition of the stomach bug which afflicted Gordon Banks in Mexico in 1970, while the players came to know the road to Lilleshall for training as well as the M1. Clough would not have concerned himself unduly with any of that. He told Bobby Robson he was wrong to closet the England players in an hotel soon after a hard league match, in preparation for an international in midweek. 'They should be with their loved ones at the weekend, instead of a plush hotel where they finish up kicking their heels, drinking, gambling, running up phone bills – bored. I never believed in training camps before a big game. Preparation should mean relaxation. Save it for when you really need it.'

Spoken like the man who broke off his holiday in Crete to win the European Cup in 1979, and returned there as soon as Forest won in Munich. It is hard to imagine Clough the England manager resembling a Revie who became neurotic under the strains of the job, a Robson sprouting grey hairs by the month, or a Taylor whose rambling sentences defeated the best efforts of the most efficient shorthand writers in the media circus. Clough's *sang froid* might have been just what England's players needed, as they relaxed into the smooth passing game that was second nature to all Clough's successful teams. He would have been happy to keep his distance from his élite players.

Peter Taylor was less committed than Clough to the idea of running England. He thrived on the daily grind of club management, doing a deal, winding up players, motivating his partner through his wildly contrasting moods. Taylor loved living on the edge, planning the next stage of rebuilding, whereas Clough was lazier, aware that his unique powers of man-management depended on a certain scarcity and remoteness. Clough, disappointed at playing only twice for England, took this second rebuff harder than Taylor, who sympathized. 'In any walk of life, the top job should go to the one with the best credentials. That was Brian – no question. He soon forgot about it, though. We were top of the league at the time.'

The other candidates lacked the calibre of Clough at that time. Lawrie McMenemy had won the FA Cup the year before, and was impressive in his efforts to transform a Second Division club into one good enough to compete with the major ones, a task he accomplished over the next few years. Bobby Robson, two years older than Clough, had steered Ipswich to second place in the First Division, showing the same kind of foresight as Clough and McMenemy in transforming a provincial club. But he had not won anything yet – the FA Cup and the UEFA Cup triumphs were in the future. Allen Wade's presence on the short-list can only be construed as *pour encourager les autres* after 14 diligent years as the FA's Director of Coaching. A series of thoughtful pamphlets and articles by Wade on the game's shortcomings was not the first qualification that springs

to mind for motivating international players. That left Greenwood. He was not officially on the short-list for the excellent
reason that he was already the man in harness. After Revie had
opted for his lucrative contract in the Middle East, Greenwood
was asked to fill the breach in a caretaker capacity for three
matches. The third was an encouraging 2–0 win at Wembley
over Italy a few weeks before the FA gave the job to him. Yet
England failed to qualify for the 1978 World Cup, missing out
on goal average. The damage had been done under Revie's
stewardship, but England still had a chance if they had scored
enough goals against Luxembourg, Greenwood's second game
in charge, but they only managed to win 2–0. After Italy had
been beaten in the next qualifier, it was shown that three more
goals in those two matches would have sent England to the
World Cup Finals.

A timid, tactically confused performance by England in the
1980 European Championships was followed by an unimpressive
run in the qualifying games for the next World Cup. England
lost three of their eight matches, including the ones in
Switzerland and Norway, and they sneaked into the Finals
because Rumania contrived to lose at home to the Swiss.
Greenwood seemed uncertain about the most desirable formation, alternating between Peter Shilton and Ray Clemence in
goal, and denying Glenn Hoddle, the oustanding young English
talent of his generation, a settled run in the side.

It was even more depressing in the 1982 World Cup Finals,
when England were eliminated on goal difference after drawing
their last two games 0–0. For the West Germany game, England
needed to win, so Hoddle was dropped. Afterwards, Greenwood praised Graham Rix and Kenny Sansom for stopping
Manny Kaltz from advancing from full-back. Kaltz could not get
in many dangerous crosses because England had beavered away
on the left wing. So that was fine, then – it did not matter that
Rix hardly made a run into the German half to try to create
something, or that England's supporters could hardly credit the
passionless, vapid performances against West Germany and
Spain.

The litany meanders on. Under Bobby Robson, England
failed to qualify for the 1984 European Championships, played

abysmally and tepidly four years later, flattered to deceive in the 1986 World Cup Finals, and were lucky to get as far as the semi-finals in 1990. Subsequent performances under Graham Taylor can only be discussed in sepulchral tones, with lowered eyes. So under a succession of safe, decent managers England have underachieved in the important tournaments since Brian Clough was rejected in 1977. He might have done better, he would surely not have fared worse. At least there would have been a thread of consistent purpose under Clough, where the players would have known clearly what was expected. Given his tolerance at club level of gifted playmakers who did not sweat buckets – Alan Hinton, John Robertson, his own son, Nigel – it seems inconceivable that Glenn Hoddle would have been in and out of the side. Clough knew the importance of imagination, the killer pass, the necessity for accurate distribution in counter-attacks and composure in front of goal. He knew that the hewers of wood and drawers of water would be needed in certain parts of the field, but like Ramsey, he would incorporate those and his gifted players into a simple strategy that did not tax their mental powers. A manager who beats the best in Europe two years in succession, who gets to the European Cup semi-final at the first time of asking, has talent in abundance. Like Ramsey, he won the First Division championship the year after being promoted. You do not accomplish such feats if you are simply a braggart with tyrannical tendencies. Players win you trophies and the best managers inspire those players.

It was Nottingham Forest's gain and England's loss when Brian Clough was turned down in 1977. Within a few months, he had become only the second manager after Herbert Chapman to win the First Division championship with two separate clubs, the kind of achievement that ought to be rewarded with greater recognition than the job of running the England youth team.

10

The Years of Plenty

'A critic is a man who knows the way but can't drive the car' –
Kenneth Tynan's aphorism could easily apply to those who gave
Brian Clough no chance of any honours at the start of the
1977–78 season. Nottingham Forest had scraped into the First
Division, courtesy of Wolves; they had signed just one player –
Kenny Burns – and consolidation was their only credible aim.
Yet those pundits had ignored recent history. In 1969, Clough
had taken Derby up from the Second Division with a side of
ageing players and raw talent. Yet Derby played some thrilling
football, sweeping more illustrious sides off the park and
finishing fourth in the table.

Eight years on, Clough was delighted to be back after a three-
year absence from the top flight, convinced he had proved his
credentials again as a manager after the traumas at Leeds, and
the partnership with Peter Taylor was working brilliantly.
Within a month of the start of the new season, Peter Shilton and
Archie Gemmill had been signed. Forest just swept to the title:
after November, they lost just one game in all league and cup
competitions, the championship was secured by a margin of

seven points (two points for a win in those days) and Clough had achieved his aim of getting back into Europe. He recalls: 'We were young, fresh and happy. It was all coming together. Signing Peter Withe was an absolute masterstroke by Peter Taylor and Larry Lloyd too. Larry emerged from the shadows and was a rock in defence for us. So was Kenny Burns. A bit of a lad but Peter said he could handle him, and he did. He turned up to sign for us in a car without tax or insurance – it's a wonder we weren't arrested. Archie Gemmill was a brilliant deal, only £20,000 plus our goalkeeper John Middleton. If Archie had cost a million, he would've paid his dues. Peter Shilton wasn't a particularly popular young man to sign because he was expensive. But he was talented and he knew it. Stoke had just been relegated and needed the money. Their chairman said Shilton would get me the sack because of his high wages and I told him, "He's not good enough to get me the sack." As the years went by, I used to remind Shilton that I'd rescued him from playing in front of 5,000 people. What he and the back four gave us was solidity. We had a firm belief that if we scored, there was no way we'd lose because they wouldn't score against our defence.'

At the time, Shilton's presence in goal was estimated to save at least 12 points a season and the facts bear that out. Forest conceded only 24 goals in 42 league games and Clough could purr over 25 of his beloved clean sheets. Forest won their first four games, conceding just one goal, but then lost 3–0 at Arsenal. The smart money would not be placed on Forest for the title after that display, particularly when Clough fined Burns and Lloyd for offences on the field that had not been seen by the referee. It seemed that Clough would have problems with those two hothead defenders, both of whom had reputations that frightened off many other managers. Burns enjoyed a drink and a flutter, but Taylor was always superb at sniffing out a player's social weakness and then ensuring the player realized he owed a debt to Taylor for keeping faith in him. It worked a treat with Burns, who curbed his temper, improved his concentration and was named Footballer of the Year later that season. As for Lloyd, he came perilously close to the sack after that Arsenal match. In the team meeting a few days later, Clough and Taylor suggested he had ducked out of a physical challenge on Frank Stapleton as he beat him to a cross to score. To someone of Lloyd's physical bearing and macho pride, that was tantamount to a white feather in wartime and Lloyd erupted: 'I jumped out of my chair and I was within two inches of chinning the pair of them. Peter told me later I'd have been out on my ear if I had. I realized that you couldn't thump your manager but they knew my reputation. I think they liked having a couple of hard men around like me and Kenny. We weren't cloggers – we could play a bit, but we were there as an insurance if it got rough. All successful defences have a bit of nastiness in them. Clough used to shout at me "Hey! Big 'Ead! Win the ball and then give it to someone who can play with it!" That hurt a bit, but I could see what the bugger meant.'

It was an important psychological victory over Burns and Lloyd, two players who had not done themselves justice because of their volatile temperaments. Clough and Taylor showed to the others that they were strong enough to take on any player and if the team is winning, there is little room for argument. When Kenny Burns was fined that season for playing a square pass across his penalty box he paid the £25 without demur. Liam O'Kane, one of the Forest coaches, was sent to organize the fine, and the envelope was waiting for Burns in the dressing-room at half-time! Only Clough could get away with such unorthodoxy while making two serious points – that he wanted his defenders to play a certain way and that he was the boss.

Soon a wider audience was starting to appreciate the vibrancy of Nottingham Forest. The television cameras began covering most of their games, as the public waited for the bubble to burst. When Forest hammered Manchester United 4–0 at Old Trafford in December, the 'Match of the Day' cameras were there to transmit a thrilling display of counter-attacking football. Archie Gemmill's scurrying, selfless style fashioned out a host of chances for Tony Woodcock and John Robertson. The speed and precision of Forest's attacking play was breathtaking. John Robertson believes it was the best team performance he played in for Forest. 'We'd been murdering sides at home but at Old Trafford, we really showed them. We were buzzing in midfield, our passing was brilliant, and we thought we could score in every attack. At that time our team meetings were fantastic, Clough and Taylor were making us laugh and convincing us we were the best players around. We started to believe them.'

In the Old Trafford dressing-room, Taylor told his players, 'It's two points for a win in December, the same as April. We can do it.' Taylor and his partner were too experienced, too successful to be dismissed as purveyors of hype. They had done it at Derby in 1972, against all odds; their self-belief was infectious. One other member of staff was convinced by now that the title could be won. John O'Hare was in that Derby side of '72, had been in that dejected dressing-room at Highbury when Alan Durban issued his call to arms. By Christmas 1977 O'Hare was convinced that Forest's five-point lead was enough to win the title. 'I'd seen how Clough and Taylor had motivated us at Derby and they were still tremendous at this time. They had the players, the place was buzzing. I told the lads we would win it. Players like Martin O'Neill and Larry Lloyd may not have liked Cloughie, but they would've run through a brick wall for him that season.'

Forest were attacking trophies on all fronts, yet when they got to the League Cup Final, they were distinct underdogs. Liverpool were the opposition, the outstanding English club side, a battle-hardened unit recently strengthened by the artistry of Kenny Dalglish. To widen the disparity between the teams further, Forest would be seriously below strength. Colin Barrett was injured, while Archie Gemmill, David Needham and Peter Shilton were cup-tied. In Shilton's place, Chris Woods – aged 18 and 124 days – was drafted in, and played heroically in a drab, goalless game at Wembley. Liverpool were far superior and the only plaudits coming Forest's way were for pluck and perseverance.

Clough and Taylor knew they had been lucky, but their first priority was to find the right way to lift their players, to stop them fretting about Liverpool for the Old Trafford replay. They took them away for some bracing sea air to Scarborough, shared a few drinks and more of Taylor's priceless one-liners. As the replay loomed, the players were told there was to be a slight alteration in tactics. John Robertson would be pushed deeper to play on the left side of midfield and the shape would be more

compact, to stop the supply line to Dalglish. John O'Hare came
in for the injured John McGovern with orders to shore up the
midfield and hit Liverpool on the break. It worked, and
surprised those who said Clough and Taylor never concerned
themselves with tactics. They did whenever Liverpool were the
opponents.

The only goal came from a Robertson penalty, when O'Hare
stumbled under a Phil Thompson tackle and fell inside the
penalty area. Referee Pat Partridge stood firm against Liverpool's protests, even though television action replays later
showed the offence was committed outside the area. O'Hare
agrees that he would have been aggrieved if the decision had
gone against Forest but points out that in similar circumstances
today, Thompson would have been sent off for the so-called
'professional foul'. Clough found the proper response afterwards: 'It was a penalty. The referee gave it and we stuck it in.
After that, there are no ifs and buts.' Students of dubious
penalties awarded in Liverpool's favour in front of their beloved
Kop shed no tears. Admirers of Clough's stance over dissent
drew their own conclusions as Liverpool besieged the referee,
while the neutrals concurred that beating such a team without
Shilton, Burns, Gemmill and McGovern was a remarkable
effort.

Clough took the view that at least Forest had qualified for
Europe, something that had appeared highly unlikely the
previous August, and he had learned something to his tactical
advantage from the defeat of Liverpool. John Robertson did not
miss its significance either. 'That Liverpool win showed us the
way to win in Europe. Till then we had rampaged at sides,
sweeping them aside, but Clough knew we'd get murdered if we
tried that in Europe. We had to be more patient, tighter in
midfield, less inclined to attack on all fronts. Once we got a goal
we were very hard to dislodge and we started to play cat-and-
mouse, especially against Liverpool and in European games. I
don't think we were ever as attractive again in my time, even
though we were so successful. I think the Forest team in the late
eighties were better to watch, a better passing side – but we
were meaner.'

Martin O'Neill who had to slave so hard on the right side of midfield, agrees: 'We had no fear in that first season. We attacked away from home, there was none of this stuff about soaking up the pressure, we just ran them off their feet. At home we were straight in at them, just paralysing sides. Clough was at his very best at keeping us on our toes and we believed we could beat anybody. It was a crusade for Clough and Taylor.'

The players undoubtedly enjoyed being part of that crusade, but it did little for their bank balances. For winning the championship in such style and against all odds, their bonus was precisely – nothing. Their contracts for the season had not included the possibility of winning the title or the League Cup, so the players missed out. The following season, they had their revenge after negotiating a bonus system with Clough. He agreed to pay them £1,000 a man for every point above 53 points in the 1978–79 league season. Forest had won the title with 64 points, so Clough reasonably felt they should be rewarded if they got anywhere near that figure. Forest ended up with 60 points, but Liverpool stormed to the championship by eight clear points. The club had to pay the first-team squad £7,000 a man for finishing second, which did not amuse Clough. His negotiations were rather more circumspect after that!

Even such a money-conscious manager as Clough, though, would surely acknowledge that his players deserved a handsome bonus for their work in the 1978–79 season. Liverpool were an outstanding side that season – conceding just 16 goals in their 42 league games – and it took a team of their stature to inflict a defeat on Forest that ended their unbeaten league run of 42 games, since the Leeds defeat the previous November. Clough is prouder of that feat than of many others in his career. He has always viewed the league as his overriding concern and it was no disgrace finishing second to Liverpool.

He still had his sweet moments against them that season. When the two sides drew each other in the European Cup's first round, Forest were the underdogs. They had started the season scratchily. Peter Withe had been sold to Newcastle in one of Clough's more bizarre transactions. His replacement would either be Steve Elliot or Gary Birtles, both young and untried. Birtles played at Arsenal in the 2–1 win, and Clough told him he would be the first name on the team sheet for the first leg against Liverpool on the following Wednesday. Birtles scored the first and made the second for Colin Barrett, as Liverpool lost 2–0. Clough had found himself another striker and a good squash partner into the bargain.

For the return leg at Anfield, Forest's preparation was typically unorthodox. Clough and Taylor knew it would be a tense affair, so they plied their players with drinks at lunchtime. Ian Bowyer thought it was a masterstroke. 'When we sat down to lunch, all these bottles of Chablis were on the table but we didn't question it, we piled in and I certainly slept well that afternoon. We were relaxed, played well in front of 40,000 screaming Scousers against an excellent side and got a goalless draw. Clough and Taylor had such an air of command that we followed their lead, we felt they knew best. The only predictability was their unpredictability.'

Clough was at his most eccentric in Athens for the next European Cup game, and he decided to take on Larry Lloyd. Clough usually operated on the basis that every fortnight or so, he would pick on someone over a comparatively trivial issue, just to keep the players sharp, to ward off complacency. In Athens, it was Larry Lloyd's turn. Forest had won capably enough against AEK Athens the night before and the party reported outside the hotel for departure the next morning. Lloyd was conspicuous in jeans and a casual jacket, whereas the rest of his team-mates were in official blazer and flannels. He had already checked with his captain John McGovern about the designated dress for the flight home, so he had packed his club blazer and was amazed to see that everyone else was in formal gear. Meanwhile, Clough had turned up in his customary green tracksuit top, but disappeared when he saw Lloyd. He returned ten minutes later, in blazer, shirt, tie and flannels. Very smart. He told Lloyd to do the same but he refused, saying his luggage was now in the coach compartment and he had not been told to wear his blazer initially. The row between Clough and Lloyd, in front of the players, was in their finest tradition, one of Vesuvius proportions, and it festered throughout the flight home, then at the City Ground the next day. Clough told Lloyd he would be fined £1,000 for a breach of club discipline, Lloyd refused to pay and he was dropped for the game against Ipswich the following day. On Monday morning, he stormed into the ground with a transfer request, only to find that Clough had drawn his sting. 'The bugger had gone off on a week's holiday! By the time he came back, I had cooled down. The bottom line is that I paid the fine and withdrew my transfer request. All my fines used to come back to me in some form, because they went into the fund for our trip abroad at the end of each season. I reckon I paid for all the drinks for the lads every trip!'

There was an amusing sequel to the blazer incident. Larry Lloyd's wife was as unimpressed as her husband at Clough's autocratic behaviour and when the carrot replaced the stick – with flowers sent to the Lloyd home after a decent interval – she rang up the club and left a message, telling the manager to stick the flowers where they rarely grow.

So Lloyd stayed in the Forest side and by the end of the season he had a European Cup winner's medal to place alongside all those envelopes containing fines. They really won it in the semi-final, an epic encounter against Cologne, two matches that showed the depth of Forest's resilience. They drew 3–3 at home in the first leg, clawing their way back into the game after being two down, then seeing an uncharacteristic error by Shilton giving Cologne a late equalizer. Cologne's three away goals meant they were the overwhelming favourites for the return leg. It was hard to argue with the sight of the Germans snapping up bargain package tour offers for the final outside their stadium just before the second leg, especially with the absence through injury of the inspirational Gemmill. Peter Taylor told Forest's players they would win and they turned in a tactical performance that was straight out of the Liverpool blueprint for winning games in Europe. They rode out the expected early barrage from Cologne, with Shilton superb in goal, then frustrated them with their calm possession play. Midway through the second half, Birtles flicked on Robertson's corner and Bowyer headed the winner from six yards. Forest were in the final. It was not the buccaneering, red-blooded display of the previous season, but it was ideally suited to the situation. Taylor's dogmatic confidence had settled his players and their performance again gave the lie to the theory that Clough and his partner were tactically gauche.

A month later, they had a problem for the final. It was a dilemma that would test their motivational powers. The opposition, Malmö of Sweden, were on a par with an English Second Division side and Taylor, who had watched them, was particularly worried. Forest ought to swat them down without any great effort and Taylor knew that they might struggle against the underdogs, they might be dragged down to Malmö's level. Injuries to Gemmill, O'Neill and Clark complicated selection and a place had to be found at last for Trevor Francis. He had been signed for a million pounds in February but was ineligible for the European Cup until the final. Surely the most unorthodox of management teams would not leave out Francis? They bowed to convention, and Francis scored the only goal of a dire match – hurling himself forward to head in Robertson's cross just before half-time. It was the only time Francis had the chance to show his talents as a striker, because he was used as a midfield man, joining the attacks late, to try to spring Malmö's obsessive use of the offside trap. Only one team seemed interested in looking for goals that night in Munich and if the performance disappointed, the result and the achievement by a provincial club that had been in the Second Division two years earlier were remarkable.

Clough and Taylor had deployed all their wiles to distract and relax their players before the game. On a hot, sultry evening, Clough had noticed that young Birtles was looking particularly tense as the team gathered in the hotel foyer before the trip to the stadium. He told Birtles to go and have a shave before he could get on the coach. Birtles mildly protested that he always liked a day's growth of stubble before a game, but Clough insisted. He told Birtles to use his shaving gear, he borrowed Chris Woods' after-shave and after 20 minutes, a fresh, clean-shaven Birtles emerged. Later he understood why his manager had been so insistent. 'There I was, a young lad about to play in the biggest game of my career and he saw I was fretting. I had no idea why he was so bothered about me getting a shave, but that 20 minutes calmed me down, stopped me worrying about the match.'

Two crates of beer were loaded on to the coach by decree of

Clough. He told his players, 'Climb in, lads – but get rid of the bottles when we're near the ground!'

It was not the first cup final that season in which Clough had enlisted the aid of alcohol to calm his players. Two months earlier, Forest had checked into their London hotel around mid-evening, the night before they were due to play Southampton in the League Cup Final at Wembley. Clough told them they had to be down at reception as soon as they had dropped their bags in their rooms. They could not believe it would be for a team talk – that sort of attention to detail was the province of other managers – but when they saw a waiter stacking up champagne bottles in a partitioned lounge, they knew what was in store. Clough told the players that no one was going to bed until the 12 bottles of champagne were drunk. Those who said they preferred beer were liberally supplied, those like Archie Gemmill who preferred a coke and an early night were told to sit down and listen. For the next three hours, Clough and Taylor wandered down memory lane, telling their players hilarious stories of their early days together at Middlesbrough, then at Hartlepools when they clipped the wings of Ernie Ord, their first chairman. They admitted some of the strikes they had pulled to get their own way, one or two kites they had flown to winkle money out of directors and fool the press and how they had outwitted a few managers. It was a brilliant double act, each feeding off the other's prompting, with Taylor's poker-faced mimicry at its most devastating. Most of the players were up till one o'clock and they fell into their beds, still laughing. Later that day, they beat Southampton 3–2.

They had sailed close to the wind, though. Southampton were leading 1–0 at half-time and it took some hard work in the interval by the comedy act to shake the players out of their lethargy. Alan Ball unwittingly helped them in that direction. In the build-up to the final, Ball had made himself a few bob by forecasting in a newspaper that Southampton would win and that Clough was not that special a manager. Lawrie McMenemy, Southampton's manager, groaned when he saw the article because he knew that his great friend would make some mileage out of it. McMenemy remembers: 'When we scored, Bally ran all the way down the touchline, waving at the two benches and I got up and really gave him a lashing. It wasn't what I wanted, not just because of my respect for Brian but because I knew that would work against us. Sure enough it happened. I've never seen a team run out like they did after half-time. They sprinted from the tunnel out to the middle of the Wembley pitch, and that's a fair way. They were motivated all right.'

Clough had not finished with McMenemy that day. At the final whistle, the beaten Southampton manager was watching the medals being presented in the Royal Box when he felt a tug on his arm. It was Clough.

'Come on, follow me.'

'What are you doing?'

'We're bloody going up those steps.'

Clough had been annoyed that the Football League had vetoed his plan to walk out alongside Peter Taylor at the head of Forest, so he let Taylor do the pre-match honours. When the teams were walking around the Wembley pitch after the match, Clough saw his chance and dragged McMenemy with him up the stairs to the Royal Box. Alan Hardaker, the formidable secretary of the Football League, hissed, 'What the bloody hell are you doing here?' but had the presence of mind to thrust two empty boxes at the two managers, as if they had been included in the post-match presentations. Another first for Clough – the first winning manager to penetrate the Royal Box at a Wembley final. Not even Alf Ramsey managed that in 1966.

Clough was in his element after that League Cup win, telling the press that he had a million-pound tea-boy in his dressing-room, as well as a pretty good side. That was Clough at his most mischievous, but mercifully the object of his barb – Trevor Francis – had already proved to be an equable character who knew that Clough needed his fantasies to keep the media happy. As Trevor Francis explains: 'I couldn't believe that the press swallowed Clough's tongue-in-cheek remarks about me. I just laughed them off. The point about the tea-boy remark is that he wanted everyone not in the side who was in the dressing-room to develop a family atmosphere, to make the selected players feel relaxed. I wasn't eligible for the early European Cup rounds or the League Cup Final, and I was very happy to make the tea. When he spoke to the press, it came out that he was cutting me down to size. He liked to show players that Nottingham Forest came first when you come to the club, whatever you cost. I understood that and just smiled.'

It was Taylor who had pressed Clough to break the million pounds barrier to sign Francis. Birmingham City were haggling for extra cash, so that they could placate their supporters by being the first English club to fetch a million pounds for a player and Taylor understood that better than Clough. 'Pay them,' said Taylor. 'Stop pissing about, it's only another 25 grand.' In later years, Clough has rationalized the Francis deal satisfactorily enough. 'I was worried early on for Trevor, but I soon saw he was the type to carry it off, he seemed to thrive on it. If it had been me as a player, I'd have been worried by that price tag. We had the money available, and it was either going to sit in the bank or it would get us a player. Trevor's flair was an extra ingredient for us at the time, with Europe on the horizon. He was an exceptionally good investment. He provided instant success, something few players can do. Trevor could turn a game with a pass, a run or a goal. He should've advertised instant coffee, because he was an instant footballer.'

Yet Francis still had to undergo the usual crash course in awareness at Forest in his early days. He made his début for the third team on a parks pitch, in front of 40 spectators and at half-time, he had his first rebuke from Clough. 'Listen, young man – everyone who plays for me wears shinpads. Now go away and get some before the second half starts.' A fortnight later, Francis made his first-team début at Ipswich and by his own admission did not play very well. In the second half, he was getting frustrated and the choruses of 'What a waste of money' were beginning to disconcert him. When a cross came over from the right, Francis, aware that he could not get his head to the ball, handled it and the ball trickled over the line. A foul for hand-ball and end of story. Not quite. In the dressing-room afterwards, Clough raged at his new signing: 'Don't ever try that again. This is a professional outfit, not Roy of the Rovers stuff.' He continued to berate Francis if he felt he was being cavalier. 'He called overhead kicks and long-range shots Mickey Mouse football. He told me he wanted shots on target. As an outstanding goalscorer himself, he was hard on me. According to him, any sort of chance around the penalty area was a good chance.'

Francis never knew where he stood with Clough during his two and a half years at the City Ground. Before he joined Forest, he had unwittingly contributed to an amusing moment when he was presented with a Player of the Year trophy by Clough on behalf of the Midland Soccer Writers. While handing over the trophy, Clough had chided Francis with the words, 'Take your hands out of your pockets, young man.' For someone like Clough to lecture anyone on sloppiness of deportment was tantamount to Bob Geldof railing against designer stubble, but Francis did as he was told. While the laughter echoed around the room, Francis replied 'Yes, sir' to make the point that Clough was being a shade schoolmasterly. 'I didn't mind about that, it was all in good fun,' Francis explains. 'Typical Clough, wasn't it? You just take that from him, especially in the dressing-room where he was lord and master. That's as it should be. But there were other times when I was prepared to speak my mind.'

The first example of the steely resolution in Trevor Francis came in August 1979 when he returned to Forest with a groin injury, sustained during a summer playing in the United States. Clough thought he should have been resting, rather than fulfilling a lucrative contract, and he refused to pay Francis any wages for the first six weeks. Francis called in his union and the dispute was resolved but he made it clear that matters of principle were more vital to him than shooting a line to the press about inconsequential things.

In May 1980 Clough reacted to Francis snapping his achilles tendon by ordering him not to travel with the team to Madrid for the European Cup Final. Francis had played superbly in the previous rounds, particularly in the semi-final against Ajax. He was hurt by Clough's decision: 'He was wrong, he should've given me the option. I'd played my part in the run-in to the final and I wouldn't have moped around, getting on the lads' nerves. But he didn't want to know you if you were out of the team.'

Francis had been given that message to stay away fully three weeks after snapping his achilles against Crystal Palace. Clough did not contact him at all during that painful period, as Francis

contemplated disruption to his international career, missing out
on the European Cup Final and a long haul back before he was
fit enough to play again in the First Division. It was to be
another seven weeks before Clough contacted him and then it
would be a peremptory summons to the City Ground, just as he
was leaving home to visit his parents in Plymouth. Helen Francis
sat in the car while her husband hobbled into the office on
crutches to be met by champagne and the Clough charm
beaming forth on full wattage. He fussed over Francis for an
hour, told him to take his parents for lunch at Clough's expense
to a friend's restaurant on Dartmoor and ushered him benignly
out of the door. Not a word of apology for his indifference in
the previous weeks.

Clough and Taylor both felt Francis lacked a certain
aggression, that devil which separated the likes of Denis Law
from other strikers. They did not think he was strong enough to
play central striker, to take the knocks and turn with the ball.
They believed Francis was on the floor too often to be a leader
of the line like Kenny Dalglish. 'Wait till you get kicked before
you fall down,' they would roar at him. With his blinding pace
and uncanny ability to cross the ball at an acute angle, Francis
was better suited to the right side of midfield, in their opinion –
the only opinion that mattered at the City Ground. So Francis
had to persevere wide on the right, no doubt reflecting that his
success in that position against Malmö had rebounded on him.
With Woodcock and Birtles playing so well in the middle, and
Robertson still outstanding on the left, the only place where
Francis could be accommodated was on the right, where he was
told to run at defenders. When Woodcock was sold to Cologne
for £700,000 midway through the 1979–80 season, Francis
assumed he would be moved to his favoured position alongside
Birtles but he was continually switched around. He had played
poorly in the League Cup Final when Wolves scraped a
fortuitous 1–0 victory and Clough made a point of criticizing
Francis' contribution at Wembley.

It was a crisis time for Forest. They had already lost the first
leg of their European Cup quarter-final at home to Dynamo
Berlin and with the return leg due a few days after Wembley,
speculation was rife that Francis would be sold to ease Forest's

financial problems. Geoffrey McPherson, the Forest chairman, made it clear that a continued presence in Europe was essential for the well-being of the club, otherwise some of the best players would need to be sold. Gates were simply not large enough, with the capacity of just 36,000 rarely met. With Forest adrift in the league, out of the FA Cup, beaten in the League Cup Final and one goal down to Dynamo Berlin, it was a tense time for Clough and Taylor.

Francis told Clough he was unhappy at being singled out as the scapegoat for Wembley's disappointment and when asked where he would like to play in Berlin, replied, 'Up front – alongside Birtles.' Clough replied, 'OK, then play there – and stay there.' Francis responded with two goals in the first half-hour, a sharp, mobile performance, and Forest won impressively 3–1. Afterwards, Clough told the media, 'Francis made the important breakthrough, and went on to have a brilliant 90 minutes. I know I criticized him after Wembley, but he put his house in order.'

Francis played brilliantly in the home leg of the semi-final against Ajax, scoring the first of Forest's two goals. A disciplined away performance saw them through to the Final on a 2–1 aggregate, but Francis still had to stick to his guns about his favoured position. After being told to play in a wide position against Middlesbrough, he stalked into the manager's office and demanded a meeting straight after the game. Other players might get away with such an approach at other clubs but that was unprecedented at the City Ground in the time of Clough and Taylor. Not even Larry Lloyd would have tried that. Yet Francis penetrated the inner office, gave the management a considerable piece of his mind and, for extra emphasis, slammed the door when he left. The day before the next game, Francis was told to report to the office and he went there, expecting to be either transfer-listed or verbally abused. He was met by a smiling Taylor. 'Hang on a minute, Trevor, the carpenter's just fixing the door you broke the other night,' and Francis laughed with him. He adds: 'Their reaction completely floored me. They saw my anger as a positive form of aggression at last, they wanted to see that I passionately cared. After that, I played up front for the rest of my time at Forest.'

Clough and Taylor were masters at disconcerting players, then making them laugh in almost the same breath. On the eve of their return leg against Ajax in the European Cup semi-final, they took the entire squad for a stroll around the back streets of Amsterdam. Taylor led them into the red-light district and purported to organize a discount – 'there's 17 of us, you know' – and then they sat outside a café, listening to Clough and Taylor yarning, enjoying a few drinks, putting the imminent game into perspective. Who else would prepare the players for the 1980 European Cup Final by taking them on a week's holiday to Majorca, banning training and encouraging some enthusiastic drinking? Hamburg were spending a week in a training camp, Forest were lolling around, with no curfews and several hangovers. Martin O'Neill, now one of the brightest young managers around, still cannot believe that Forest got away with such a relaxed approach. 'We won two European Cups and we never practised a free-kick. "Just give it to Robbo," was the cry. Brazil practised set pieces, despite their quality, but not Forest. In the final against Hamburg, we were dead on our feet after being in Majorca. I'm sure that we'd have lost if they had equalized.'

That 1–0 victory over Hamburg was a much more satisfying one than that of a year earlier against timorous, craven Malmö. Hamburg were a fine side, thorough in a typically Germanic way, with the European Footballer of the Year, Kevin Keegan, expected to dominate. Yet Burns soon let Keegan realize that he would be snapping at his ankles and as Keegen was pushed further back, Forest snatched a goal. Birtles nicked the ball back to Robertson and he scored from just outside the penalty area. After that Forest shut them out. Birtles soldiered on alone up front, the five-man midfield was reinforced by Gary Mills – and who else would have such faith in an 18-year-old, putting him in for the injured Francis? – and Shilton and Burns performed heroically in defence. John Robertson admits it was a performance light years removed from the quixotic attacking of yore, but they had to cut their tactical cloth accordingly. 'Without Trevor Francis, we were the complete underdogs. We were short of players – John O'Hare was a substitute and he was 34! We didn't intend to defend so much, but our five-man midfield held them at bay for long periods. It wasn't just a case of hanging on, we never lost our shape or our passing. We held on to the ball and they didn't hurt us as much as they should.'

So a smallish club in a smallish city in the East Midlands had won the European Cup two years running, even though they plainly lacked the support, the financial depth and the infrastructure of Manchester United, Liverpool, Everton, the major London clubs, or Celtic and Rangers. It was a remarkable achievement, even though both performances had been from the pragmatic book, rather than the cavalier approach that had been so captivating in the winter of '77. It had been a triumph for a style of management that was idiosyncratic, yet effective.

On the night of Forest's return match in East Berlin, Taylor was on the pitch, eyeing the Dynamo players as they came out to examine the deteriorating conditions. It was freezing, the atmosphere was distinctly hostile, and Forest trailed 1–0 from the first leg, yet Taylor had seen straws in the wind that encouraged him. He had noticed that the Germans wore gloves and tights as they warmed up. Taylor went back to the dressing-room and told the players that the Germans had no chance, they did not want to play, their body language spoke of tension. Forest played brilliantly and were 3–0 up at half-time. As they filed excitedly into the dressing-room, trying to thaw out, Clough told them, 'None of you say a word.' They had to sit there for ten minutes in total silence. Clough later admitted he was so proud of them that he did not want to say anything until after the final whistle. They were still only three goals up at half-time, after all.

At times, Clough was unstinting in his praise and generous with the club's money. On other occasions, he was maddeningly perverse, obdurate beyond reason. After the 1980 European Cup Final, he refused permission to the players to meet up with their wives and girlfriends for a celebration. The previous year, they had all gathered in the same hotel in Munich and relished the occasion. This time, the players and management were installed in an hotel an hour's drive from Madrid and their partners. Clough refused to lift the curfew afterwards, possibly because Larry Lloyd of all people had led a deputation pleading for a change of heart. John Robertson also argued with Clough and that exchange was only curtailed when the manager threatened violence to the player who had won the Cup with his opportunist goal. In the end, Robertson and several others slipped out, commandeered some taxis and made sure they were back early the following morning while Clough was still in bed. Perhaps Clough knew they would ignore the curfew whatever he said, but it seemed bizarre that he should be so dogmatic, when his players had performed so magnificently for him.

It was no more bizarre, however, than his usual demand at the end of Forest's training sessions alongside the River Trent. When he was bored – and that was sometimes after ten minutes – he would shout, 'Right, let's go through the nettles,' and the players would have to run through a 25-yard square of long grass and nettles. Players valued at more than a million pounds, and experienced internationals would join with the most junior squad member in running through the grass and wincing as they were stung by nettles. Clough, Taylor and Taylor's black labrador Bess would view the proceedings with varying degrees of interest as the players ran through the equivalent of a brick wall. Then they would all run into the same net, to see how many the net could accommodate, with the last to get in ending up with a forfeit. Gary Birtles soon got used to the mayhem. 'It was all a laugh, done just to relax us. Imagine – 15 grown men trying to squeeze into the same small net and then getting stung by nettles! It didn't happen at other clubs. But we didn't mind that because we had such a great spirit in the team then. We played such a lot of games that Clough didn't want us to leave our energies on the training pitch, so we just fooled around a lot of the time. The lads would go out for a night together, and the manager knew all about that. He knew we would never abuse the privilege.'

Clough was just as enigmatic with opposition managers as with his own players. Although he always expressed solidarity with fellow-managers when directors started flexing their muscles, he was sufficiently competitive to try exerting psychological pressure on the opposition's manager before a match. Clough always wanted to win – within the rules of course – but he would not be averse to playing mind games. When Forest played Wolves in the 1980 League Cup Final, Clough was miffed to discover that John Barnwell had pipped him for a favoured hotel in north London for the usual preparations. On the morning of the match, Barnwell was idly looking out of the lounge window, ruminating that he could not have done more to get his players right for the day, when a coach from Nottingham drew up outside the front door. The wives and children of the Forest players then spilled out of the coach and filed into the reception area for a pre-arranged meal. Barnwell knew who was behind the ruse. 'Cloughie had sent them there to disconcert me. He knew that I'd want peace and quiet for my players, not a bunch of kids screaming in the foyer. I went berserk, demanded a partition for my lads. He'd disturbed me and he would've known that I'd be thrown off my job. A few hours later, I tried to get my own back. I thought I'd leave them waiting in the tunnel, till we were ready to go out with them. "I'll let Cloughie kick his heels," I thought. At the third time of asking, I led my players out of our dressing-room into the tunnel and I went to the head, looking for Cloughie. Blow me, he'd done me again – Jimmy Gordon was to lead Forest out and Cloughie was already sat on the bench by the halfway line!'

In the end, Barnwell had the last laugh. Wolves stopped John Robertson from exerting his usual influence by playing Peter Daniel on the right wing instead of in his usual midfield role. Daniel's tackling was decisive and it was from his deep cross, and after David Needham and Peter Shilton had collided in a comical tangle, that Andy Gray put in the easiest goal he had ever scored, the only one of the game. Significantly, Forest were outmanoeuvred by the long ball and the frequent use of the deep cross, a tactic that would become more and more successful against them for the rest of the Clough years. Larry Lloyd's absence that day at Wembley emphasized his importance in the air; he and Burns were never surpassed as a pairing at the heart of the Forest defence throughout the next 13 years in the First Division. The increasing emphasis on the physical, the knock-downs from long clearances and the preference for aerial assaults on Forest would combine to reduce their effectiveness. By now it had dawned on other sides that siphoning off the supply lines to John Robertson diminished the threat from Forest. Wolves were the inferior side that day at

Wembley, but Peter Daniel's example had shown the artisans how to combat one of the most influential club players of that era. Many of Daniel's ilk would prosper at Forest's expense.

No one knew it then, but the 1979–80 season marked the end of Brian Clough's great years as a manager, even though he was only 45 years of age. Forest had lost 18 games in all competitions that season, compared with four in each of the previous two years. A total of five major trophies in three seasons was remarkable, but it would be another nine years before Clough again held a cup aloft. With hindsight he should have allowed his players to let their hair down on that warm Madrid evening after beating Hamburg. There would be scant excuse for a knees-up over the next few years.

11

On the Slide

Within two years of Forest parading the European Cup around
the Bernabeu stadium in Madrid, they had become mid-table
mediocrities, with little hope of halting the downward spiral. It
was a stunning decline, reinforcing fears that a provincial club
like Nottingham Forest lacked the means to compete with the
big names, season after season. By the summer of '82, Brian
Clough was facing one of his sternest tests as a manager. He had
lost most of his best players and his partner Peter Taylor had
retired. Clough was alone – and in trouble.

Taylor's dealings in the transfer market were disastrous around
this time, a fact which contributed to the emerging strains in their
relationship that led to Taylor's eventual resignation in 1982. But it
was Clough who earned most of the plaudits during their halcyon
period, so he has to shoulder the blame. He agrees: 'There
should've been a period of stability at that time, but we wobbled
more than we should. There was a slight case of panic, we ought to
have taken longer to sign players and a bit of ego crept in as well.
The standard of players we bought wasn't as good as before, and I
must take the blame for that.'

The turnover at the City Ground in the early eighties was bewildering. In the year after Madrid, Gary Birtles, Ian Bowyer, Martin O'Neill, Larry Lloyd and Trevor Francis left, and the next 12 months saw the departure of Kenny Burns, Frank Gray, John McGovern, Peter Shilton and Gary Mills, and the retirement of John O'Hare, David Needham, Frank Clark and Peter Taylor. Thirteen players of great experience and an assistant manager who had been an integral part of Clough's best days in charge. The bulk of the replacements confirm that Clough and Taylor had taken their eyes off the ball. Justin Fashanu, Ian Wallace, Peter Ward, Mark Proctor, Willie Young, and significantly three foreign players – Einar Aas, Jurgen Rober and Raimondo Ponte – were not in the same class as those players who had won so many trophies a year or two earlier. Clough and Taylor had not previously expressed much interest in going abroad for players, feeling that they lacked the essential British phlegm and grit to survive in the First Division, but now they were looking for bargains and were not too picky to go for foreigners. The trio managed fewer than 100 league games between them, so they were hardly a success. The same could be said for the three strikers – Wallace, Fashanu and Ward – who cost a cool £2½ million, enough to buy two players of Trevor Francis' quality.

The fate suffered by Francis encapsulates the odd decisions by Clough and Taylor between 1980–82. After working slavishly hard to recover from his achilles operation, Francis recaptured his England place and, in his opinion, played better than at any time of his career so far, week in week out, for Forest. Then Fashanu and Wallace were bought in the summer of '81, with Fashanu agreeing to join Forest so he could play alongside Francis and Clough assuring Fashanu that he would be staying. Yet Francis found himself playing wide on the right of midfield when the new season started, a sure sign to him that his days were numbered at the City Ground. He did not want to leave, with a year left on his contract, but he was soon transferred to Manchester City, for a slightly higher price than he had fetched two and a half years earlier from Birmingham City. Perhaps it was felt that Francis was now more vulnerable physically, that his pace would be blunted by the damaged achilles, that a million-pound deal was good business. He was still playing a decade later in the First Division with the suspect achilles holding up pretty well.

Francis was not that surprised at being frozen out at the City Ground. He had experienced Clough and Taylor's ruthlessness a year earlier when he was still recovering from that serious injury. While recuperating on holiday in the South of France he read that he was going to Barcelona for £1.5 million – even though his leg was still in plaster. He went to Spain for three days of medical tests and negotiations, but the deal fell through. It was a salutary warning to Francis that no player should expect to put down domestic roots in the Nottingham area.

Justin Fashanu certainly discovered that. Although he had impressed hard defenders like Larry Lloyd and Kenny Burns whenever Forest played Norwich, there was little evidence that Fashanu would offer much sophistication or consistency to his new club, despite a spectacular goal against Liverpool that was broadcast regularly on television and voted Match of the Day's Goal of the Season in 1981. Fashanu could not be called a success at Forest and Clough was dismayed at his apparent reluctance to play football. In the end, he barred Fashanu from training, a wholly illegal action that had the players' union frothing. Fashanu refused to leave the training ground. The players were secretly hoping that the massive Fashanu, a boxer of genuine potential, might take the matter into his own hands and reward Clough with a right hook, but Clough brazenly faced him down and won yet another test of wills, though it was only after police intervention that the hapless Fashanu was led away. Soon afterwards, Fashanu was sold to Notts County and one of the most embarrassing transfer deals by Clough and Taylor had drawn to an ignominious close.

Larry Lloyd witnessed the transformation at the City Ground first-hand, before he left to become Wigan's player-manager and he feels that Forest ought to have followed the example of his old club, Liverpool. 'At Anfield, they used to tinker around with the machinery, get rid of one player a year and replace him with someone who had done his time in the reserves and knew all about the style of play. Ian Rush did a year in the reserves after being signed from Chester, you know. Major surgery was avoided at all costs. That should've been Forest's way, but the team was broken up far too quickly. I'm sure I could've played another season but Clough told me he wanted to bring down the average age. Then he signs Willie Young, who was older than me, as my replacement!'

Ian Bowyer, one of the first from the successful team to be sold, was back at Forest within a year of going to Sunderland. Clough admitted he had been wrong to sell him, but Bowyer soon knew that things had changed very quickly. 'The turnover had been too fast. Some of our older players were over the hill but the experienced replacements were not as good as people like Larry Lloyd and Kenny Burns when they were signed. The younger ones like Colin Walsh, Bryn Gunn, Steve Wigley and Stuart Gray never quite made it, even though they all had great potential. Clough and Taylor hadn't managed the changeover well, and they were at fault. They got the benefit of the doubt because of their earlier successes, but they weren't at their best towards the end.'

Their major distraction was money. In Forest's championship season, home gates averaged around 36,000 but they were down to under 20,000 four years later. By the 1985–86 season the average was just 16,800. It was a constant frustration to Clough that crowds did not flock to the City Ground and it was a major problem for a provincial club such as Forest, as they tried to attract new players and trim the wage bill, with the likes of Shilton and Francis enjoying a handsome pay packet. The new Executive Stand that was opened in August 1980 added to the lustre of the City Ground but it cost nearly £3 million and interest charges on the bank loan for that would hamper Forest for a number of years. Elimination in the first round of the European Cup in the autumn of '80 was another financial blow; Forest did not compete in Europe for another three seasons. Even then the players did not receive one penny extra in bonuses for reaching the 1984 UEFA Cup semi-final, a run that included two cash bonanzas for the club against Glasgow Celtic.

Money was a constant bone of contention between management and players during that period. Forest seemed to be dashing all over the world to raise cash by playing in lucrative

friendlies, the European Super Cup or the World Club
Championship. They played 75 first-team games in the 1980–81
season, including a ridiculous schedule in the summer of '80 that
was designed simply to generate cash. Martin O'Neill still
cannot believe an itinerary that took in the United States,
Canada, South America and Holland. 'It was a journey Marco
Polo wouldn't have taken on – all for money. Three days in
Vancouver, four in Florida, then down to Colombia where we
lost 5–0. Clough wasn't on the tour, sensible fellow, and at half-
time in the Colombia game, we went spare at Peter Taylor.
Peter Shilton said, "Pete, we're a laughing stock here" and the
crowd certainly thought so. When we got to Quito, we were told
that they didn't want us to play after all in Ecuador, because we
had been so awful in Colombia. That trip was when it all started
to go down the pan. Clough and Taylor thought they were
immortal, but they were driving the players to ridiculous lengths
– all before the start of a hard English season. And we started to
bitch about money among ourselves. We started to lose our will
to win.'

The club chairman, Geoffrey McPherson admitted he was
having difficulty generating more money through the boardroom.
'We will support the management as far as possible in every
way. If funds can be provided they will be. But there has to be
realism. We are faced with declining attendances. If the people
of Nottingham would support us, it would be much easier to
provide money for transfers. We might possibly be able to
increase our loan from the bank, because it is secured by the city
council, but it is imperative that we tread carefully.'

Forest were no longer successful enough to attract large
crowds to the City Ground. It was a classic Catch-22 situation
and Clough kept selling players to balance the books, while
leaving him just enough to bring in replacements, who proved
inadequate. He recalls: 'I got very little back for Ward, Wallace
and Fashanu when I sold them and it crippled the club for a
number of years. It was very dodgy for a time and I had to
scrimp and save. Many young managers don't know about that
aspect of management, but finding a star for nowt gives me
greater pleasure than landing someone of obvious quality.
Sometimes judgement is more important when the sum isn't all

that much, but is a hell of a lot to the club. My judgement was
at fault a few times.'

Clough's frustration spilled over with his directors. He
thought they should have found more money to fund his
rebuilding programme and he fired off a volley about them in his
newspaper column. For a time it looked as if the board might
demand his head on a sacrificial platter, but he eventually issued
an apology, which by his standards, was a major grovel. Such a
sensible climbdown by Clough indicated that he knew his
ground was no longer totally secure.

Seventh in the First Division, twelfth the following year, the
lowest until relegation in 1993. Beaten 4–1 in the League Cup by
Second Division Watford, defeat at home in the FA Cup by
Third Division Wrexham – the wheels were coming off quickly
at the City Ground. John McGovern was on the transfer list one
day – by decree of Taylor – then off it the following day, on the
authority of Clough. The players were bitching about a lack of
spending money on overseas trips which were solely to make
money for Nottingham Forest. A gruelling journey to Tokyo to
contest the 1981 World Club Championship was hardly the ideal
way to prepare for the fifth round FA Cup match against Bristol
City, with Forest desperate for a run in the Cup to boost the
coffers. The Football Association and the Football League
would not co-operate with postponing domestic games either
side of the Tokyo trip, so Forest's players just kept ploughing
on. If this is Monday, it must be Tokyo.

The hassles were clearly affecting Taylor, who had a history of
heart trouble, and in the last days of 1981, Clough was struck
down. He complained of chest pains after shovelling snow at
home and he spent a few days under observation at Derbyshire
Royal Infirmary. He was given the all-clear after exhaustive tests
in the coronary unit, and spent the next three weeks recovering
at home. It was a salutary warning to a man in his middle forties
who had prospered at the sharp end of a highly competitive,
neurotic profession. Managing a football club seemed to be
getting harder for someone who had appeared physically
indestructible over the previous 16 years in the job. He was to
be tested even further in the forthcoming year.

12

A Public Separation

Brian Clough was never the same manager after a conversation in his office on the night of 5 May 1982. Forest had just lost at home to Manchester United when Peter Taylor sat down wearily and announced he was retiring. For the greater part of the next 11 years, Nottingham Forest would play attractively, gracing Wembley under Clough's leadership – but he did not flourish as spectacularly as he did when Taylor was at his side, working at their peak. It is impossible to imagine a Clough team being relegated with Taylor alongside him in the dug-out, even when their relationship had become as strained as it was by the time of Taylor's retirement.

Both men had felt the pressures of a disappointing season for Forest. Clough felt Taylor had let him down in the transfer market, that he was losing his touch, while Taylor believed his partner was not motivating his players enough, that the policy of divide-and-rule was rebounding on him. A few years later, Taylor told me, 'It went sour in that last year and I could see the club suffering. I was tired and the players weren't happy. It was the right time to go.' Clough confirms the break-up was civilized enough and that he helped Taylor negotiate a satisfactory pay-off from the club, an issue that always perturbed Taylor, who maintained he got no more than his entitlement under his contract. That was a minor quibble: the bad blood would really flow a year later.

It was entirely understandable that someone like Taylor, who lived on his nerves, and prided himself on his thorough professionalism, should want to retire at the age of 53, with money not a problem any more. The special talent he brought to the partnership stemmed from years on the road, looking at players in the most obscure places, checking, double-checking, ringing contacts. It took its toll, and no wonder. 'I was always too tense. Brian used to despair of me trying to set up the next piece of business when he said I should be relaxing, enjoying our success.' It was made clear to Taylor that he would always be welcome at the City Ground and with so many race meetings nearby, a contented family life, and the prospect of seeing his grandchildren grow up, it was the right decision to go, once he had lost his self-motivation.

In that case, why turn up six months later as the manager of Derby County? He was bored. Taylor missed the wheeling and dealing, the excitement of match day, the pleasure of turning raw material into a player of quality. He did not miss Brian Clough – respect for him had diminished over the past year or so. They had had a few spats over money. Taylor felt Clough had over-reacted when he published a book (*With Clough by Taylor*) that yielded money for just the assistant, not the big name in the book's title. Clough had not known about the book and complained he should have been given a cut, but Taylor stuck to his guns, pointing out that Clough had earned a small fortune over the years with his newspaper columns, without giving Taylor a slice. A return to football, now that the batteries had been recharged, would suit Taylor. He had turned down Clough's offer to return to Forest at the start of the 1982–83 season but he could not resist the call from Derby County. They were near the foot of the Second Division, in serious financial strife, but Taylor had always been a romantic for Derby and loved the idea of restoring the club's prestige. Against his better judgement, he was asked to sound out Clough for a possible return and after a tense meeting, Clough abruptly ruled it out. They would now be rivals, separated by 15 miles.

The fates must have been in a playful mood in December 1982 when the balls came out of the velvet bag at Lancaster Gate for the FA Cup third round draw. Out came a home draw for Derby County – against Nottingham Forest. Every possible ingredient was in place for a dramatic day. Taylor had recruited men very familiar with Clough's personality – Archie Gemmill, Kenny Burns and also Roy McFarland as his team manager – while Clough had Colin Todd in his ranks, returning to the ground he had graced a decade before. In the build-up to the match, both Taylor and Clough were models of discretion. In a brief interview with me, Clough would only say, 'I've missed Peter Taylor since the day he walked out on me,' and he mentioned that McFarland was a good neighbour. They both knew that fur would fly in a feverish atmosphere that would recall the most dramatic occasions at the Baseball Ground. In front of 28,000 impassioned supporters, Derby won 2–0, with the first coming from Archie Gemmill. Clough kept his own counsel afterwards when asked for public comment and, an hour after the final whistle, Taylor was still in an intensely emotional state. As I prepared to interview him for BBC Radio, he warned me, 'If you ask me about Brian, I'll blow you out – I'm not here to talk about him.' No mercy in the hour of victory – and no sign of a thaw in the cold war.

Four months later, the relationship foundered for good. The unwitting agent of its destruction was the man who had been such a brilliant player for Clough and Taylor, who had genially taken all the gibes thrown at him – John Robertson. When Taylor heard that he had become a free agent at the end of the season, he moved for Robertson and snapped him up. Quite why he thought that type of subtle player would help Derby's plight in the lower reaches of the Second Division will remain a mystery. It was bad enough to have Taylor running Derby, just a few miles from his Quorndon home, but for Clough, it was the last straw when Robertson was spirited away from him, without a courtesy call. Clough was on a charity walk in the Peak District to raise money for a wheelchair for a Derby hospital when he phoned home, to be told the news by Barbara. Alan

Hill was with him and remembers what happened: 'We were in a little pub and when he put the phone down, he went to the bar, ordered a bottle of whisky and slumped down beside me. "That bastard, I'll never speak to him again," he said. "He's bought Robbo and he never had the decency to tell me what he was up to." '

Clough says it was the lack of courtesy that angered him. 'Just a thirty-second call. "How's the Walk going? Are you all right? By the way, I want to sign Robbo." We'd known each other so long, and it had come to that.' He says that he was having to work very hard at Forest after Taylor had let him down in the transfer market. He wanted to keep Robertson, because he at least was a class player, unlike many of those on his books at the time.

Taylor always felt that the Robertson signing was a red herring; it was his presence at Derby as manager that infuriated Clough, he could not bear the thought of Derby overtaking Forest in prominence. After all, Taylor had willingly covered for Clough over the years; who was minding the shop at the Baseball Ground while Clough swanned off to the television studios? They had often argued in front of their players. About money. About status. About the best time to get to the ground, particularly on European trips – Taylor liked to get the players there early, while Clough liked to leave it till the last minute, convinced that the players would get bored and lose their edge. That was always a matter of aggravation between them. Yet they needed each other and woe betide anyone who dared to criticize one of them within earshot of the other. They reserved the right to disagree with each other, but they presented a united front to the rest of the world. Away from football, they did not spend a great deal of time together, although Taylor had a genuine soft spot for Clough's three children, especially Nigel. After Robertson's transfer to Derby, they would exchange just a few words on the phone before Taylor's untimely death in October 1990.

Robertson also felt the backlash from Clough. He was barred from the City Ground for a time, although he returned to play a handful of games in the mid-eighties. He admits that the incident did not reflect very well on him, he had not shown the 'moral bravery' his two mentors often lauded. 'I should have had the courage to go and see Clough, but at the time I was frightened. He had caught me at a vulnerable time. I was worried about my security, because I was out of contract and Clough was making it hard for me. I had done my knee at Old Trafford in the January and as I limped to the coach after the game, he said, "What a bad time for that to happen, Robbo – with your contract up soon!" I was thirty and needed another contract and Pete caught me at the right moment. Deep down I wanted to hurt Clough for that remark in January. He should've known how I felt, because injury had finished his career as a player. That move to Derby really finished my career – if I'd stayed at Forest, I'd have been playing European football next season, instead of struggling in the Second Division.'

After Robertson's signing, Clough poured forth the vitriol towards Taylor. He over-reached himself when he announced in his column that if he saw Taylor hitch-hiking along the A52 between Derby and Nottingham, he would run him over. It was tasteless and shocking and Taylor's family was deeply hurt. Clough refused to help out Derby with any player loans, even though Derby desperately needed an injection of new, talented blood and Forest's wage bill could have done with a reduction. Clough would only refer to Taylor in public by his surname, whereas Taylor at least preserved the façade of respect by calling him by his Christian name. 'I'll never understand the things Brian said and did in my second spell at Derby, it was criminal really. It affected Derby County more than me. People working with me couldn't understand the lack of co-operation he gave us. It's not as if we were in the same division! Brian has to live with that. He has to find peace of mind, take stock of himself, he's wrapped up with too many people who blur his judgement. I now realize life's too short to hold grudges. Brian and I had some great times together, travelling the world at someone else's expense. We laughed, we bullied, we cried and succeeded. I'd love to sit down and have a private chat with him now.'

Those words were spoken to me after Taylor's second spell at Derby had ended anti-climatically in 1984. He was sincere about his desire for a rapprochement with Clough, but it never happened. Despite the lure of lucrative offers, Taylor resisted the chance to tarnish Clough and his reputation. He contented himself with glowing comments in public about Nigel's progress and how proud of him his father must be.

Clough ingeniously defends the newspaper articles in which he castigated his old partner by pointing out that the money raised bought 50 wheelchairs for local hospitals, rather than the one he was trying to buy on that fateful walk in May 1983. Nobody with anything more than a passing acquaintance with Clough doubts his sincerity on charitable issues, the thoughtful generosity which is one of his most admirable characteristics, yet his intemperate outbursts over Taylor were ill-judged. He is a good hater as well as a loyal, unswerving friend and sadly, Peter Taylor never had the chance to heal the wounds on either side.

Clough's attitude towards Taylor over the next year or so was sadly hostile. Liam O'Kane, one of his coaches, was suspended for a week because a strong Forest reserve side did not give Taylor's Derby an expected hammering. David Pleat bumped into Clough on holiday in Majorca, and over a drink, expressed admiration that he still had the drive to keep going. 'I'll tell you why I keep going,' Clough told him. 'To beat people like you and that Taylor.' He used to say to his Forest captain, Ian Bowyer, 'Get me down the tunnel, pal,' in the immediate aftermath of Taylor's departure. Bowyer believes Clough was vulnerable at that stage: 'For a couple of years, he wanted to walk out with us, so that the cameras wouldn't focus on the fact that he was alone, without Pete. I think he was lonely and he wanted the spotlight to be on the team. He knew the media were saying, "He can't do it without Taylor," but I don't believe he thought that for a second. Don't forget he also lost Jimmy Gordon at the same time. The gaffer respected Jimmy a lot and when he retired, that was another gap. Jimmy was quiet and discreet but gave both of them great loyalty and advice.'

Lawrie McMenemy recalls meeting Clough when he was at a particularly low ebb in the first season after Taylor's departure. Southampton had won 2–1 at the City Ground and McMenemy was looking for his old mate. He found him alone in the bath. 'He was very low. I sat on the edge of the bath and he told me a few things about the break-up. I could see a resolve in him, as if to say, "I'll show you lot I can do it on my own," but I wondered if he really wanted to carry on. I had no doubts about his talent, but he was very morose. I'm glad he saw it through and the fact that he's kept Forest up there for so long since Peter left just shows the kind of manager he was.'

At their best, Clough and Taylor were unstoppable. They had a common purpose, a desire for victory and a galvanic aura about them that imbued confidence. They knew how good they were, and encouraged other managers to aim high. They told David Pleat when he first went into management at Nuneaton Borough, 'Don't be frightened by it – there aren't many good managers around, there's room for you.' Every player that prospered under them pays tribute to the laughs they had. Trevor Francis described them as 'football's Morecambe and Wise' and wished he had managed to tape some of the team meetings, as they passed the beers around and listened to the tall tales. For Larry Lloyd, Taylor was like Tommy Cooper – 'You knew the punchline, but it didn't matter, his timing was so good.' Alan Durban thought Taylor was matchless at getting new players assimilated into the special management style: 'He'd look at a newcomer and say, "I don't know what you're thinking, but you're dangerous." He used to think that a bad character was better than someone who had no character. He was very popular with the lads. Pete couldn't lie straight in bed, he was always up to something, talking out of the corner of his mouth, giving us his racing tips.'

Durban agrees that the Clough/Taylor double act was usually too much for any player who thought he had a grievance. 'After we won the First Division, I went in for a pay rise. I was on £80 a week and wanted £100, it was my last chance of a decent contract at my age. Clough said, "You're having nothing, but I'll double your appearance money," and I knew that meant he wasn't going to play me much next season. Peter rounded on him and said, "You shithouse – after all he's done for you." All of a sudden it's a game and it's like watching a tennis match. I walked out with an extra £8, not the £20 I wanted. They'd done me. Usually Clough was the frightener and Pete put his arm round your shoulder, but they'd really confuse you sometimes by reversing the roles. Too much for us.'

Gary Birtles is particularly fond of Peter Taylor's memory because he made him laugh so much and also because he is sure that Taylor went in to bat for him when Peter Withe was transferred. At the time it was a toss-up between Birtles and Steve Elliot to replace Withe, with Clough favouring Elliot. But Taylor had been impressed by a drag-back by Birtles that had wrongfooted a Coventry defender in a reserve match and pushed hard for Birtles. 'Amazing, isn't it? One second playing for the reserves got me the nod! But the gaffer had great respect for Pete's judgement of a player, and he would allow himself to be talked round by him.' In fact, Taylor's record in signing strikers was more impressive than that of one of the great post-war strikers, Brian Clough.

Peter Withe, Trevor Francis, Peter Davenport, Roger Davies and Birtles were all Taylor captures and put his judgement handsomely in credit, despite the later aberrations over Fashanu, Wallace and Ward that strained his relationship with Clough. Taylor used to explain: 'I think I was better than Brian with strikers because it was all instinctive with him when he scored so many goals. I was a goalkeeper, so I studied them more, they were nearer to me than Brian up the other end. I knew what to look for.'

It seems likely that Taylor would have found good enough players to get Clough out of trouble had he been alive and still working with him in 1993. There would have been none of the second-guessing that Clough indulged in with his backroom staff. Towards the end of the eighties, Clough used to toy with retirement, but postponed it because he felt he had a good enough squad of players to have a tilt at the championship. In fact, he was always a couple of players short, but Taylor at his best would have found them. Decision-making would have been more rational, less prey to the whim of Clough and there would have been enough defensive cover to avoid playing Roy Keane and Nigel Clough in the back four, robbing the side of its creative flair and midfield drive. Brian Clough's success since 1982 has been admirable, a reward for persistence, self-belief and the integrity of his principles – yet his secure place among the managerial greats was obtained with Taylor at his side.

There may never be another Clough but equally there will never be another Clough and Taylor.

Roy McFarland, who played for them at Derby, then worked alongside Taylor on his return to the Baseball Ground, believes that the older man was essential to Clough's success. 'It was a partnership that fed off each other. Pete was in the background, suggesting things that Brian reacted to. They saw things quicker than anyone else.' McFarland, who has a touching affection for Clough, has lived in the same village for a number of years now, and he grieves that the pair never made it up before Taylor died. He thinks that Clough has not been the same since, that he is sorry he missed the opportunity to offer the olive branch. Alan Hill thinks that they might have made it up, and that his old partner's death hit Clough hard. Mutual friends were not surprised to see Clough slip quietly into the back of the church at Taylor's funeral service after interrupting a club tour abroad; he also made a phone call to the Taylor family. When Clough received the Freedom of the City of Nottingham in March 1993 it was gratifying to hear him say some kind words about someone, who unlike him, had been born in Nottingham – Peter Taylor. It was left to John Sadler to put his finger on why their relationship worked when he wrote in his column in the *Sun*, 'Whatever else Clough is missing from Taylor now they have split up, I know one thing – he's not laughing very much.' A few days later, Clough told Sadler, 'A lovely line, that – and absolutely true.'

What a shame they could not share some laughs in retirement. William Makepeace Thackeray once wrote, 'A good laugh is sunshine in the house,' but it was very dark at times at the City Ground after Peter Taylor left.

13

Fighting Back

With Peter Taylor gone, Clough set to work on rebuilding Forest and his work over the next ten years gave him immense pleasure and pride. Any other club manager would have been delighted to have achieved the same, up to the disastrous relegation season of 1992–93, and it is only because Clough was so outstanding so early in his managerial career that his later years were thought an anti-climax. Relegation hurt him deeply but as the pain eases, he can content himself with the knowledge that he left Nottingham Forest in sound financial hands, with a vastly improved stadium, a flourishing youth policy and a deserved reputation for footballing integrity.

Throughout the eighties the gap between the major clubs and the others became bigger than ever. The home club was now allowed to keep the bulk of its receipts from a match, so that the ones who had enjoyed a handsome pay day for trips to Anfield, Old Trafford, Highbury or Goodison were left to find alternative ways of building revenue. Usually that meant selling their best players, concentrating power still further in the small coterie of wealthy clubs. Nottingham Forest continued having to sell in Clough's rehabilitation years – with Viv Anderson, Peter Shilton and Peter Davenport all going – but Clough kept polishing up young gems, with the help of Alan Hill as youth development officer, and soon they were holding down a first-team place and playing with remarkable assurance.

Take Roy Keane. Ron Fenton, Clough's assistant, discovered him playing for Cobh Rangers in County Cork and signed him for £20,000. Clough took one look at him, could not believe a 19-year-old had such mature talent and put him straight in the first team – at Anfield! Keane had not met his first-team colleagues when they assembled at Anfield and was introduced to some of them on the pitch before the Liverpool game. Clough has always maintained, 'It doesn't matter how young he is – can he play?' and soon Keane was looking the ideal midfield player for the modern English game – strong in the tackle, excellent in the air, with extraordinary stamina for one so slight. Three years after making his début for Forest, Keane reluctantly left after relegation, but not before making it clear he owed his career to Brian Clough.

Stuart Pearce was another. He was signed for £250,000 from Coventry within two years of coming into the professional game at the age of 22, because Clough saw a hunger in Pearce that appealed. He has always liked his defenders to have a hard edge if necessary and Pearce's aggression seemed demonic at times. Yet Clough knew that his defence was rather too Corinthian and that Pearce would bind it together by example and leadership. Soon after signing Pearce in 1985, Clough forecast he would be an England player. 'He's got every chance, provided he stands up when he tackles, always helps his colleagues out – and gets his hair cut. The first thing I noticed about him was his competitiveness.'

It was to be another 18 months before Bobby Robson gave Pearce his first cap, but then he blossomed into an authoritative international and confounded those who thought his raw aggression would leave him exposed at the highest level. Pearce eventually captained his country, confirming that the sleekest model does not always capture the top prize. As club captain, he may have been diffident in his public relations, but his influence in the dressing-room was as positive as on the field. His brilliant, swerving free-kicks from a range of 30 yards if necessary also gave Forest an extra attacking dimension. Pearce's success with those free-kicks gave the Forest backroom staff even less reason to work on set pieces. Instead of 'Give it to Robbo,' the tactic now was 'Give it to Psycho,' the affectionate nickname donned on Pearce by the Trent End.

Clough's awareness of what makes an international player was not dimmed during the later years of his managership. A year before Des Walker won his first cap in 1988, he forecast great things for the sleek, athletic defender with that extra burst of speed which made him such a supreme defender in English club football. Walker had cost the club nothing after being turned down by a number of London clubs and at the age of 22, he was being lauded by the hard taskmaster who had first-hand experience of what makes a top central defender. 'He's very experienced for one so young, he's got the temperament and the pace. If he ever gets into trouble, his speed can get him away. He's well balanced and composed. Bobby Robson should be putting him on the subs bench for the full internationals now, rather than playing him in Under-21 internationals.'

Less than three years later, Walker was outstanding in the 1990 World Cup, leading finally to a lucrative move to Sampdoria. His absence was probably the decisive factor in Forest's sudden decline. There was no Walker to mind the shop, to cover for the other defenders with his astonishing pace, thereby allowing Pearce to make those surging runs forward from full-back. Even before Pearce was ruled out for the final third of the relegation season, he was struggling to come to terms with the absence of Walker. There had been times when Pearce could play as a left-sided midfield player, although nominally a full-back, because Walker's covering skills were so wide-ranging across the back four. That extra surge of power and speed from Pearce was a potent attacking weapon for Forest, who at times looked lightweight going forward. But without Walker, Pearce was having to re-define his role as full-back and without Pearce, Forest became even more pallid.

Clough's knack of converting players to different roles was still considerable, even after Peter Taylor's departure. Neil Webb had played up front and on the right wing for Reading and Portsmouth, until Clough converted him into a midfield player on the right side. Soon Webb's stylish displays for Forest got him into the England team. In his first spell at the City Ground, his stamina in the middle of the field was impressive; one coach of another club calculated that in one game he watched, Webb made 23 runs of more than 40 yards. Add that to his goalscoring ability, his intuitive understanding with Nigel Clough and his subtle passing and you have the ideal midfield player for a side such as Forest. Webb's equable character helped him concentrate on his game amid the midfield maelstrom, and to ride with the verbal punches Clough threw at all of his players at some stage. His first meeting with Clough alerted him to the prospect of some bizarre stories. Clough had barely exchanged a couple of sentences with Webb before he brought him to the player's table in their north London hotel, where they were preparing for a match at White Hart Lane. Clough told several of the players, 'This young man will be taking your place – or your place – or your place.' Even though Webb had not even discussed terms and was undecided whether to go to Aston Villa or Queens Park Rangers. The next time the pair met, at the City Ground, Webb was still undecided. An exasperated Clough said, 'Look son, go and walk around our pitch and when you come back, I want your answer – yes or no.' Webb returned with an affirmative and Clough opened a bottle of champagne.

'I don't drink champagne,' said Webb.

'You do now,' he was told and then Clough took him to his favourite Italian restaurant just up the road from the ground. Webb was so taken by Clough that he ended up signing a blank contract after the meal. 'When I got home, I couldn't believe what I'd done: he could've stuck any terms on that contract now he had my signature on it. But he didn't and next day he said to me, "If I'm honest with you, I want you to be straight with me." Negotiations were very simple – he told me what I was getting and that was it. But he was straight. People like me who thought Nottingham was a suburb of Birmingham signed for Brian Clough, because he was the Messiah. I was an average player when he signed me, then he turned me into a First Division player, then an international.'

Webb soon had a painful introduction into the Nottingham Forest way. Playing in the County Cup Final against Notts County just after he had signed, Webb tried to chip the goalkeeper from the edge of the penalty area, but the ball sailed wide. As he ran back to his place in midfield, Webb was told to come off by Clough. The game was only about 20 minutes old and he had already been substituted. Afterwards, Clough told him, 'You don't do that at this club, son – you pass it to someone who's better placed.' Webb never did that again. Nor volunteer to go in goal. 'In one of my early games, Hans Segers got injured against West Ham and I volunteered to go in goal, and we ended up losing 4–2. After the game, Cloughie said, "No wonder we lost, we've got a midfield player trying to keep goal." He dropped me for the next game because he thought I was too keen to go in goal. In your first year, he tests out your character. I was dropped three times in my first season, but I never knocked on his door to find out why. I asked the advice of the older players and they told me just to keep my head down, he was testing me out. I'm glad I kept quiet. He stopped me playing what I call "the wonder ball", when you split the defence and everyone raves about the pass. He told me I was trying to be too clever, that I was giving the ball away. In training, he'd stop the play and say to me, "Son, you're doing this wrong," and patiently talk to me. He was brilliant at treating you like an adult in a football sense, at not cluttering up your game. If you had the right attitude, all the other daft things didn't matter, in fact they were a laugh.'

Lee Chapman was 29 when he came to Forest, with ten years' experience of playing in the Football League – but Clough made him a better player in the space of a few months. His first touch improved with the experience of the six-a-side matches in training, he learned to turn with the ball and his near-post headers became an important part of his game. Chapman was fascinated at the relaxed approach at Forest ('the walk back to the ground from training was often longer than the training session'), at the insistence that energy should be saved for match day, at Clough's absence from a week's pre-season training in France, when he was used to his other managers being particularly hands-on. After a year at the City Ground, he was dropped, even though the leading scorer, and he realized that he was now expendable to Clough. After 15 months with Forest, he moved on to Leeds where he won a championship medal and showed how much he had improved as a target man. He gives Clough a great deal of credit for that and, despite an erratic relationship, speaks of him with respect. He particularly enjoyed his actress wife, Leslie Ash, being called 'My Beauty!' by Clough. Wives of Clough's players have often wondered why their husbands sometimes despair of their irascible manager, but they only get the flowers, chocolates and the honeyed words – not the earbashing at the most unusual times.

There were periods in the eighties when Forest were just a couple of players short of winning the championship, Clough's main aim. He enjoyed his trips to Wembley, ached to be back in Europe, but for him, winning the league has always been his priority. For long periods, though, he lacked the financial clout to be a major player in the transfer market. In any event, Clough has not been a great success when bids of a million pounds are discussed, he is far better in the small-to-medium range of transfer. Not enough supporters came through the turnstiles at the City Ground to finance concerted transfer activity in the mid-eighties, so Clough had to soldier on with a mixture of old sweats, youngsters and square pegs in round holes. Even in the 1986–87 season, when Forest played particularly attractive football, the average home gate was just over 19,000 – and that was a leap of 2,000 from the two previous seasons.

Forest's successful run in the UEFA Cup in 1984 helped put the club back on a reasonable financial footing and if they had managed to get through the semi-final against Anderlecht, the final against Tottenham would have been a genuine money-spinner. Clough was disappointed with himself over that narrow defeat by Anderlecht. He blames himself for alienating the Spanish referee with his pre-match comments and admits he might have picked the wrong team. He took a chance on Hans van Breukelen in goal, even though he had recently broken a finger. He was at fault for two of Anderlecht's three goals in the second leg and afterwards, Clough told Steve Sutton, his reserve goalkeeper, 'I should've played you, Sooty.' He also decided to play two wingers, Steve Wigley and Colin Walsh, but then brought them back into a five-man midfield, leaving Peter Davenport to forage alone up front. Echoes of Hamburg and the 1980 European Cup Final, except there was no Larry Lloyd, Kenny Burns or Peter Shilton to shore up the defence and no John Robertson to calm things down and retain possession. The game ran away from Forest near the end, their neat, slight midfield players were overwhelmed by the brilliant Enzo Scifo and although unlucky with a couple of refereeing decisions near the end, they were well beaten. Ian Bowyer captained Forest that night and his mind went back to previous tight encounters in Europe: 'I wondered about that formation in Brussels. Cloughie had been agonizing over his formation – he even admitted that to you blokes – and I just got the feeling that if Peter Taylor had been with him, there would have been no hesitations. Pete was great at making swift decisions and sticking to them. Brian needed the old Taylor that night.'

At least the UEFA Cup run yielded one vignette that was vintage Clough. The two games against Glasgow Celtic were, as expected, titanic battles. Celtic were clear favourites after coming away from the City Ground with a goalless draw. Clough had noticed a fondness for vodka by the Celtic manager David Hay when he visited his office at Forest and he filed away that information in his capricious mind. When Forest arrived at Glasgow, Clough noticed en route to the hotel a sign advertising 'David Hay's Bar'. He tracked down the pub, ordered a round of drinks for everyone and informed Hay's brother-in-law and pub manager, 'David's paying for this because he drank a bottle of vodka at my place. I'll have another round and this time, I'm paying.' The following morning, he told the players, 'If you want to go and play golf, fine. The rest of you come with me.' He took the players for a walk around Ibrox – the ground of Celtic's great rivals, Rangers – then on to a boys' club in Airdrie, which had a connection with Forest. Then back to the hotel, where he told the players to go for a walk as a gentle loosener for the match that night. Forest beat Celtic 2–1 in front of 60,000 roaring Glaswegians. It was another example of Clough's uncanny ability to take the players' minds off an important game by doing different things. Strolling around Ibrox was more diverting than going early to Parkhead and thinking about the game ahead.

By 1986, Forest were playing some dazzling football. Webb and Pearce had settled in, Franz Carr was at his most dangerous on the right wing, before he started to think about what he had done instinctively at speed, and Nigel Clough was knitting together midfield and attack with his subtle passing and ability to hold the ball, waiting for faster players to support him. Gary Birtles, restored at Forest for his second spell, was playing effectively at centre-half (another old dog being taught new tricks by Clough), and Johnny Metgod was making stylish, inventive contributions in midfield. They put six past Chelsea and Aston Villa in successive games and a glorious home game against West Ham marked a triumphant assertion of the principles of both managers, Clough and John Lyall. It was a match of charm, intelligence and the acceptable brand of commitment, won for Forest by Metgod's astonishing, swerving free-kick. More importantly, it was matches like that one which lodged in the memory bank of the most jaded reporter and helped to explain why so many Forest fans roared out Clough's name after his final game in May 1993.

Another game from that period still lodges in this reporter's mind. Forest went to Old Trafford and beat Manchester United 3–2 after being one down at half-time. United were top of the league after starting the season with ten straight wins and losing only three before Forest came to call in January 1986. Clough was so delighted with his side's performance that day that he asked the BBC's 'Match of the Day' programme to run off some videos of the match, and he presented all 11 players with a copy each. That same month, he was rather less charitable. Forest lost to Second Division Blackburn 3–2 in an FA Cup replay and he was so annoyed that he insisted the coach should return to Nottingham in darkness and in silence, with no food for the players. It was a long couple of hours for the chastened team.

The average age of the Forest team around that time was just 24, with Steve Sutton the oldest at 27. He remembers that period with particular fondness. 'We were inexperienced, but we had a wonderful camaraderie. We had the same interests away from football, we knocked around together socially and it was a pleasure to be at Forest. The gaffer was still in good nick and he was very supportive, knowing we were bound to make mistakes because we were so young. But it was terrific standing in my penalty area, watching us play some lovely stuff.'

Clough clucked over his young team with paternal pride. He was so upset by Jimmy Greaves' forecast at the start of the '83–84 season that Forest would be relegated that he wrote to his old mate, telling him he would be proved wrong. Forest finished third and that forecast had sparked him off. 'One thing you never do in football is write off good management and good players.' Over the next few years, Clough would proudly point to the high standards his young players were reaching. 'We play good, clean football. Referees like coming to us and I like that. My lads are gorgeous young men and I'm proud of them. The physical side of the modern game is a problem for them because we play so many matches that a young man's frame can't always cope with that. But I've got people like Webb, Walker and Pearce who could walk into any of the top teams in the league, and the rest of my players are all good enough for any of the other sides in the First Division. That type of thing makes the rebuilding all worthwhile.'

Across the road at Meadow Lane, the Notts County manager John Barnwell echoed the thoughts of many in the game when he said, 'If you ever get fed up with football, go and watch Forest reserves. There's no pressure on them, other than learning how to play the game properly, no abuse of the ref. All that's down to one man.'

Yet Clough was getting frustrated towards the end of the eighties. He was aware that his idealistic brand of football was not winning him trophies. The praise showered on himself and his team was gratifying, but Clough the manager was just the same when he played cards, tennis or squash – he wanted to win. He knew that many felt he would never win a major trophy again, without Peter Taylor's assistance. Being drawn against a brilliant Liverpool team in two successive semi-finals of the FA Cup strengthened the feeling that Forest might be fated to be the nearly men. The dreadful events at Hillsborough during the second of those semi-finals against Liverpool put the quest for the FA Cup into perspective, but Liverpool's subsequent demolition of Forest only confirmed the gulf between the two sides. Clough knew he was tantalizingly short of a breakthrough. 'It's no good a season-ticket holder going on about us winning nowt for a few years. I know that better than him. It's my pride, my expertise he's talking about and I feel it more than anyone. But there's only one way I can manage, I can't change now.'

Perhaps it was this frustration that saw him flirt with the idea of managing Wales in 1988. That episode was another one of Clough's cameos where he appeared to encourage an approach then reject it while offering a scapegoat – even though the truth was some way from the official version. Clough mulled over the offer to manage Wales part-time, but then pulled out, saying that Forest's directors would not allow him to combine the two jobs. He says he thought about resigning from Forest, but his experience at Derby had hardened him against resignation; besides a new manager at Forest would then capitalize on all his foundation work. So he stayed with Forest and aimed a few public barbs at his directors for presuming to stand in the way of his international ambitions.

One of Clough's fellow-managers feels it was all a ruse to lure back one of his trusted confidants. John Barnwell, the manager at Notts County at the time, had appointed Alan Hill to build up County's youth policy after Hill and Clough had had one of their periodic spats. Hill was happy at County, enjoying a fruitful working relationship with the manager but Barnwell still felt that Hill would eventually find Clough's siren song too powerful. So it proved, when Hill told Barnwell that he was going to be the Wales assistant manager under Clough, working at the City Ground. When the deal fell through on the apparent dictate of Forest's directors, Hill stayed on at Forest as youth development officer. 'So Cloughie got what he wanted,' says Barnwell. 'I knew Hilly would go back to him eventually, they had this love/hate relationship.' Clough's actions cost Forest £19,000 because County took them to a tribunal, alleging breach of contract and the case was settled out of court. An expensive show of backbone by the Forest board, then – or did they really have a say in the Welsh job?

Alan Hill thinks not. He also believes that it was all a smokescreen to restore him at Forest. Clough had told him he would only take the Wales offer if he came as his assistant. 'You've got ten minutes to think about it,' he was told. They shook hands on the deal and when they told the Forest chairman, Maurice Roworth, he was perfectly amenable. Hill and Clough met the Welsh FA delegation at the Holiday Inn, Birmingham, talked about salaries and cars, and that night Clough rang Hill to say the Forest board had agreed to everything. Hill was told to present himself at the City Ground for the news conference in two days' time. 'I got there and Cloughie slammed the door behind us and said, "Those bastards won't let me take the job, they've had a rethink." I said I'd left Notts County for the job, and that left me with egg on my face. He said he'd sort me out a new contract at Forest if he decided to stay. It got very bitter with County. I think the Forest directors were innocent. I reckon Brian had talked it over with Barbara, and she influenced him to turn the Wales job down. It would've meant extra work for Brian, no matter what he said about just being at the matches. There would've been more travel, extra hassles from the press and more work to do on getting to know the Welsh players – as well as still running the show at Forest. He was getting no younger, either. In the end, I reckon he just went off the idea.'

Clough would only say, 'I wanted the job and my chairman stopped it.' Perhaps the identity of County's chairman is relevant. Derek Pavis had been a Forest director, a thorn in the side of Clough who had rallied shareholders' support against him. Pavis had been voted out but made it clear that Clough held no terrors for him. It would appeal to Clough's manipulative streak to infuriate Pavis by snatching the services of a man for whom he had great personal affection and professional respect. If it meant lining up his own directors in the coconut shy, that was perfectly agreeable – in Clough's eyes that was their main function in football.

They did give him support when he needed it a year later, though. Clough offered to resign immediately after television cameras caught him punching several fans who had run on to the pitch, after Forest had beaten Queens Park Rangers 5–2 in the League Cup. There was no excuse for a manager getting involved in such an incident, it was a matter for the police, whom he used to praise ostentatiously at matches. Some Rangers supporters had been taunting the Forest fans but a handsome victory in brilliant style was surely the perfect answer to a mild outbreak of moronic chanting. Clough has always guarded the playing area of the pitch zealously, and he was outraged at the sight of several hundred youths capering over it, but he ought to have stayed out of it. He knew that as soon as he had walked down the tunnel, after swinging a few right hooks, some of which found their target. He apologized to his chairman, offered to resign, but Maurice Roworth would hear nothing of it.

The following morning, Mr Roworth's performance in front of the media suggested a disturbing lack of awareness, and a blind faith in his manager that was almost touching. The manager did what he thought was best at the time, the fans had no permission to be on the turf, local radio calls were 90 per cent in favour of Mr Clough's actions, if some of those fans had been given a clip around the earhole when younger, this might not have happened – and so on. When it was suggested to Mr Roworth that his manager deserved to be sacked, he replied, 'Sack? No way, he's got us into another semi-final.' So that's all right, then. If he had been in charge of a struggling team that had lost a League Cup quarter-final, he would have been dismissed? Such is football's realpolitik when the manager is infinitely more clever than the directors who ostensibly employ him.

Clough took his medicine, a £5,000 fine and a ban from the touchline for three months. Despite sporadic outbursts of paranoia from sections of the Forest staff on the day of the FA Commission's ruling, it was a comparatively light sentence, given that Clough could have been prosecuted for assault. Two of the fans who were thumped by Clough then participated in the final, amazing twist to the affair. They were fêted at the City Ground, apologized for being on the pitch and pledged their undying loyalty to Forest and the manager – all in front of the television cameras. So much for the iniquities of trial by television. Clough was shrewd enough to use the instrument that had spotlighted his aberration two days earlier and turned it into a classic photo opportunity, which was picked up by the rest of the media. When Clough ended the meeting with a request for a kiss from the two young larrikins – a request they readily obliged with – the television cameras recorded the moment. Even Clough's most bitter enemy had to admire his chutzpah.

Two months after that incident, Clough at last led out a side again at Wembley for a major final. They overwhelmed Luton 3–1 in the Littlewoods Cup after a sticky first half, relishing Wembley's open spaces to play their controlled passing game. Breakthrough for the father, and for the son. Nigel won the Man of the Match award, displaying his skills to a wider audience and taking a substantial step towards becoming an outstanding footballer, irrespective of his famous surname. Clough senior granted me an interview perched on the edge of the dressing-room bath and when I introduced my producer, Andrew Parkinson, he was delighted to yarn about his famous father, Michael. 'Tell your dad he's an old bugger and I haven't seen him for too long. But tell your mam she's gorgeous. Be sure and tell her,' was the most telling of his reflections immediately after winning his first trophy in nine years, the first without Peter Taylor. Later, the pleasure of it all washed over him. 'We all got home in our various ways and I stuck the Cup on top of the TV and all the family, and Nigel's girlfriend, sat down and smiled. It was nice that Nigel stuck one in. I left the Cup on top of the TV for a couple of days so I could keep going back for a peek in case I thought I'd been dreaming.'

A few weeks later, Clough was back at Wembley, as Forest beat Everton to take the Simod Cup, a spurious competition designed to make money and overload the players further – but still another trophy. They won the Simod's successor, the ZDS Cup, three years later, again beating First Division opposition in Southampton. Another successful visit to the Twin Towers for the 1990 League Cup was matched by two failures, the League Cup against Manchester United in 1992 and – the saddest – the FA Cup in 1991.

By the time Clough finally got to the FA Cup Final, for the first time as manager or player, he was acquiring the status of football's Queen Mother. It seemed everyone bar Tottenham supporters wanted Cloughie to lift the trophy, in the same way that Stanley Matthews and Gordon Richards had been willed to their winner's posts in the Coronation Year of 1953. In the build-up to the final, Clough had been low-key, denying rumours of retirement if he won the Cup. 'Win or lose I'll be back at the City Ground in August. This will be a nice occasion and I'm pleased we got there to reward a year's hard work, but I haven't given it a passing thought till we got all our league games out of the way.'

Nigel Clough made the reasonable point that no one else in the Forest dressing-room had won the FA Cup, but there was never a chance that attention would be deflected away from his father. It was to prove a sad occasion for both Cloughs.

When confronted with a 'what if?' question or an 'if only' observation, Brian Clough tends to snort derisively and say, 'If me auntie had balls, she'd be me uncle.' His fertile, challenging mind does not permit flights into the unknown, he is not a man for hypotheses. Yet he must have considered since that he would have won the FA Cup if somebody other than Roger Milford had been the referee. Milford felt the way to have a good football match was to develop a chummy rapport with the players, and trust to their good sense. That was not a good approach with Paul Gascoigne on hand in May 1991. Gascoigne had been widely hyped since a successful World Cup the previous summer and there was now a serious danger that he believed all the favourable publicity. Tottenham's precarious financial position had tested the expertise of Terry Venables and Gascoigne was determined to impose himself early in the final and win the Cup for Venables, to secure his position at the club. Gascoigne's antics before the match were immature. In the tunnel, he was kicking the ball against members of the band of the Royal Marines and when he ran on to the pitch, eyes popping, he carried on baiting the band while playing up to the television cameras. When the game started, he left his studs on Gary Parker's chest early on, with the ball an irrelevance, and then he caught Gary Charles with a wicked late lunge that could have finished the young full-back's career. From the resultant free-kick, Stuart Pearce scored and as Forest celebrated, Gascoigne was being wheeled away on a stretcher, his right knee smashed in that second tackle. So began an obsession in the media over the state of Gascoigne's knee that over the next year spawned a wave of sympathy that was totally out of proportion. It was Gascoigne's fault that he was seriously injured, a fate that could easily have been shared by Gary Charles. He should have been booked for the first offence and Milford ought to have flourished the red card over Gascoigne as he was helped on to the stretcher.

Gascoigne's departure and replacement by Nayim seemed to work against Forest, almost as if they felt the game was in the bag. If Gascoigne had not been injured, there is no reason to doubt that Forest's concentration and commitment would have been sharper and they would have won. Had Milford booked Gascoigne, Tottenham would have faced the last 70 minutes with ten men and a goal adrift. Cue Clough's observation about aunties and uncles. Clough was more prescient than most observers at the match, when just after half-time, he tapped Alan Hill on the knee and said, 'We're going to get done here, pal.' At the time Forest were still ahead, but Tottenham were pressing, with Paul Stewart a dominant force in midfield. Clough suddenly realized that his young side lacked experience of the big occasion, that the tension was sapping their energies. That morning, he had sounded out his aides about the team and carried on in the coach on the way to Wembley. He was unsure about Roy Keane's fitness and whether to play Steve Hodge instead in midfield. In the end he opted for youth, picking Keane (20), Chettle (22), Woan (23), plus three aged 21 in Charles, Glover and Crossley. The experienced Brian Laws and Hodge were the substitutes. Now the particular pressures of playing in a Cup Final had drained the youngsters and Clough knew that his initial instinct to trust in experience had been correct. Tottenham simply got stronger, winning 2–1 after extra-time.

At the end of the ninety minutes Clough had one last chance to rouse his team, but chose not to take it. As the players slumped on the pitch, waiting for the start of extra-time, Venables dashed out to his Tottenham players and exhorted them on to greater glory. Clough stayed on the bench, leaving the hands-on work out on the pitch to Ron Fenton, Archie Gemmill and Liam O'Kane. Surely a few words from Clough might have matched the influence of Venables? Clough will have none of it. 'They didn't want my big head around them then, they knew what they had to do. Once they're out on the pitch, you can't do any more. They gave me everything I asked for and we couldn't do it. Wembley's not a place to go and lose, but they deserved it.'

Steve Sutton, wise in the perverse Clough ways, thinks he did not go out on to the pitch simply because it was expected of him and so he stayed put, just to be different. A risky way to underline his idiosyncratic approach, surely – and there are enough examples over the years to confirm that, without putting the destination of the FA Cup at risk. Perhaps Clough preferred that his particular version of management's black arts should be confined to the privacy of the dressing-room. This was the first time the cameras would have homed in on the way he motivated his players, an intimate occasion for Clough at all other times. Woe betide anyone else who interrupted Clough or his players with about a quarter of an hour to go before a game, or at half-time. It may be that he felt inhibited by the thought of the public looking on at him, as he walked from player to player.

He did it his way and the FA Cup slipped through his fingers, never to be grasped again in Clough's career.

So he ended up as the only one in the élite group of great post-war club managers who did not win the FA Cup. It would have been interesting to see how he would have viewed his career had he won it in '91. Those close to him – including his son Nigel – feel he would have probably retired.

As it was he carried on, still thinking he could possibly compete seriously for the championship, but the side lacked consistency, experience and depth despite the regular daubs of delightful brushwork on an increasingly fustian First Division canvas. Perhaps his best side in that final decade was the '88–'89 vintage, with five internationals – Hodge, Walker, Webb, Clough and Pearce – a speedy outlet on the right wing in Franz Carr, a solid, professional full-back in Brian Laws, a tenacious midfield ball-winner in Terry Wilson and an improving target man in Lee Chapman. Yet Webb was allowed to go to Manchester United in the summer of '89 when he was happy to stay at the City Ground. 'I just got the impression he didn't want to keep me. He kept pressurizing me for a decision during the season, but I wouldn't commit myself to a decision until the summer. Then he sent me the same contract he offered me in March, but you always turn down the first one as a negotiating tactic. Later, Cloughie said if I'd taken down my son Luke when I was looking to negotiate, he would've given me anything I wanted, but that might just be talk. He was very fond of Luke, though. We just never got round to serious discussions in the summer and I felt he wasn't too upset at losing me. But the deal would've been fine for both sides. It was strange.'

Not that strange to any connoisseur of Clough transfer dealings, particularly as he disapproved of players having agents, especially one as streetwise and resilient as Webb's agent, Jon Holmes. It may be that Clough did miss Webb and his family – certainly he often praised Webb's contributions and character – but Clough junior definitely missed him. They had an excellent understanding on the pitch, clearly on the same creative wavelength, with Webb's strong running from deep positions the ideal foil to Clough's imaginative passing. They contributed handsomely to an extremely attractive side.

Lawrie McMenemy knows a thing or two about trying to keep a provincial club hanging on to the shirt-tails of the big guns, with their strong playing squads, huge support and directors with large cheque books. He did a noble job for a few years with Southampton, the pinnacle being second place in the First Division and an FA Cup semi-final place the same year, 1984. For him the post-Taylor period was an impressive part of Clough's career. 'He stayed hungry, showed his character by keeping going and did tremendously well to keep Forest in the forefront. It's really hard for a provincial club to keep that up, and it can only be done by good management. Brian showed he wasn't as big a dummy as he said when it came to judging players after Peter left and he had all those trips to Wembley. If we hadn't been banned from Europe for a time after Heysel, he would've loved playing again in Europe.'

Clough finished third in the table on three occasions in the eighties, and the last two would have meant a European place, had it not been for the ban. Until his final season, Clough's Forest were never out of the top ten in the division after Peter Taylor left and he got them to Wembley six times in four seasons, winning four trophies. Add to that a UEFA Cup semi-final and two FA Cup semi-finals, and a steady production line of young players becoming internationals, and it is hard to see how any manager could have fared better in testing circumstances. Since Forest won the title in 1978, the subsequent champions have all been major clubs – from Liverpool, north London, Manchester and Leeds. Title hegemony became more and more concentrated in the hands of the big fish, while the minnows just tried to keep swimming, staying in the pool. Nottingham Forest managed that better than anyone else in the last decade of Brian Clough's career.

14

The Number Nine

A couple of years after Brian Clough joined Nottingham Forest in 1975, regulars at the City Ground became aware there was more than one Clough on the premises when the manager was working. During time off school, Simon and Nigel Clough would spend hours kicking a ball around in the car park, watching the Forest players return from training, wondering what it was like to be a professional footballer. One of them would find out in 1984. The other, Simon, had his potential nipped in the bud by a cruciate ligament injury, the same knee problem that ended his father's playing career.

Nigel and Simon had already been spotted by the television cameras, smiling cheekily up at their dad as he affectionately tousled their hair in various dug-outs up and down the country. Nigel kept him company at times as he drove up daily to Leeds during his nightmare period and he was lucky enough to witness the special pressures of playing from a very early age. He remembers going to Turin for the 1973 European Cup semi-final against Juventus, when he was just seven, and by the time Forest were on their European jaunts, Nigel was an old hand at drinking in the atmosphere. It was to prove a useful experience when it came to acquiring the psychological steel necessary to thrive on the big occasion.

By the late seventies, Nigel was joining in with the Forest players in six-a-side games if there was a spare place, and Ian Bowyer remembers the day when he realized the small, intelligent boy had genuine talent: 'It was 1979, on a pre-season tour to Amsterdam and Nigel joined us in a kickabout. At 13, he was passing the ball as well as any of us. He was controlling it easily, passing it well, just doing all the right things. He had a football brain. When he joined the staff a few years later, there was no question of it being nepotism. He didn't take long to convince us he was in there on merit.'

Both Nigel and Simon stayed on at school for their 'A' Levels, so Nigel was 18 before he registered with Forest as an amateur. He had been playing a bit for Heanor Town and AC Hunters, a team started up by his brother. They played Sunday league football in the Derby area and Clough senior rarely missed a game. It was therapy for him as his close friend, Colin Lawrence remembers: 'My son David played and Nigel started turning out for them when he was 14. Brian and I used to go and cheer them on and he found it very therapeutic, whatever happened to Forest the day before.'

Even after Nigel graduated to the Forest first team, he would act as linesman for AC Hunters on Sundays, as they made their way impressively through various leagues. Nigel says the football talk around the family table was always about their team, not their father's: 'Forest didn't get a look in, we wanted to talk about our games. If Forest was ever mentioned it was only in passing – you'd have thought AC Hunters was the important team, not Forest. He never talked to us in any depth about what it was like to be a manager.'

How much of a burden was it having such a famous father? Nigel recalls: 'I remember me and Simon were teased at school about Forest because we were at a school in Derby and there's a pretty intense rivalry between the two clubs. When he was at Brighton, we were teased a lot. I had nothing to compare my experience with, it doesn't dawn on you in the early years, he was just my dad. It was only when I came to Forest that I experienced what it was like. He never talked to me in any detail about the job, or my own role. I knew what I had to do, and I got the same amount of advice as any other striker. He was good on things like coping with a bad trot, when you're not scoring. He'd say, "Keep getting into the positions and one will hit you on the knee and go in." Obviously, he had great knowledge of what was involved as a striker, but he hardly ever talked about his playing days to me. He was unpredictable at work and didn't change just because I was now working for him. I got praised sometimes but I was always just the number nine on the team sheet and that's the way I wanted it.'

Nigel first wore the number nine shirt for the Forest first team against Ipswich on Boxing Day 1984 – a significant day in his father's playing career as well. Clough had been pestered by his backroom staff to blood him for a few weeks, but he held back: 'I wasn't sure. The timing had to be right. Whatever anyone thinks of me, it's got nothing to do with the centre-forward. The sins of the father shouldn't be heaped on the shoulders of the son.' Nigel did not know he was playing until an hour before the start and his father had been shrewd enough not to give the press a steer in that direction either. It made sense to catch the media cold and slip him in for his début when most of the press box were more concerned about hangovers and getting away from the ground early for further festivities. Just to make sure of Nigel's anonymity, Simon was deputed to chaperon him after the game and whisk him home before the media tracked him down.

Gary Birtles watched Nigel's début from the stand, as he nursed an injury, and he recalls some supporters' scepticism about the débutant. 'But then he curled one of those lovely passes to one of our lads and they soon shut up. Everybody in our dressing-room got on with Nigel. They respected his ability – and that's always the most important thing with players – and he liked you to join in with jokes about the gaffer. He called Nigel "the number nine" and he copped his fair share of bollockings as well. The players would've resented it otherwise.'

Steve Sutton says Nigel was always objective about his father with the rest of the players. He would tell them if he thought he was going through a dodgy patch, when his behaviour could be extremely irrational. 'He wasn't really one of the lads, but that was his prerogative. Nigel didn't drink, so he'd miss out on the socializing, but no one slagged him off for that. Nigel enjoyed the banter in the dressing-room and there was never any jealousy. Nigel's a super lad and the way he's come through everything is a credit to himself and his family. His mum deserves most credit, she's a lovely lady.'

Nigel says there was never any danger that he would be perceived as his father's spy in the dressing-room and he was quick to dispel any doubts in that direction. 'I joined at a time when players were still there who had European Cup medals, so I was well aware that I was just a small part of that set-up. It was important to me to win their respect and to let them relax in front of me, that I wasn't going to be running back to my dad with gossip. Nobody ever held back when talking about him and I'm glad of that.'

Clough senior never referred to his son by name either in interviews or with his staff. It was always 'the centre-forward' or 'the number nine' even in team meetings, or with his coaching staff. He admits that in the early days he was particularly hard on Nigel because he had to be seen to treat him with no favouritism. On the rare occasions he would allow himself to be drawn into public comment about his son in those early years, Clough would content himself with something along the lines of 'he's got a chance', but within three years of his début, he had relaxed his guard. 'Now he's proved himself, I don't need to be so hard on him. His colleagues rate him and opposing centre-halves certainly rate him. He's the exact opposite to me as a person and player. He's cultured, I was the up-and-under type, greedy to bang 'em in. I was in at the keeper all the time, hustling him, whereas he wouldn't dream of imposing any physical pressure on them. He imposes himself with the ball at his feet and then he's not afraid of anything. He does have an obsession with perfection, though. He thinks that if he plays 100 balls in a match, they've all got to be spot on, otherwise he gets frustrated. I think that's daft but he'll grow out of it.'

Just occasionally the impassive mask would slip and the father's pride would appear, as distinct from the manager looking for the job to be done. Once at Luton, Nigel scored the winning goal near the end and David Pleat recalls Clough jumping out of the dug-out, clapping his hands above his head and declaring, 'Nigel – you're as genuine as your mam' to no one in particular.

Ian Bowyer sat in the dug-out one day and he was interested to hear Clough expressing his admiration for the enthusiasm for the ball shown by 'the number nine'. 'Cloughie said, "Knock him down 20 times and he'll keep coming back for the ball," and he was so proud of him. From an early age, Nigel was the master of the ball, with the ability to pass it, but I never again heard his father say so much about him, that was kept under wraps.'

As Nigel became more and more important to Forest on the field, his father occasionally had a dart at the England management on his behalf. He said it was unfair that Bobby Robson did not give him another chance after his international début against Chile. When Graham Taylor replaced Robson, Clough took up the cudgels again on his son's behalf, wondering in his *Sun* column why Nigel was not getting a game. Lawrie McMenemy, Taylor's assistant, rang Clough to set the record straight. Clough told his friend that it seemed daft to go halfway round the world to sit on his backside in an hotel and then on the bench during the match, while McMenemy pointed out that Nigel always wanted to go on those England trips, whether or not he played. According to McMenemy, 'Underneath it all, Brian burns with pride every time Nigel gets another cap. I remember after one international in which he played I said to Nigel, "Well done, and tell your dad that's another cap you've won," and Nigel smiled and said, "Yes, that's another one more than he got," and we both had a laugh. I told Nigel I wouldn't say that to Brian and I advised him not to!'

Nigel says he was never aware that his father was especially proud of him playing for England, although he used to talk about his disappointment in only getting two caps. 'I got praise sometimes but only along the lines of "Well done the centre-forward" and that was it. I got as many rollickings at the ground as any other player who deserved it – and a few more at home. At least the other lads escaped that!'

Were they totally dissimilar as centre-forwards? Certainly

Nigel is slighter, easier to knock off the ball, despite the adept way he shields it with a defender right alongside him. His father appeared to have the greater hunger for goals, while Nigel seems to be the better all-round player, with a greater awareness of his colleagues around him. In his best position, just behind the front two strikers, with space to use his creativity, Nigel is one of the most interesting English players at a time when muscle and speed are beginning to be more relevant than brainpower. He sizes up options very quickly, switches the play adroitly, and with players alongside him who are both quick in thought and movement, Clough is a gifted playmaker. He and Neil Webb were an excellent combination and his one-twos with a rampaging Stuart Pearce could unpick the firmest of locks. Lack of an extra yard of pace may be his major weakness at international level but his football brain more than compensates at club level.

Clough's transfer to Liverpool in June 1993 certainly represented good business for both the club (a fee of £2.2 million) and player. It will be interesting to see how he fares in his new challenge and whether he can be as influential with good players around him as he was at Forest.

Brian Clough is wrong just to dismiss himself as a goalscorer, little more than a robust predator. Newsreel films of his playing days reveal tantalizing glimpses of calmness under physical pressure, and some imaginative passing. Alan Brown, his old manager at Sunderland, noticed a similarity between the Cloughs when he first saw Nigel's composure and passing skills. 'I remember seeing Brian play once at Huddersfield, when he controlled a ball on his chest deep in his own half, turned quickly and swept a beautiful ball out to his right winger in an instant, almost without looking. It was a 40-yard pass and it split the defence. That's always been one of Nigel's great strengths and when I next talked to Brian, I reminded him of that pass I saw him strike all those years ago. He was very pleased to be compared to his son.'

The Cloughs are poles apart temperamentally. The elder may have learned the value of discretion late on in his career, but he has been more than happy to impart his views on most aspects of football, and a few more besides. Almost as soon as he started playing for Middlesbrough, he had the ear of the local football writers and as the electronic media grew in influence, he was ideal for television and radio. Sometimes too popular; his mother used to turn off the radio whenever she heard her son pontificating, after he had become Hartlepools manager in the mid-1960s and started drumming up local interest. Sally Clough said she was worried what Brian would say next!

Nigel, in contrast, is self-effacing with an inner resolve – according to family friends, much more like his mother. He kept away from the media for a long time after he broke into professional football and it was only after he became an international in 1989 that he submitted to the occasional interview. Towards the end of his Forest career, he collaborated in a weekly column in the local evening paper, that was a model of restraint and common sense; his father's previous outpourings in the same paper were much spicier! Nigel's public diffidence at the start of his career was construed by many to be the result of advice from his father, or even concern that anything he said would be blown out of all proportion. According to Nigel, this was not the case. 'I've always preferred to live a quiet life and I'd rather not say anything, but that's down to the type of person I am, rather than who my dad is. He in fact used to say it would do me no harm now and then to do some interviews, but a low profile suited me.'

His introspective persona added to the favourable impression made by Nigel Clough during the last painful days of his father's career as Forest slid towards relegation in 1993. He had accepted without murmur the need to play in defence on several occasions in the spring ('All part of the learning process. Gary Birtles did it, so why should I be any different?'), but still ended up Forest's leading scorer in a miserable 1992–93 season. He was appalled that a Forest director, Chris Wootton, had talked indiscreetly to a journalist about his father's alleged drink problem, that a subject which had caused the family private anguish should now be airily discussed in newspapers at a time when the Cloughs felt that Brian at least deserved to go with dignity of his own accord.

The statement issued before the penultimate game by Barbara Clough and her three children, deploring the timing of the announcement about Brian's decision to retire, was all the more effective because they had always stayed out of the arena of publicity. One member of the clan has gathered more than enough fame over the past five decades. Barbara has been the ideal foil for her turbulent spouse, following after him with the metaphorical poop-scoop after his umpteenth gaffe, while going about her tireless charity work with admirable anonymity.

Barbara can be justly proud of her son's quiet dignity in those last few weeks of his own career at the City Ground, before he went to Liverpool. He had been captain of the side for the last third of the season in the absence of the injured Stuart Pearce and he still managed to turn in an acceptable level of performance through the final months while all about him was disintegrating and relegation loomed. On 1 May, the day when Forest's fate was sealed, Nigel still had the courtesy to stand and applaud the fans before he trailed mournfully off the pitch after losing to Sheffield United. Afterwards he had the decency to apologize to the Forest faithful for relegation and to thank them for their astonishing support during such a difficult season. He knew it would be his last season at Forest, because Chris Wootton was refusing to resign from the board of directors, and he felt so strongly about the way his father had been treated that he could no longer remain if Wootton stayed put.

Nigel has often wondered what it would have been like as a player at the City Ground when his father was younger. 'I'd have been interested to have copped him and Peter Taylor when they were at their peak, producing teams that beat the best in Europe. You look at teams like AC Milan and Marseilles today and realize that Forest were beating their equivalents in the late seventies. I was on some of those trips but I was too young to take in their significance. But you think about a small provincial club from Nottingham winning the European Cup two years on the trot with those two in charge. They must have been good.'

They were, and it was pleasing to hear the reference to Peter Taylor, who had always been fond of Nigel and regularly praised him in print after the sad split with his father in 1982. Nigel says he hopes that his mum can enjoy some peaceful years away from the pressures of life with the game's most famous ex-manager and start enjoying together as normal an existence as possible.

Certainly Barbara Clough deserves more serenity; it cannot have been easy at times in that household, keeping the lid closed on such a volatile character during a marriage dating from 1959. It is a tribute to both parents that their three children are warmly praised by family friends and people from inside the game. Only one of them has peeked above the trench of privacy and only then because of his outstanding talent as a public performer. There have been enough insights gleaned into his character to know that any parent would be proud to have a son like Nigel Clough.

15

How Did He Do It?

If Brian Clough could be bothered to turn up on time at
conferences for a few hours a week in his retirement, he would
make a fortune telling managers in other professions how to get
results. He could be another John Harvey-Jones, albeit with a
rather better taste in ties and a superior hairdresser, breezing in
and out of stagnant companies, doling out unpalatable truths.
Shooting from the hip and the lip has been second nature to
Clough and he would be the ideal man to advise jaded
executives on how they could achieve results faster and with less
expenditure. If nothing else, it would be fun to observe Clough
pricking a few balloons of pomposity and complacency. His
cavalier attitude to punctuality might be an amusing sideshow as
well.

Every player or member of staff who has worked for Clough
has a story about him, a fact which should gratify a man of his
massive ego. One view about him does not change, no matter
who is reminiscing. Everyone agrees Clough was remarkable at
man-management. He had that magic touch which makes staff
give more than they thought was possible, a priceless asset

which breeds success. No one will ever know if Brian Clough just winged his way through a working day, by doing it off the cuff – perhaps he did not know himself – but the fact is that he commanded respect and loyalty by being totally self-indulgent. He enjoyed himself more than most in his working life by earning the right to please himself. That right flowed from his success and the self-confidence that resulted from getting it right more than others did in his chosen profession. It would be impossible to try to follow his highly distinctive method of working but the key was the sure-handed way he steered the Good Ship Clough between the Scylla of ruthless self-preservation and the Charybdis of looking after his staff.

In his Derby days, he used to tell players who had given their all for him on the field, 'You sit there, son – I'll take your boots off for you,' and the biggest name in football, with the ego to match, would also haul the shirt off his exhausted player's back. He once told Roy McFarland, 'It's nice to be liked sometimes, Roy,' a rare admission from someone who seemed fully aware that popularity was one of the more irrelevant considerations in football.

McFarland once shaped up for a showdown with Clough that could easily have led to the transfer of his defender, but saw him offered a holiday in Spain instead. He had read in the evening paper that Clough was to fine him £100 for getting suspended. He was furious. This time Clough had gone too far. McFarland was told to wait until after training before he could see the manager and then Clough began by saying, 'You're no use to me sitting in the stand.' Then he told him to look inside an envelope on his desk. In it were two plane tickets for McFarland and his girlfriend. 'Typical – I went to fight him and ended up in his debt. There was always a cushion alongside his clenched fist, whether it was flowers for our ladies or he'd come in the day after a match and say to a player, "Son, I was wrong to take you off." He just disarmed you.'

Did Clough rule by fear? Not according to the majority of his players. But Trevor Francis, who suffered more than most in his two years at the City Ground, points out there was a thin dividing line: 'It's nonsense to say Forest were ruled by fear, because he was so good at relaxing the players, allowing us to express ourselves. But you are aware you must give him everything. You know that he might belittle you. Getting bawled out by Brian Clough isn't a pleasant experience. He spotted things, he could tell if you didn't fancy running that extra ten yards to get in a tackle.'

The Clough memory was phenomenal, and not just for the smallest incident in a match that he would turn to his advantage, either at half-time or at the next team meeting. He once embarrassed Ian Bowyer by referring to an incident in Majorca four years earlier that had never been mentioned since. He made sure that the other players were all listening at the time.

England internationals in his side were never spared the lash, if he felt they deserved it and even if they did not. Steve Hodge had several running battles with Clough in his two spells at Forest, one of the last at Barnsley in a Zenith Data Systems trophy game. 'We were all very tired after a hard FA Cup replay against Crystal Palace, and at half-time, he really tore into the established players. "You think you're an England player – you're garbage!" he shouted at me. I was dying to have a go back, but he knew how to wind me up. In the second half, I played a short ball and he gave me unbelievable stick from the dug-out. I put my hands on my hips, we stared at each other for several seconds and we were both thinking, "We don't really like each other, but we'll just have to make the best of it." He gave me stick again after the game. He always won those battles.'

Clough had no time for self-pity in the dressing-room, he insisted that his players' body language should be bright, happy and positive. Steve Sutton had a harsh introduction to that philosophy when he looked morose at half-time on a pre-season tour to Spain. Peter Shilton had just been transferred from Forest to Southampton and young Sutton was desperate to make a good early impression to get Shilton's place. He had let two goals in, and was thoroughly down about it at half-time when a clip around his ear from Clough brought him back to reality. 'Grow up son – it's a big world out there!' Sutton played excellently in the second half, but all Clough said to him afterwards was, 'Son, that's good management.' No praise for the player. On his first-team début for Forest, Sutton thought he had had a good game, even though Liverpool had beaten them, and he was reflecting on that afterwards in the dressing-room, relishing the special atmosphere and feeling good about it. Clough spotted that and roared, 'Hey! What are you smiling at – we've lost a bloody match here!'

The players never knew what to expect in the dressing-room, apart from a few minutes of calm relaxation and a request for smiles just before going out. In Clough's squash-playing days at Forest in the late seventies, the door would be flung open around 2.30 and he would step into the bath chuntering about his partner Gary Birtles' luck on the squash court. Sometimes, he would bring someone in to make a point to his players. It might be someone from his own playing days ('Now this man could play, lads'), or one of the 'suits' ('Without this gentleman's firm, there would be no sponsor of our league, and not so much money for you lot'), but there was always a reason. After he stopped playing squash, he would lock himself away for half an hour, just thinking about the game ahead. Then he would be ready for his players. Alan Hill, who saw Clough at close hand for many years at Forest, says he kicked every ball in the match and had to steel himself not to impart his tensions to the players. 'I've never seen a man go into a dressing-room, say so little and get so much from his players,' is Hill's verdict.

Clough certainly earned his money at half-time in the 1989 League Cup Final, when Luton were leading 1–0. Clough was furious and the players waited for the blast. They were not disappointed. 'Gentlemen, we are absolute crap. They are playing to the best of their abilities. Now my wife's in the stand, so are yours, so are your relations and friends and all those lovely people from Nottingham. So please – go out and show them what we can really, really do. Because you are fucking garbage. Go out and show them! Please, gentlemen.' The rasping voice had built in a crescendo of power until that final sentence, which was carefully spoken, and he ended with a smile. That was the sum total of his team talk. Forest came roaring out, played superbly and won the Littlewoods Cup 3–1.

Sometimes, when they might be expecting praise after a good match, he would rant at them, just to disconcert them. When it suited, he would turn anything to his advantage. Once he came back from holiday to supervise an FA Cup replay at Queens Park Rangers. Clough was never one to dedicate himself to an entire season without a family break and at half-time he told the Forest players what he had given up to return for this game. 'And you're playing crap when I should be on holiday!' he shouted and slammed the door. Nothing else was offered by the manager during the interval. Forest ended up the winners, Clough opened the door and said, 'Thank you, gentlemen,' and went back to Majorca.

He could also be totally reasonable after a bad performance either by the team or a player. His teams were rarely locked in the dressing-room for a tedious post-mortem lasting an hour. He knew – and expected – his players to be suffering enough without an immediate bout of soul-searching. Clough thought the time for positive action was during the match, not afterwards and his way of helping a disappointed player would be to sit on the edge of the bath and say quietly, 'Now son, should you have done that?'

Steve Sutton will never forget the kindness shown by Clough after a match at Middlesbrough. It was the week after the dreadful scenes at Hillsborough in April 1989, when so many died on the terraces during the Forest–Liverpool semi-final. During the minute's silence at Ayresome Park, some of the Middlesbrough fans behaved disgracefully, throwing pies and other objects at Sutton in his goalmouth, and chanting obscenely. Sutton was dreadfully upset and broke down in tears afterwards. Clough sent for a whisky and sat with his arm around Sutton, just the two of them left in the dressing-room. He told him to go home to his family – 'because they're the most important ones' – and come back to work in time for the next game. 'He was like a father to me,' says Sutton. 'There was no need for him to do that, he was on his home patch up there and could've gone to see all sorts of people. I was thinking about retiring that day. That's the Brian Clough I remember with most fondness. He could reduce the strongest character to tears but they'd never turn round and say "I'm going". He really did like you to be settled and happy at home.'

Yet he would toy with players. They could never be sure about him. On one of Derby's trips to Majorca in the early seventies, Alan Durban was looking forward to a night out with his mates, and got himself spruced up for the occasion. Clough walked into his room and asked, 'Where are you going? You're looking after my bairns, I'm going out tonight,' and Durban did as he was told. So did Peter Shilton when Clough told him to pour the drinks for the rest of the Forest players at a function just after he had signed him in 1977, for what seemed an enormous amount for a goalkeeper at the time. No swollen egos at the City Ground from any new signings. At the same function, Ian Bowyer had drunk half of his beer and had the glass to his lips when Clough shouted over to him, 'Off you go to the bath, son,' and Bowyer, still in his training gear, put the glass down immediately and did as he was told. So did David Needham, when told by Clough he should have a lager. 'I don't want a lager,' said Needham, but he did not prevail. 'David, you're a lovely lad, you've got a lovely wife, lovely house and you've got a brilliant contract. In life sometimes you have to do the things you don't like – you'll have a lager.' He had a lager.

Towards the end of their time together, in the mid-eighties, he would call Ian Bowyer 'pal'. Did he feel that was a true reflection of their relationship? Bowyer exclaims: 'You're joking! But I think he respected me for putting in a fair amount of years for him, and being honest. In our first year together, in 1975, I took Forest to a tribunal over my contract and I got more than he was prepared to give me. I think there was a bit of respect from him after that because I'd dug my heels in and stood up to him.'

Clough did not like losing, whether it was at a tribunal, at cards or at tennis. He liked to drive a hard bargain over contracts and bonuses with his players. At Derby, the players were all on just one-year contracts, designed to keep them on their toes, and at Forest he could be very niggardly. When Forest reached the Simod Cup Final in 1989, the players asked for clarification of the bonus situation just two days before the Wembley game. They were told in no uncertain terms that they would be getting nothing. After Forest beat Everton in a thrilling game, Clough had a rethink. They each got a box of chocolates with a ten pound note attached.

When dealing with other clubs over a transfer, he was

ruthless, as Ian Bowyer discovered when he went to Hereford as player-manager and looked to his old boss for a helping hand. 'He was ice-cold in his dealings with me, determined to get the best deal.' Another young manager fretted for days before he plucked up courage to ring Clough with an enquiry for his striker, Paul Wilkinson. He even stood up when he was put through to Clough on the phone, and called him 'Mr Clough'. He was totally disarmed when he was told, 'Call me Brian, young man – and what can I do for you?' He asked if the player was available and started the ball rolling at a fee of £100,000. 'A hundred grand?' Clough spluttered. 'A hundred grand? More like five hundred grand – and call me Mr Clough, young man!'

Clough liked to see his players gather round the team sheet to check if they had made the first team. That was particularly so at Derby, despite players such as Colin Todd and Roy McFarland being automatic choices, even in Clough's mind. But he told them all that if a player did not jump up to look at the team sheet he would not be in. Complacency was a bane to Clough. This applied also to his backroom staff. When Alan Hill secured for Forest the services of Gary Mills, Clough was delighted that he had captured a boy who had been coveted by all the top clubs. Clough told his youth development officer to bring the contract to him when it was signed by Mills, at any time, wherever he was working. It so happened that Mills signed on match day and the contract and the lad were duly paraded in front of the first-team players in the dressing-room, with the inevitable threat that Mills would soon be taking the place of one of the seniors. Clough effusively told Hill to crack open a bottle of champagne for himself, and when they shared a glass afterwards, Clough instantly stopped Hill from being too pleased with himself. 'Cheers, Hilly, well done – but never forget, that's your job!'

Hill says that in his first six months working with Clough at the City Ground, he learned more about how to organize a club and handle people than in the whole of his career previously. He always marvelled at Clough's ability to praise and disconcert you in the same sentence: 'On my first day, he took me to see Forest play at Oldham. We were in the hotel, having the pre-match meal when he shouted over to me, "Hey! Have you organized a room for these lads to watch the TV? No? Well get off your arse and do it – that's your job." I wondered what I'd let myself in for. He told me to sit, listen and take it all in. He was an amazing man. We'd go anywhere for him, even though he could wound you with just a few words.'

It was Hill who secretly organized a farewell to Clough from his staff soon after he retired. The chairman Fred Reacher flew back from his holiday in Cyprus and sixty-one people attended an emotional lunch at the Kedleston Hall Hotel. Clough thought he was just having lunch with his son Simon and grandchildren, but when Tina Turner's *Simply the Best* blared out over the public address system and he looked around at the people who had worked for him at the City Ground, he was overcome. 'I didn't realize I had so many friends after the bollockings I've given all of you.'

It was rare to see Clough disconcerted. He was the one who would calmly announce to his players, 'We're off to Spain for a break tomorrow, lads,' and be certain that no one would raise an objection. On one of those trips, Forest shared an hotel with Southampton, a side containing a fair amount of experienced internationals at the time, and some fiery characters – like Alan Ball, Mick Channon and Peter Osgood. The Southampton players were enjoying a drink at a roadside bar when Clough walked past them, on his way to a game of tennis. One of them shouted out, 'We wouldn't play for you, Mr Clough,' and thought the object of the derision would simply keep on walking, as his team-mates tittered. Not a bit of it. Clough walked over and said, 'Is there a problem?' and he sat down and had a drink with them. As he was leaving, he shouted back, 'You know what you were saying about not playing for me? Well I've got news for you – I wouldn't pick any of you bloody lot!' The Southampton players loved that, because he had shown the strength of personality not to be outfaced in front of so many players he did not know, and he was sharp enough to have the last word.

Clough never got too close to his players, but the nearest was at Derby, where the age difference was very slight, particularly in the late sixties. He took a proprietorial interest in the welfare of his players. Roy McFarland recalls being bawled out early in

his Derby career because he was emulating too closely the
lifestyle of Dave Mackay. He was living in the same hotel as the
legendary character and Clough hauled McFarland into his
office and told him he was living 'like an alleycat' and that his
career was on the line. 'I went away with my tail between my
legs, but I sorted myself out. He was right. If any of us had
problems, he'd try to sort them out for us.'

If the players had disappointed him socially, he would be
merciless. In April 1972, Derby won the Texaco Cup, beating
Airdrie 2–1 in the second leg. Clough was absolutely delighted
and phoned several of his players, who had been rested for the
run-in to the championship. After the fourth call, he finally got
hold of one of them, Alan Durban. 'I'm bloody glad I've got
you in, unlike some of the others I've rung,' he told Durban.
The following morning, Clough was in a foul mood, as Durban
remembers: 'He played hell with us, especially those who
weren't in when he called from Scotland. He wanted to share his
pleasure with his lads and there was hardly anybody at his beck
and call. He looked as if he needed a good row that morning, so
the sensible thing was just to keep our heads down.'

Some players waited in vain for praise from Clough, for the
crumbs from the rich man's table. Martin O'Neill finally
received a commendation from him for the first time after three
years of waiting. It came when he least expected it, after Forest
had been knocked out of the FA Cup by West Brom in 1978.
'Not our day, lads, but I thought you did magnificently today,
son,' he said, turning to O'Neill. He then suggested O'Neill
should be the only player entitled to be measured up for the
special shirt the players would be wearing for the forthcoming
League Cup Final at Wembley. 'He said I was the only one
certain to play. We all knew that was guff, but I promise you, I
walked out of that dressing-room ten feet tall, even though we'd
just been knocked out of the FA Cup.'

O'Neill had to wait another two years before he was praised
again, and it came in the European Cup Final against Hamburg.
At half-time, with Forest one up and holding the favourites,
Clough told O'Neill he was thinking of pushing him further up
front, alongside Gary Birtles – 'But I'm loath to, because you're
playing so well.' Yet just a few months earlier, in February

1980, O'Neill had been told he was to be transferred to Coventry City in an exchange with Mick Ferguson, even though he did not want to go. At some time during the day's negotiations Clough went cool on the idea but O'Neill had by then agreed to go. He signed three blank sheets of paper and told officials of both clubs to sort it out because he was going home. Clough told O'Neill he was still a Forest player and to be on the team coach the following morning. 'To this day, I don't know why Clough decided against the deal. I just felt a commodity, an object for bartering.'

That O'Neill/Ferguson episode was just one of many bizarre transfer deals that have involved Clough. Take the Asa Hartford transfer. He was at Forest for just 63 days in the summer of 1979, and after playing in the first three games of the league season, which were all won by Forest, he was transferred to Everton. The management announced that Hartford was not suited to the Forest style, even though they must have known what they were getting when they moved for Hartford after deciding to sell Archie Gemmill. Hartford now smiles at the memory of his two months there. 'At least I can say I played for Brian Clough, even if only for a short time. It was different – some days he couldn't do enough for you, others he'd just ignore you.'

John Sheridan and Gary Megson had the same experience. Clough was astonished to discover that Megson's pre-match nerves meant he was often sick in the dressing-room, and the process was sometimes repeated at half-time. 'He doesn't do that in my dressing-room' was the sympathetic response and Megson was swiftly shipped out. The same with Sheridan. Clough did not appreciate Sheridan's downbeat attitude, his reluctance to smile, a body language that appeared sullen. When he failed to say a bright 'good morning' to the manager and look as if he was enjoying life at Forest, his time was up. It did not matter if you were the best player in your division – if you were not smiling and looking positive before a game, Clough would not keep faith in you.

Clough would not stoop to bending the rules, but he wanted to win at all times. Not at all costs, but he would be displeased if his players failed to do themselves justice. 'Winning matches keeps me going, no matter what level of standard we're playing in. Winning with style is the icing on the cake, but that goes out the window when your backs are against the wall. My players are brought up to play fairly and cleanly, but they're also expected to win.' Both Liam O'Kane and Archie Gemmill from Clough's backroom staff were suspended when the Forest reserve side under their authority did not play well enough in the manager's opinion.

When Clough signed Justin Fashanu in the summer of 1981, he decided to take him on the pre-season tour to Spain. It meant one player had to drop out, and it proved to be the youngest, Steve Sutton. He had been eagerly anticipating his first overseas tour with Forest but Clough told him to get his kit out of the team coach, because he was being pulled out at the last minute. His parting words to Sutton were, 'That's the way it goes, Sooty.' The priorities were clear, with the million-pound signing edging out the inexperienced goalkeeper. Sentiment was not a factor, nor was the bad news sugared.

He was even more ruthless when it came to injuries. The trauma of Clough's early retirement in 1964 clearly bit deep, because he would rarely get close to a player who was injured. His attitude was that they were no use to him and that it was up to the player and the medical back-up to bring him back to the manager's attention. When Forest brought their full side down to Southampton to play in a testimonial, John McGovern went down injured and the referee Clive Thomas blew the whistle immediately. It was a few days before the European Cup Final and Thomas did not want any Forest players injured in what was just a run-out. Nevertheless McGovern struggled to his feet as soon as the referee stopped the play. 'I've got to get up, ref,' he said. 'Otherwise he won't pick me for the Final.' Thomas was astonished to hear Clough admonishing his player from the dug-out, rather than worrying about a possible injury. It was clear that the manager expected the same level of commitment in any game and that thoughts about an important game on the horizon were secondary. If you were injured, that was your hard luck.

Trevor Francis experienced Clough's cold attitude to injuries when he snapped his achilles tendon in 1980. Francis is baffled that the press made much of his own man-management problems when he was in charge of Queens Park Rangers. It was hinted that Francis was aping the custom and practice of Clough when some of the Rangers players were being fined and transfer-listed. Francis snorts at the suggestion – 'No one who had met us both would've written that' – and says that Clough's desire to win was very intense underneath all the bravado. His presence alone at the training ground had a salutary effect on the players. 'From the moment you saw him walk towards us, the difference in our effort was remarkable. If we were playing six-a-side, the tackles would start flying in, players would run around all over the place. He just transformed us by being there.'

To Clough, it was always a simple matter of paring down the job to its essentials. 'I manage the same way as I did when I first started at Hartlepools. I look for honesty and I'm not afraid to tell people when I don't see honesty. Some managers are better talkers in their own office than in the dressing-room, but I think I'm consistent in both. Sometimes my staff ask me why I get so upset when watching my players train in six-a-sides. I tell them there's a right way to play football and I believe mine is the right way. If it doesn't happen on a Monday morning or a Thursday morning, then it might not happen on a Saturday afternoon. That's when I get uptight. If you've cracked it, why settle for second best?'

In his later years at Forest, Clough became more paternalistic towards his players, especially the young ones. He was proud of their good manners, short haircuts and good disciplinary record. If he saw an apprentice slouching along, looking glum, he would shout, 'Hey! Head up, son! Up there the stars, down there the mud!' There was never any doubt who was the boss though, despite a perceptible softening from the doting grandfather. Young players who would want to find out why they were out of the team or not getting a pay rise would be wrong-footed immediately by Clough asking, 'How's that lovely mam of yours, son?' and he would be delighted if he heard the lad was getting married, or about to become a father. A few minutes later, he would be ushered out, without any extra cash or none the wiser as to why he had been dropped. Apart from his bloody-mindedness about money, Clough was very understanding about the pressures on young players. 'You must never send out young players saying, "You've got to do this or that," that's a terrible way to approach a game. It freezes them. It's wrong to go out and think a draw is enough, you must approach every match with the intention of winning in style. If you have to settle for a draw, that's different – much better than losing 3–0. But you must relax your players before the game, otherwise they can't give their best for you.'

Geoffrey Boycott has watched Clough's man-management at close quarters and admires the way he appears to act spontaneously. 'It must have been amazing for those young players. One day he was God, the next the Devil.' Boycott had personal experience of Clough's ability to motivate. One day at Chesterfield, Boycott had got out early on a perfect batting wicket and our Geoffrey was less than pleased at watching his team-mates fill their boots for the rest of the day. Clough was at the game, and after a decent interval, came along for a consoling word with the distraught Boycott. Clough came straight to the point. 'You're right to be upset, because it's your profession, but don't be down all day. See all these players – they're all worried if they'll ever make runs. You'll always make runs, if not today, then the next day or next week. There's no substitute for class.' Boycott soon snapped out of his misery and never forgot the advice. A decade later he was still scoring runs by the bucketful for Yorkshire and England. 'He was very clever that day with me. He didn't tell me any lies, he told me the truth in such a way that I felt like a giant, ready for anybody, even though I had failed that day.'

Brian Moore was always fascinated by Clough's insight into the mental aspects of football whenever they commentated together for television. 'I'll never forget the night that Aston Villa won the European Cup in Rotterdam, when Brian gave a remarkable assessment of what was going through the minds of Tony Barton, Villa's manager, and his players. He was never a man for research, but absolutely brilliant at the psychology of it all. After all, he'd won the European Cup twice and he knew what the players and manager were thinking. That night was his peak as a co-commentator and I don't think I've ever worked with anyone better.'

Like many others, Brian Moore has been overwhelmed by Clough's generosity, a quality in his character that has been as consistent as his unpredictability. When Moore's wife was ill a few years ago, Clough bombarded her with flowers and phone calls. Once Clough organized a charity dinner in Derby and was so embarrassed by the standard of the food that he gave everyone a refund of five pounds. After a local journalist asked Forest if she could do a bucket collection for an ambulance to help Romanian refugees, he rang up immediately and pledged £1,000, half from the Cloughs and the other half from the club's directors. He took a shine once to two youngsters from Sunderland who had asked him for his autograph at the team hotel. They were from a broken home, so he brought them down to the Clough household now and then for weekends, and paid for a new pair of glasses for one of the boys. When Alan Hill left Forest for the first time to start up his hotel business, Clough bought him a cooker for the pub restaurant as a farewell gift. Clive Thomas cannot speak too highly of the man who helped him so much in his refereeing career. Clough drove to Cardiff from Derby one afternoon to help Thomas launch his autobiography and then suggested he should speak at a dinner to raise money for local boys' clubs. He refused to take a penny for his day's work and contented himself with some sandwiches for the journey home that night. Another time, he made a 420-mile round trip to a lunch in the Rhondda Valley to honour Thomas. The fee? Just another round of sandwiches.

Clough has rarely forgotten those who helped him in the early stages of his career. That includes journalists. Contrary to received wisdom, Clough does not regard the whole of the species with disdain. Doug Weatherall, the *Daily Mail*'s man in the North-East for many years, has known Clough since he was a player at Middlesbrough. When Clough heard that Weatherall's wife was in hospital for a heart operation, he sent her a dozen red roses. He was fairly busy that day in 1972 – he bought David Nish for a then record British transfer fee – but still managed to remember an old friend.

Harry Storer's influence on Peter Taylor in the fifties has already been documented and Clough shared Taylor's admiration for the fierce old disciplinarian, once he got to know him.

When Storer was dying, Clough visited him in hospital and promised to look after his widow, Kathy. She was always invited to Derby's games, and Clough would ensure she was picked up at home, given a good meal at the ground, cared for during the game and driven home whenever she wished. He was equally thoughtful to Gordon Turner, a former Luton player who played alongside Clough for the Football League. Through a mutual friend, they met up again after a long interval, just as Gordon was starting to suffer from motor neurone disease. Eventually he had to take to a wheelchair, but whenever he could get to the Baseball Ground, Clough would make a fuss of him. One night, he organized the usual comfortable vantage point for Gordon Turner, so that his old friend could enjoy another great European Cup occasion at the Baseball Ground. Clough did not mention that he had just driven down from Middlesbrough, after being up all night at his dying mother's bedside. He managed to contain his grief, get back to Derby for the big match, and still find time to look after Gordon Turner in his wheelchair.

He was such an unorthodox mixture, Brian Clough. Too eccentric and too clever for his players when in his prime. Roy McFarland now freely admits that 'I love the man', but that is not a common opinion among those who worked for him. Most did not like him, yet they did not expect to. Football is like that. The doctrine of *sauve qui peut* runs through the harsh, unsentimental sport and the players are inured to the boss being isolated, taking unpopular decisions. Clough seemed to relish that part of the job at times, while he could also disarm a player with a thoughtful, unheralded gesture. In the end, it was respect Clough wanted and he got it in abundance. Those like Larry Lloyd, Martin O'Neill, Steve Hodge and Steve Sutton, who never managed to develop a consistent rapport with the man, are the first to confirm how much they respected him. Ian Bowyer tells the story of a dispute in a hotel bar in Magaluf in the early eighties between Clough and his tempestuous defender Willie Young. Money quibbles and Clough's desire for everyone to have an early night were the seeds of the row and at one stage it looked as if punches would be exchanged between player and manager. Bowyer is convinced that Clough would have been supported. 'To a man, we would have jumped on Willie Young, because we respected the gaffer so much. You didn't have to like him. Despite all the eccentric things he did, he treated us like adults for most of the time and we knew how much we owed him. He deserved our respect.'

He was either lucky to have so many docile players under his thumb or a genius at man-management. There have been so many references from his former players to brick walls they would run through for him that it is a safe bet that Clough knew instinctively how to set the mood of the day. He had no intention of bottling the magic elixir and selling it, he was far too competitive for that. Much better to dress it all up in the flim-flam of provocative comments and decisions that were apparently irreconcilable. No one was better for so long at growing so much from apparently infertile ground. Yet Clough knew how much seeding, watering and nurturing was needed. His harvests yielded bumper crops for many years.

16

The Final Curtain

No contemporary evidence suggests that Christopher Wren knew much about the game of football, but the superb architect knew a thing or two about greatness in its enduring form. His tombstone in St Paul's Cathedral bears the inscription, 'If you would see his monument look around.' Quite so, Christopher; your cathedral remains a handy memorial to your creative talents. Will we be able to say the same about Brian Clough, now that he is no longer running the City Ground with his unique brand of benevolent despotism?

The stadium and its facilities are a vast improvement on the situation when Clough arrived in 1975, with Forest now hoping to stage a few games in the European Championships in 1996. The transfers of Nigel Clough to Liverpool, Roy Keane to Manchester United and Gary Charles to Derby for a combined total of seven million pounds, mean the club is on a secure financial footing, even though relegation means an estimated shortfall of two million pounds. Forest's youth scheme continues to flourish, but how many parents will choose bigger clubs, now that they are not being charmed by the eccentric paterfamilias who would guarantee their son would encounter the smack of firm discipline? There must have been a host of fathers who persuaded their boys to sign for someone they saw score so many goals a few years back, someone they had always wanted to meet. Cloughie stories went down well at the local pub, when your lad had signed for him and you and your missus had been exposed for a day to the Clough charm.

Frank Clark, Clough's successor appointed in May 1993, was right to praise the legacy but also to maintain that there must have been something wrong at Forest in that last desperate season. They were, after all, hardly ever out of the bottom three, and long before the season's end, their pretty football was also punchless, lacking in confidence and character. On the harshest, most exacting standards, Clough had failed, in the process exposing the myth that a particular side is never too good to go down. Tell that to Manchester United in 1974, Tottenham in 1977, Leeds United in 1982, and West Ham every alternate year. Forest's demise under Clough in 1993 was nasty, brutish and short. He was certainly thrown by it. As late as January 1992, he was telling me that the trophy cabinet would soon be extended. 'With all these young players coming through, we are in incredible nick. You can look forward to another ten great years here. It gives me a buzz to keep getting three points but also see these young men doing so well. That Roy Keane – he jumps higher than Red Rum, an incredible header of the ball. What a smashing player. I like being in charge, there's not a prayer of me retiring and I'm going to win a few pots.'

Eight months later, Forest were in a run of six straight defeats and Clough was baffled. He remained baffled for the rest of the season, but at least had the character to take the blame. Of course, he should have retired earlier, but that is easy for the uncommitted to state. Football was the core of Clough's professional career, despite his talented dabbling in other fields, despite his genuine pleasure in family life. There are only so many walks he could undertake, cricket matches he could attend and media contracts he wanted to fulfil. Football management was his particular forte and if he did lose the recipe for success in the final years, at least the meals remained palatable. Bland but not inedible.

It is not as if the other major managerial figures in the English
game enjoyed untroubled success throughout their careers. Bill
Shankly did not win a trophy for Liverpool for a six-year period
until 1973. Stan Cullis was sacked by Wolves in the year they
were relegated. Matt Busby flirted with relegation in the
1962–63 season, before Manchester United won the FA Cup.
Bill Nicholson resigned from Tottenham after a bad start to the
1974–75 season, when he clearly lacked support at boardroom
level and could not motivate some of his top players. Clough's
main failure came right at the end of a managerial career that
spanned 28 years and several major acheivements. On four
occasions, he won two trophies in the same season (see
Appendix, pp. 230–31). Like Busby, he won the European Cup,
like Revie he won the championship twice, he shared with
Ramsey the achievement of the First Division title immediately
after promotion in 1977–78. Only Herbert Chapman has
matched Clough's feat of winning the title with two different
clubs, and in Chapman's case, doing that at a major club like
Arsenal does not compare with doing it at provincial outfits like
Derby and Forest, 40 years later. Not even Clough's biggest
detractors could quibble at his place in the élite group of great
managers in English football.

It would be wrong to overstate Clough's crusading zeal for
style and panache in his football teams. Peter Taylor, as one
would expect from a former goalkeeper, drummed into Clough
the necessity for a tight defence and there were times at Derby
and particularly at Forest, when the team chiselled out narrow
victories in utilitarian fashion. When Forest won two successive
European Cup Finals, they did not convert many neutrals to the
quality of their play, even if there were extenuating circumstances – effete opposition in the first game and injury
problems for the Hamburg final. What both Derby and Forest
under Taylor and Clough always did was play with a coherent
strategy, respect for the laws of the game, with neatness,
precision and honesty. Once Taylor had left, Clough imposed a
more cavalier approach, with passing a dominant theme. He
managed to win a number of trophies in the late eighties, but it
was the purity of Forest's play, with the emphasis on passing and
intelligence that illuminated those years. They were lightweight,

the combative Pearce apart, and their defence never seemed too secure, despite the redoubtable Des Walker. A championship was always beyond them, because they were the kind of side that would lose 4–3 away from home, having led for most of the game. That was their attraction for football fans, rather than those purblind enough to swallow the cant from managers about 'getting a result' irrespective of the means deployed. It was the way Forest played that evoked those remarkable scenes in May 1993 at the City Ground and Ipswich, once it was certain Clough was taking his farewells and Forest were going down. He had become an anachronism among managers, preaching constructive football in his hansom cab, while the macho philistines roared past him in their Range Rovers. The tears for Clough were not those of frustration at relegation, but a recognition that the most powerful and respected advocate of the art of the possible was leaving the stage at a time when the snarl, the gritted teeth and berating of referees were the accepted norm on the field.

Forest's gates continued to rise from the late eighties and they usually attracted a sizeable chunk of neutrals when they played away. When they lost 4–3 at Queens Park Rangers in the final month of the relegation season, it was a hammer blow to their chances of staying up. The reaction from the Rangers supporters that April day spoke volumes for the respect Forest and their manager engendered from other camps. It had been a vibrant, gripping game with Forest at last showing something like their true pedigree. They were unlucky to lose and the reception the Rangers fans gave them was a heartening affirmation that some clubs still have an awareness that there are wider issues at large than the cold-eyed pursuit of three points. If Forest had won that day, they would have been cheered off the pitch by the home supporters. The warmth of the tributes from both the Sheffield United and Ipswich sections of the crowd on the final two Saturdays of Clough's reign only served to confirm that a major force for the good was leaving football.

Many current managers pay lip service to Clough's insistence on playing the game his way. 'If God wanted the game played in the air,' he used to say, 'why did he put grass on the floor?' Other managers would smile indulgently at the old boy, express pious hopes that Forest would continue to prosper, and proceed on their own cynical path, perfecting the offside trap, the knockdowns from long clearances, and the systematic reduction of the referee's authority. Then they would purport to be baffled at England's poor international performances, refusing to see a connection between the type of play that was becoming the vogue in the top division and the lack of technical skill displayed by England players. There are some managers who are more sincere in their admiration for Clough's methods. David Pleat is one. 'There was always a balance to Clough's sides, they didn't run around like blue-arsed flies, like so many other teams. They made shapes and triangles, they knew where to pass the ball. His players were told they had to cope on the field. They took up relevant positions and their brains told them when to pass it short or long, or to knock it into the penalty area, while avoiding predictability. He also had an excellent attitude to dissent, an incredible stance when you see what goes on elsewhere and the advantage that is sometimes gained by it. You never saw his players surrounding the referee, verbally abusing him. A lot of managers have become winners by allowing that to go on.'

The referees were sorrier than most at Clough's retirement. Alf Grey is now a referee's assessor for league matches after 23 years officiating in the Football League. He used to look forward to Forest's game for weeks. 'You'd go into their dressing-room and Cloughie would have them all sat down, waiting for a word from the ref. They'd listen and show respect. Other managers wouldn't care – they'd let their players stay in the toilet or wander around, sticking their backsides up at you. Cloughie and his players were a delight to deal with. If all managers were like Cloughie, the ref's job would be so much easier.'

Jack Taylor, who refereed the 1974 World Cup Final, has been associated with football for almost 50 years, and on Clough's retirement, he wrote to him. It was the first time he had ever written to a manager. 'I felt I owed it to him on behalf of all referees and also for the many kindnesses he showed me. A great man, Cloughie.'

Neil Midgeley retired from the list in 1992 and is now the

President of the Association of Football League Referees and Linesmen. He believes Clough's best quality was allowing the referee to arbitrate, without pressure. 'All my colleagues say the same – he's never given a ref the slightest problem. You were always looked after at Forest and one of his staff would always come in and thank you afterwards. If any of his players were booked, Cloughie himself would come in and apologize!' In one game, Stuart Pearce allowed his formidable aggression to spill over just before half-time and he exchanged words with Midgeley. Just before the re-start, Midgeley was waiting at the top of the tunnel and Pearce came up and said, 'Sorry about that, ref – out of order.' After Forest had lost at Leeds in 1991, Midgeley was surprised to see Clough standing at his door. He came in after knocking, put both hands together under his chin and said gravely, 'I cannot believe, I *really* cannot believe – how well you refereed that match this evening. Thank you, young man.' Midgeley thought that for once Clough was going to complain – 'but it takes something to say that after you've lost. Different class, Cloughie.'

Clough could not see why so many managers and players allowed themselves to be sidetracked by referees. To him, it was a matter of priorities. He deplored losing a player through suspension, when it was caused mainly through dissent. Operating with small squads, he saw it as self-defeating and unprofessional. 'I love 90 minutes of blood and guts, honesty and skill – and no moaning at referees. I like to put a smile on everyone's face with the way we play. Some sides annoy me with the way they moan at the referee when someone has the audacity to take the ball off them. They let their club down. Every day of the week, it's ingrained into my players that the referee is in charge when the whistle blows. You get good ones and bad ones, but it evens itself out over a season.'

Clive Thomas started refereeing in the Football League in 1967, the same year that Clough began as Derby's manager. They got on famously as soon as Thomas told the young manager to stand up when he spoke to him and to knock on his door, instead of storming in. Clough told him, 'In my opinion, you'll be the finest referee in the country and we're going to get on very well.' They did. After every game involving a Clough team, Thomas would be invited into his office and he would guide the referee through his performance. 'He was so constructive, he'd point out mistakes but also praise. He helped me understand what managers wanted from the ref. I'd argue with him, but always came away thinking he was so thorough and fair.'

Thomas was due to referee the second leg of a League Cup semi-final against Leeds at the City Ground, when fog swirled in off the River Trent. Clough's side was at full strength and Leeds had some injury problems. Clearly Clough preferred to play, but Thomas called it off. 'He rang my wife and told her I wouldn't be home that night because of the fog and didn't utter one word about my decision, even though I knew he was disappointed. Not once did he ever try to influence me before or during a game.' Clough was happy whenever Thomas booked one of his players for dissent. Kenny Burns fell foul of the Thomas notebook one day and Clough said afterwards, 'Well done – you keep doing that.'

It is safe to say that Clough will not be missed by many directors, either at Forest or elsewhere. His regular derisory comments about directors have been cherished by the media and the fans but not in boardrooms. Men who have made something of themselves in other professional fields do not take kindly to a mere football man suggesting they should concentrate on entertaining civic dignitaries and passing around the vol-au-vents. Fred Reacher, his last chairman, maintained these were just Cloughisms, that he meant no harm, but Reacher is a kindly soul, who would see good points in anyone's character. He managed to hold the ring for Clough in the final weeks before his retirement but it may be that Clough's position would have become untenable had he stayed and Forest made a bad start in their promotion push. Giving his chairman a vote of confidence was typical of Clough, but he had enough savvy to know that hanging on to have his power base limited would have been very humiliating. Donald Wolfit's dresser never told the forbidding old actor-manager to iron his own tights, and it would have been against the natural order of things for football's actor-manager to start listening to his directors.

His departure marks the end of the period when the manager

ran the club. Bobby Robson, Graham Taylor, Lawrie McMenemy and Don Revie were in the same mould as Clough over the past 20 years, albeit without his eccentric ways. They felt that important matters of club policy were too serious to be left to the directors, although they dressed up that opinion more diplomatically than Clough. Now the chairmen have fought back and their profile is getting larger as the manager finds that football is too complicated to be left to someone with little practical knowledge of finance, safety measures or negotiations with television companies. With agents whispering in players' ears that a move would be a good financial wheeze, with freedom of contract and European horizons weakening the hold on loyalty, managers in England will find the job more and more complicated. Their chairmen will reduce their autonomy, meddling in transfer deals, wooing the media and marginalizing the manager. Clough would not have handled such a transition with any degree of grace. It was a good time for the bully to pack away his conkers, apologize for the bloodied noses and leave the playground.

No wonder Clough was held in awe by so many managers. Not just for his record, but for having total control of his club. Whenever he attended a meeting of the League Managers' Association, he was listened to in silence. Any manager who has survived that long, who has the power to tell his chairman he simply has to find the money for a new player, who can manipulate the media with such dexterity – that man can hold an audience of his industry's competitors. Some of them might nudge and wink that the old boy looked tired, but even those cynics showed him ungrudging respect. Clough had beaten the system by a combination of talent, ego and durability. No one else will manage a club like him.

So many others in other professions must have envied Brian Clough. He never seemed to worry about compromising just to keep up the payments on the mortgage. Other managers under pressure in different careers would love to tell their boss where to stick the latest business plan, or to go public on something they thought was unfair, illogical or damaging. Clough got away with all that, apart from the time in 1974 when he alienated the workforce at Leeds, a particularly disputatious bunch with a pronounced public relations problem. He was so different in his methods and his attitude to his job that he made a fortune out of the profession he affected to despise – the media. It was all a game – he has enjoyed friendships with many in the media – but he was perfectly happy to play the system for all it was worth. To someone of his towering self-belief, the occasional barb from a media pundit was an irrelevance. He might even agree with the criticism. He might ban the offending reporter from the ground. It was of no account. How many others have been able to please themselves for so long in such an insecure profession?

Is that self-belief a pose? His old mentor and manager at Sunderland thinks so. Alan Brown says, 'He's as shy as I am, that brashness is just a façade.' Anyone who suffered under the yoke of Alan Brown's severe guidance in his palmy days as a manager 40 years ago, will be amused at his self-description, but it is a view of Clough shared by Brian Moore, his good friend in television. 'He is shy, I'm convinced of that. Brian's not as self-confident as he appears. In Majorca when on holiday he'd send his two sons ahead of him into a restaurant, to check there was a quiet corner, where he could eat in peace. He didn't like being bothered by the public, despite all this stuff about being the Man of the People. After all the years together, all the chats around the fireside with our wives, he still keeps me on my toes. I still don't know him intimately, still can't feel I can relax completely with him.'

Moore believes that Clough is a good deal more prone to hero-worshipping than he would admit. He loves to talk about meeting Muhammad Ali and Frank Sinatra and he was surprisingly jumpy about sitting alongside Johann Cruyff when they were on the same ITV panel for the 1978 World Cup. Moore remembers the first time Clough saw Cruyff, on the day they were due to work together: 'Cruyff came into the hospitality area, looking godlike, immaculately dressed. Brian said to me, "Is there any chance I could sit next to him, so some of that magic can rub off on me?" He wasn't joking. Each time they worked together during that tournament, Brian managed to get himself alongside Cruyff. That wasn't the action of a supremely self-confident person.'

Despite the occasional bout of name-dropping, Clough is

happiest with friends he has known for a long time, homespun people whose loyalty is unquestioned and advice respected. He has a genuine affinity with old folk and his idea of a good night is a sing-song round a table. It remains to be seen how fulfilling he will find retirement, without the buzz of telling people what to do. His wife deserves to have him restored to health and serenity and his friends in that close-knit area of Derby will continue to sustain him. Del Boy will be one of the fittest dogs in the county if Brian carries out his promise to walk him vigorously every day, and Quorndon Cricket Club will not lack encouragement from their famous local supporter. As for football, do not rule out a return in some capacity, but not management. Perhaps as an adviser to a manager he respects, possibly even as a director? Clough still has a shareholding at Nottingham Forest and he has bought season tickets for the next campaign. As a shareholder, he has fulfilled the first qualification for being a director; he also has the money and a smattering of knowledge on the subject of football! Clough as the chairman of Nottingham Forest one day? It would appeal to his mischievous mind and constitute a new challenge. He might be the first to attend board meetings in a green tracksuit top!

One of the most impressive testimonies to Clough has been the absence of tabloid tales from his former players. Once it was clear Clough was indeed retiring, the tabloids moved in with lucrative offers to anyone willing to offer Clough's head on a platter. It soon became clear that the dominant sound was the deafening clamour of praise from former players, even from those who had no affection for him. Steve Hodge pointed out that Clough made him an England player twice over in his two spells at Forest. Steve Sutton remarked that all those who played for Clough and had become managers and coaches wanted to play football in the same manner. Larry Lloyd said, 'To do what he did was a bloody miracle.'

Clough would hammer his players to do the basics the right way. He would invoke the names of sporting perfectionists like Geoffrey Boycott, Nick Faldo and Steve Davis to insist there was a proper method for everything, that professionalism did not cater for short-cuts. He would get very frustrated in training, trying to teach young players their trade, when he was too old and his knees too arthritic to permit him the chance to show how it was done. At certain times, that frustration would hamper Clough, the demons would overtake him and anyone in his line of fire would suffer. Yet he never lost sight of the need to care for his players. 'I'll tell you the best time in football for me. It's when we've played away, we're coming back on the coach and we've won. Even better if we've won in style. It's probably been a long haul, a few hundred miles, but me and the lads have done our jobs well. That feeling of team spirit is wonderful, it's a feeling that outsiders can't comprehend, it's shared by just those who were there for that game, either playing or sat in the dug-out.'

Somehow Clough would summon up that generosity of spirit when his players had almost despaired of a kind word. Instinctively, he managed to balance the ruthlessness with warmth, the threats with concern. It may be that Clough just got out of bed of a morning, with no preconceived notion of how he would do his job that day. If he had no idea of his plans, his players were certainly in the dark at all times. He was never boring, nor were his teams, and in an age of mediocrity among leaders, there are worse epitaphs for a public figure.

whelming ego. By the summer of '94, he had been cleared of both allegations and this most implacable of foes was looking for legal and compensatory redress. Like Wilson of the *Wizard*, Clough had emulated the fictional athletic hero of his boyhood: with one bound he was free.

His retirement had just reached its sixth week when the owner of Tottenham Hotspur, Alan Sugar, cast the first stone. Sugar, in the course of a High Court hearing into the events that led to his sacking of Terry Venables, had alleged that Clough 'liked a bung' in cash for his part in transfer dealings. The sale of Teddy Sheringham from Forest to Spurs was the particular example offered by Sugar but he maintained that Venables had confirmed this was Clough's usual practice. Rumours of meetings at motorway service stations, involving large sums of cash in brown paper bags, flourished. While insiders tapped their noses meaningfully and confirmed that this was common currency in the murky world of football finance, the media once more declared open season on Clough. His home village of Quorndon was swamped by journalists and photographers, yet all they encountered was a populace fiercely loyal to its most famous resident, and the principal character walking his dog in the rain, biting one of the most celebrated tongues in sport. Clough was furious that Sugar had made those comments under the protection of a statement in court ('Otherwise I'd have done the bugger for libel') and settled down for the long haul of clearing his name.

Four months later, an even more damning allegation. On the *World In Action* television programme, Forest's former ticket office manager stated that Clough obtained 2,000 tickets for the 1992 Rumbelows Cup Final against Manchester United. Andrew Plumb alleged that Clough demanded the tickets and that they'd ended up on the black market, in the hands of Manchester United supporters, leading to crowd trouble at Wembley on the day of the match. Once again, Clough was besieged by the media at home, while the morals and Spanish customs of the football world were thoroughly dissected and criticized. Nottingham Police called in the Fraud Squad to comb through the financial dealings at the City Ground, while Forest's supporters came to terms with the realization that Clough might be a fraud. After taking legal advice, Clough contented himself with a general comment – 'I've never sold one black market ticket in my life' – and proceeded to co-operate fully with the police. Three months later, he was told by the police that he had no case to answer, that Plumb's allegations were groundless. That was the cue for Clough to move back on to the front foot. He told me: 'That programme will make me even richer by the time I've finished with them. They're going to make me another million.'

Clough was equally co-operative with the inquiry set up in October to investigate questionable payments in the wake of Alan Sugar's allegations. With football's business ethics now up for debate, the Premier League's chief executive Rick Parry's reaction was commendably swift. He set up an independent inquiry appointing Robert Reid QC and Steve Coppell, the new chief executive of the League Managers' Association, to sit alongside him. Many witnesses were called, and Clough, in a telephone conversation with Reid, left no doubt that he was determined to clear his name. Despite guarantees of confidentiality not one witness gave evidence to implicate Brian Clough in under-the-counter activities. When the inquiry's report was published a year after Alan Sugar's allegations, there was no censure of Clough. Any case against him had collapsed through lack of evidence. The inquiry was at great pains to stress the importance of new guidelines concerning agents and extra payments, so that the whiff of corruption might be stifled, but no one pointed the finger at Clough. It may be that the freemasonry of football proved more durable than the probings of three men of undoubted integrity, but it is a surprise that nobody came forward who might have been expected to know where certain entrepreneurial bodies were buried concerning Clough. One thing is certain: many other high-profile managers were more than happy for Clough to take the heat of media rumour, while they hurried to make deals with the Inland Revenue for payments they had not declared in previous years.

The flood of innuendo was one of the reasons why Clough never went to a match in his first year of retirement. He knew that as soon as he was spotted, a media frenzy would ensue. That left his son, Nigel, to forge a new career at Liverpool without the visible support of the old patriarch. Clough was delighted at Nigel's excellent start at Liverpool, concerned when he was eventually dropped by Graeme Souness and consequently by England, and ended up worried how his gifted son could kick-start his career at the age of twenty-eight. Although Clough Senior professed himself uninterested in professional football any more – 'I haven't missed it for one second, sometimes I don't know the results till the Green 'Un pops through my letterbox' – old habits die hard. He kept a beady eye on the football scene, thanks to the satellite television bought him by his children, and bemoaned England's elimination from the World Cup Finals. He was loyal to Graham Taylor's efforts, and thought that Ron Atkinson would have been the ideal successor as England manager – 'they need someone who's proved himself in club management, who knows the game inside out and doesn't mind telling the players where to get off'. Clough always had time for Big Ron's expansive personality and his compulsion to produce entertaining teams and it was typical that he should ring Atkinson at home to congratulate him, the day after his Aston Villa side had beaten Manchester United in the Coca-Cola Cup Final. 'It was the first time I'd ever had a call from Cloughie at home and I was knocked out. To me he was always the guv'nor, and I was made up when he said he'd been on the edge of his seat, watching the game.'

Clough was even more pleased that Nottingham Forest bounced back into the top flight at the first time of asking. Regular visitors to the City Ground noticed a slightly more physical side to Forest's play in the post-Clough era and certainly they looked a fitter side, with a different tactical shape, playing Stan Collymore up front, as the lone striker. Yet good habits do not disappear overnight and the fact that Forest's passing game was still intact pleased the old taskmaster. 'I'm really delighted for Frank Clark. He's had a lot on his plate because of all these stupid rumours, and it can't have been easy for him to keep his eye on the job with so many journalists wanting to talk to him about things that have nowt to do with the football. But he's a charming man, a good guitar player with a sense of rhythm.' A typical Clough final sentence, that one: he had not forgotten the impromptu sing-songs with some of the Forest players in the late seventies, with Clark, one of the seniors, providing musical accompaniment.

Clark, as befits one of the most sensible and dignified managers in the game, had made it clear to his old mentor that he was always welcome at the City Ground. There was little danger of that after the events of October 28, when Chris Wootton was voted back on to the Forest board by the club's shareholders. Wootton, who had been forced out at a special annual general meeting six months earlier, after alleging Clough's managerial judgement had been impaired by alcohol, was back in the fold. Wootton and the chairman, Fred Reacher, agreed to bury the hatchet in the interests of the club, promising greater openness and improved public relations. Yet when I interviewed Wootton that night, he bridled at my comment that Clough had no time for him, and that his leaked innuendos six months earlier had destabilized the club. Wootton declined to comment on that last point, suggesting that I was 'out of order' – an opinion roughly on a par with agreeing to interview Richard Nixon without mentioning the Watergate Tapes. No director would come out and say it but the feeling was that Clough's departure was a blessing. For his part, Clough vowed he would not set foot again in the City Ground, as long as 'that Wootton' remained on the board.

Clough's moods remained as mercurial as ever during his first year away from the managerial coalface. Another grandchild brought him great joy, and he was gratified to be able to spend Christmas in the bosom of his family. England's wimpish performances against the West Indies saddened him, as he watched a succession of spineless collapses, agreeing with everything Geoffrey Boycott said about the need for greater pride in performance and sterner professionalism. Clough resisted Boycott's invitations to join him in the Caribbean for a week or so: 'I've had me fair share of airports and delayed take-offs when I was a football club manager. A trip out to Calla Millor will do me now and again.'

He became more hermitic, rationing his public appearances, apart from occasional sightings on behalf of the Labour Party or the mining community. Clough would not admit he missed football, deflecting the question with a rediscovered enthusiasm for televised rugby or a desire to spend more time with his family. His wife Barbara acted as his secretary, dealing with the avalanche of letters and flowers that showed no sign of abating. Clough gave every indication of an awareness that his time in football had gone, but surely he must have still missed some elements of a profession in which he had been so outstanding? That may partly explain the times when he supped rather too well and unwisely, as he came to terms with a new chapter in a life that was still comparatively young. His close friends worried about him after occasional bibulous sightings at the Kedleston Hall Hotel, but Brian would have none of it: 'Sure, I drink a bit too much on some occasions, but doesn't everybody?' Well, no, actually; the hope was that his sporadic excesses could be contained and marginalized. Certainly he looked a deal better than in his final few months at Forest. He had lost weight, the complexion had lost its disturbingly red hue, and he gave every indication that Del Boy, his faithful dog, had upped his fitness levels even further by dint of some rigorous walks. At least Brian looked more relaxed now, even though a feeling of depression could not be fully exorcized.

One hopes that Brian Clough's retirement proves more fulfilling than for some of the other immortal managers of his era. Both Bill Shankly and Bob Paisley struggled to come to terms with a life without the all-consuming demands of the game, while Jock Stein and Don Revie sadly did not live long enough to smell the metaphorical roses. Yet Clough has been, and remains, a well-rounded character with enough interests to sustain him once he finally gets football out of his system. When you have spent forty-one years in one particular trade, that is no easy task – the more so for a man who has spent a lifetime disproving cosy theories.

Appendices

Brian Clough

b Middlesbrough, 21.3.35

Signed for Middlesbrough as an amateur, November 1951; as a professional, May 1952.

Played six seasons for Middlesbrough, all in the Second Division; for five seasons, between 1956–7 and 1960–61, he hardly missed a game. His total Middlesbrough record:

	Appearances	*Goals*
League:	213	197
FA Cup:	8	5
FL Cup:	1	2
TOTAL:	222	204

In 1958–59, he was the leading scorer in the country with a total of 43 goals. That season, he also had the unusual distinction of scoring double hat-tricks against two different clubs: five goals in Middlesbrough's 9–0 victory over Brighton on 23 August 1958, and three goals in the 6–4 win at Brighton. He also got hat-tricks in both matches against Scunthorpe that season.

Transferred to Sunderland in July 1961 for £42,000: he stayed until 1964, making 61 league appearances and scoring 54 goals. He injured his knee on Boxing Day 1962 in the 2–3 defeat against Bury, and that effectively ended his career as a player.

His career total of 251 league goals in 274 games gives him the best post-war goals per game ratio.

Clough's effectiveness as a striker in terms of goals per game

	Season	League Games	Goals per Game
Jimmy McCrory	1922–39	397	1.004
Brian Clough	**1956–63**	**274**	**0.916**
Dixie Dean	1923–37	437	0.867
Gary Lineker	1979–92	341	0.563
Ian Rush	1979–93	405	0.523

Two England caps, against Wales and Sweden in 1959; no goals. He also won one England 'B' cap and Under-23 caps (2 goals).

Playing for the Football League, he once scored all five goals against the Irish League at Belfast in 1959.

Clough's Managerial Career

Oct 1965: Becomes youngest manager in League (30) at Fourth Division Hartlepools United.

May 1967: Becomes Derby manager.

May 1969: Derby win Division 2 championship.

May 1972: Derby win Division 1 title.

Oct 1973: Resigns from Derby, with assistant Peter Taylor, after long dispute with club directors.

Nov 1973: Becomes Brighton manager.

Jul 1974: Appointed manager of Leeds. Sacked after 44 days.

Jan 1975: Joins Nottingham Forest as manager.

May 1977: Forest promoted to Division 1.

Mar 1978: Forest win League Cup.

Apr 1978: Forest win Division 1 title.

May 1978: Named Manager of the Year.

Feb 1979: Signs Trevor Francis (Birmingham) for £1 million – Britain's first seven figure transfer.

Mar 1979: Forest retain League Cup.

May 1979: Forest second in Division 1. European Cup winners.

Mar 1980: Hat-trick chance lost as Forest beaten in League Cup final.

May 1980: Forest retain European Cup.

Feb 1989: Charged with bringing game into disrepute; fined £5,000 and banned from touchline of all Football League grounds for the rest of the season.

Apr 1989: Forest win League Cup.

Dec 1989: 1,000th league game as manager.

Apr 1990: Forest retain League Cup.

May 1991: FA Cup finalists.

Apr 1992: Losing League Cup finalists.

Apr 1993: Announces retirement from football.

May 1993: Forest relegated from Premier League.

Clough's Managerial Record Season by Season

Season	League	FA Cup	League Cup	Europe	Other
Hartlepools					
1965–66	18 Div 4	3	2	—	—
1966–67	8 "	1	1	—	—
Derby County					
1967–68	18 Div 2	3	SF	—	—
1968–69	1 "	3	5	—	—
1969–70	4 Div 1	5	5	—	—
1970–71	9 "	5	4	—	Watney Cup Winners
1971–72	1 "	5	2	—	Texaco Cup Finalists
1972–73	7 "	6	3	EC SF	—
Brighton					
1973–74	18 Div 2	1	1	—	—
Leeds United					
1974–75	19 Div 1	—	—	—	—

(At time of Clough's sacking)

Nottingham Forest					
1974–75	16 Div 2	4	2*	—	—
1975–76	8 "	3	3	—	—
1976–77	3 "	4	3	—	Anglo–Scot Cup Winners
1977–78	1 Div 1	6	W	—	—
1978–79	2 "	5	W	EC Winners	—
1979–80	5 "	4	F	EC Winners	Super Cup Winners
1980–81	7 "	6	4	EC 1	Super Cup RU
1981–82	12 "	3	QF	—	—
1982–83	5 "	3	QF	—	—
1983–84	3 "	3	2	UEFA Cup SF	—
1984–85	9 "	4	3	UEFA Cup 1	—
1985–86	8 "	3	4	—	—
1986–87	8 "	3	QF	—	—
1987–88	3 "	SF	3	—	—
1988–89	3 "	SF	W	—	Simod Cup Winners
1989–90	9 "	3	W	—	—
1990–91	8 "	F	4	—	—
1991–92	8 "	QF	F	—	ZDS Cup Winners
1992–93	22 Prem	5	5	—	—

* Forest were knocked out from 1974–75 League Cup before Clough's appointment.
Clough has also landed a record 24 managerial awards, including Manager of the Year in 1978.

Longest Serving Managers

Matt Busby	Manchester United	24 years	1945–69
Jimmy Seed	Charlton Athletic	23 years	1933–56
Joe Smith	Blackpool	23 years	1935–58
Billy Walker	Nottingham Forest	21 years	1939–60
Eddie Davison	Sheffield United	20 years	1932–52
Brian Clough	**Nottingham Forest**	**18 years**	**1975–93**

Most Successful Managers Since the War

	Major Trophies Won
1. Bob Paisley	14
2. Brian Clough	**12**
3. Matt Busby	8
Bill Nicholson	8
5. Don Revie	7
Bill Shankly	7
7. Stan Cullis	5
Kenny Dalglish	5

Most Manager of the Month Awards

1. Brian Clough	**24**
2. Bill Shankly	22
3. Graham Taylor	21

Index

George Best
with Ross Benson
The Good, The Bad and the Bubbly

'If football is an art, I was an artist . . .'

George Best's footballing genius brought him fame and fortune at the age of 19.

Less than ten years later he walked out of Manchester United – into a nightmare world of lurid newspaper headlines, wild affairs, court appearances and battles with alcohol addiction.

What went wrong?

The Good, the Bad and The Bubbly is George Best's own version of the most dramatic rise and fall in the history of British sport . . .

. . . and the first honest story from the *real* George Best.

Still – even after all that has happened – the most famous footballer in the world.

'Where's George?'
SIR MATT BUSBY
'The best player in the world'
PELE
'He was unfaithful, bad-tempered and always fighting'
ANGIE BEST
'It couldn't last'
ANGIE LYNN

Michael Feeney Callan
Richard Harris: A Sporting Life

Sinner or saint?
Creative actor or 'professional Irishman'?
Wild man or sensitive genius?
Who does Richard Harris think he really is?

He's the Irish school drop-out who became a Hollywood king. A legendary drinker and brawler whose wild exploits almost destroyed his creative talent. From his first Oscar nomination (for *This Sporting Life* way back in 1963) to his last (for *The Field* in 1990), Richard Harris's life has followed a complex and unpredictable pattern, every bit as varied as the many roles he has claimed for himself.

A Sporting Life, the controversial biography written by fellow Irishman Michael Feeney Callan, is a no-holds-barred, intimate portrait of a man who has become an institution; a man who, despite the set-backs and disappointments, will never lose his ability to surprise . . .

Dick Francis
Lester: The Official Biography

'*Lester's life is not just a tally of dazzling achievements but also the story of the development of an exceptional man . . .*'

'For Francis, Piggott has lifted the lid of reserve he has maintained towards the world at large, to reveal something of his inner motivations and private life as he has done to no one else . . . Here is the overriding ambition . . . the cold courage which has enabled him to overcome dreadful injuries and setbacks; the struggle with weight; the tension of the great occasion and his feeling towards his family and few intimates . . . A well-told story of life at the top of one of the most demanding professions in the world' IRISH TIMES

'Excellent . . . gives real insight into the character of Piggott. Dick Francis' biography is a fitting tribute to a great career' TODAY

'His gifts as a novelist and own riding experience illuminate many aspects of the enigmatic Piggott character hitherto publicly under wraps' SUNDAY TIMES

'Fascinating . . . a very good racing book indeed . . . I shall always look at this book when I want racing reminders' SPECTATOR

'Francis has the rare gift of being able to bring yesterday's horses and races to life' SPORTING LIFE

All Dick Francis' thrillers and his autobiography are available in Pan.